NUMBER SIXTEEN

The Walter Prescott Webb Memorial Lectures

Essays on American Antebellum
Politics, 1840–1860

[THE WALTER PRESCOTT WEBB MEMORIAL LECTURES]

Essays on American Antebellum Politics, 1840–1860

BY WILLIAM E. GIENAPP, THOMAS B. ALEXANDER,
MICHAEL F. HOLT, STEPHEN E. MAIZLISH,
JOEL H. SILBEY

Introduction by THOMAS J. PRESSLY
Edited by STEPHEN E. MAIZLISH
and JOHN J. KUSHMA

Published for the University of Texas at Arlington by
Texas A&M University Press: College Station

Library of Congress Cataloging in Publication Data
Main entry under title:

Essays on American Antebellum politics, 1840–1860.

(The Walter Prescott Webb memorial lectures; 16)
Bibliography: p.
Includes index.
Contents: "Politics seem to enter into everything": political
culture in the North, 1840–1860 / William E. Gienapp—
The dimensions of voter partisan constancy in presidential
elections from 1840 to 1860 / Thomas B. Alexander—Winding
roads to recovery: the Whig Party from 1844 to 1848 /
Michael F. Holt—[etc.]

1. United States—Politics and government—1815–1861—
Addresses, essays, lectures. I. Gienapp, William E. II.
Maizlish, Stephen E., 1945– . III. Kushma, John J., 1949–
IV. Series.
E415.7.E67 1982   973   82-40314
ISBN 0-89096-136-0

Manufactured in the United States of America
FIRST EDITION

In Memory of Martin Hardwick Hall
1925–1981
Historian, Colleague, Friend

Contents

Introduction   3

     Thomas J. Pressly

"Politics Seem to Enter into Everything": Political Culture in the North,
1840–1860   15

     William E. Gienapp

The Dimensions of Voter Partisan Constancy in Presidential Elections from
1840 to 1860   70

     Thomas B. Alexander

Winding Roads to Recovery: The Whig Party from 1844 to 1848   122

     Michael F. Holt

The Meaning of Nativism and the Crisis of the Union: The Know-Nothing
Movement in the Antebellum North   166

     Stephen E. Maizlish

The Surge of Republican Power: Partisan Antipathy, American Social
Conflict, and the Coming of the Civil War   199

     Joel H. Silbey

Essays on American Antebellum Politics, 1840–1860

THOMAS J. PRESSLY

Introduction

THE decades of the 1840s and 1850s and the secession crisis which ended in the outbreak of the Civil War represent to historians what mountain peaks represent to mountain climbers. Those mid-nineteenth-century historical peaks have been a challenge to historian-climbers. For almost a century and a quarter, ever since 1861, they have made the ascent and brought back reports of what they found. Experienced historian-climbers are today aware of the differing routes followed by their predecessors, aware of the varied equipment their predecessors have used in their climbs, and aware of the varied findings they have reported upon their return. Now we can read the reports brought back by this latest group of historian-climbers, published here as the 1981 Walter Prescott Webb Memorial Lectures.

All of the essays in this volume discuss one or another aspect of politics in the United States during those two crucial decades in the middle of the nineteenth century. The essays provide examples of both some of the newer approaches employed by historians in the 1980s and some of the persistent problems facing those who seek to understand the two decades. One of the most lasting of those problems may be stated as a dilemma: how to understand the 1840s and the 1850s as distinct historical periods in their own right and on their own terms, while recognizing their relationship to the secession crisis and the outbreak of war which followed. The dilemma is subtle, complex, and seemingly unavoidable. "Hindsight," as David Potter remarked, is both "the historian's chief asset and his main liability." Whatever the difficulties posed by that dilemma, the common focus of these essays upon the 1840s and 1850s provides an underlying unity to this volume despite differences among the individual essays in scope, in scale, in types of evidence consulted, in methods of analyzing evidence, and in general perspective.

Differences in scope and scale are reflected in the arrangement of the essays, those with the broadest chronological or topical scale appearing first, followed by those of more restricted scope. One of the early essays is Thomas Alexander's "The Dimensions of Voter Partisan Constancy in Presidential Elections from 1840 to 1860." Alexander is widely known as a leading practitioner of the "new political history," which emerged in the 1960s, and his essay illustrates some of the differences between that approach and more traditional ways of understanding the political developments of the 1840s and the 1850s.

Alexander describes and analyzes voting in presidential elections from 1840 through 1860, suggesting explicitly and implicitly at least three criticisms of earlier accounts of those elections. The first is that earlier accounts, using newspapers, diaries, personal correspondence, and other such "literary" sources, have described the elections one at a time, considering each as a more or less self-contained event. Alexander, by contrast, analyzes the voting returns by counties for all the presidential elections from 1840 through 1860, viewing each election as a portion of one series. His methods of analysis are also different from those of most earlier historians, since he compares voting (county totals) in one election with voting in each of the other elections. For those who know the technical terms, he describes his method as "least-squares estimates of voting behavior from county-level aggregate voting returns," involving "bivariate regression analysis." From this analysis Alexander concludes that there were indeed striking patterns in those presidential elections, one being the closeness of the outcomes and another being the continuing adherence of voters to their respective parties.

Alexander's second criticism of the earlier accounts of presidential elections in the 1840s and 1850s is that they were premised upon erroneous assumptions about the nature of antebellum voters. Previous scholars assumed that pivotal numbers of voters were uncommitted or that each voter was a free agent, independently weighing the issues and the candidates in each presidential election. In accordance with these assumptions, earlier scholars ascribed electoral outcomes to the voters' responses to the issues and policies advocated by the candidates or to the perceived personal characteristics of the candidates or even to campaign enthusiasm. Instead, Alexander suggests that which "side won was probably more a factor of chance than of anything else."

The final criticism by Alexander disputes a major conclusion reached in many earlier discussions of these presidential elections: that the 1850s witnessed a sharp realignment of political organizations and of voting, in a generally North versus South direction, to the extent that by 1860 "sectionalism had destroyed the two-party alignment of the 1840s." Instead of a sharp realignment, he finds massive continuity in voting. He agrees that some realignment did take place in the 1850s, but it was not as important as continuity.

Alexander's minimizing of the importance of North versus South political realignment in the 1850s will catch the attention of readers familiar with his book *Sectional Stress and Party Strength*. In that volume Alexander analyzed the votes cast at 1,135 roll calls in the U.S. House of Representatives from 1836 to the summer of 1860—surely one of the most comprehensive analyses of roll call votes ever published. From that study he concluded that, though division in the roll call votes along party lines was always a prominent pattern, an even more prominent pattern by the 1850s was voting along North-South sectional lines. Forces "greater than party discipline or loyalty . . . were evidently at work continuously, relentlessly forcing party to yield to section on a definable array of issues."[1] Thus, in disputing the importance placed by earlier historians on a North versus South sectional realignment of politics in the 1850s, Alexander is disputing the findings of his own earlier study. Perhaps the roll call votes show a sectional realignment while the presidential votes reported here do not show such a realignment, but it would have been helpful to the reader if Alexander had noted and commented upon the difference between the present chapter and his earlier book.

Alexander's essay stops short of linking his view of the voting patterns in the presidential elections to the coming of war in 1861, but he made that link in his recent presidential address before the Southern Historical Association in language worth noting here. The published version of that address, focusing on "the extent to which certain institutional arrangements directly facilitated the onset of the Civil War," gave prominent place to "the effective attachment of voters to political party" in mid-nineteenth-century America. Without that attachment to party, Alexander wrote, without "the carefully cultivated fidelity of

[1]Thomas B. Alexander, *Sectional Stress and Party Strength: A Study of Roll Call Voting Patterns in the United States House of Representative, 1836–1860* (Nashville: Vanderbilt University Press, 1967), 110.

rank and file to name and symbol, party managers would have found it very difficult to create a major party on issue positions taken by the Republican party in 1856, and even more difficult to attract the necessary accretions to achieve an electoral-college victory in 1860. Without that fidelity, rival Democratic party leaders in 1860 would not have dared risk the defection of their followers by their apparently suicidal division of the party, and any ensuing secession movement probably would have been the tantrum of frustrated leaders that Lincoln first took it to be."[2] In another portion of the address Alexander described secession as "a step so drastic and so contrary to the fervor of American nationalism that it could never have been made persuasive to a majority of voters on the basis of arguments that individuals could readily associate with their own well-being. Only through the vehicle of the Democratic party was secession possible."[3] Without the lasting attachment of voters to their political party, he seemed to say, there would have been no secession and no Civil War.

Some readers may think that Alexander finds such a "massive continuity of voter alignment" in the presidential elections from 1840 through 1860 by doing with statistics in 1982 what party leaders and voters did not do in those elections—that is, by combining into one statistical unit the votes cast for separate candidates and parties in certain elections. One example is his combining the votes cast for the Free-Soil party with the votes cast for the Democratic party in 1848, but not in 1852. Another example is his consolidation of the votes cast for the two separate branches of the Democratic party in 1860 and his combining the votes cast for the Republican party with the votes cast for the Constitutional Union party. But one may hazard the guess that even readers who raise those objections will find Alexander's essay original, provocative, and worthy of close study.

Quite different from the main thrusts of Alexander's essay are the perspective and emphasis of "'Politics Seem to Enter Into Everything': Political Culture in the North, 1840–1860," by William Gienapp. The essays by Gienapp and Alexander cover the same chronological period and employ quantitative analysis of voting, but the two essays are not congruent in other respects. Gienapp's concept of "political culture"

---

[2]Thomas B. Alexander, "The Civil War as Institutional Fulfillment," *Journal of Southern History*, 47 (February, 1981), 14.

[3]*Ibid.*, 20–21.

(not defined) encompasses more than voting in popular elections; the evidence he uses includes personal correspondence, diaries, newspapers, and accounts by foreign travelers, in addition to election statistics, all focused primarily on the northern United States. Although the studies by Gienapp and Alexander have different geographical boundaries and employ different sources, it is still striking that two subjects described in both, voters and voting patterns, are portrayed so differently. The voters described in Alexander's essay were so wedded to party labels that they were "almost impervious to rival appeals of candidates or issues," and they "had little sensible choice to make" in the presidential elections of 1856 and 1860, other than to follow either Democratic or anti-Democratic figures. The voters described by Gienapp, however, combined both a high degree of loyalty to political party and the capacity to "make meaningful political decisions" about such issues as the expansion of slavery.

The differences between the voters described by Gienapp and those described by Alexander are matched by dissimilarities in the descriptions of voting patterns by the two historians. Alexander found a pattern of "massive continuity of voter alignment" in the presidential elections from 1840 through 1860, in which "constancy" of voting was more important than change and realignment. Gienapp, on the contrary, finds that a "mass-based party realignment" occurred in the 1850s, a realignment in which the nonsectional Jacksonian party system collapsed and was replaced by the "decidedly sectional," North versus South, Civil War party system.

The bulk of Gienapp's essay is a detailed description of various facets of the political culture of the North in the 1840s and 1850s. That northern political culture is contrasted with the political culture of today; Gienapp notes among other things that politics played a more central role in American life then than it does now, as shown by much higher turnout rates for eligible voters and higher rates for other forms of participation in political activities. It is also likely, he writes, that the electorate then was "more committed, more informed, more issue-conscious" than today.

After describing the northern political culture, Gienapp relates his description to what he calls "the larger analysis of American politics and the coming of the Civil War." He concludes that the political realignment of the 1850s toward a North-South sectionalism was a key development, and he describes the political cultures of North and of South, despite some commonalities, as "strikingly different" in "important ways." Explaining "the ultimate collapse of the normal political process in 1861," Gienapp writes that "one important contributing cause was the interaction between each section's political culture," leading to a "growing sectional crisis." That sectional crisis had to be faced within the country's political system, some aspects of which "weakened the ability of moderate leaders to check the growing forces of extremism in American society." But the basic factor in Gienapp's description of the coming of war appears to be the interaction between the "strikingly different" political cultures of North and South.

Although differences between North and South are also an underlying theme in "Winding Roads to Recovery: The Whig Party from 1844 to 1848," Michael Holt challenges the emphasis traditional historians have placed on them. Holt's masterful broad synthesis, *The Political Crisis of the 1850s*, has already attained the status of a classic, but his focus in this present essay is more restricted than that of Gienapp and Alexander.[4] Holt, in tracing the varying strategies by which different Whig leaders and supporters sought to revive the fortunes of their party during the four years after the defeat of Henry Clay in the presidential election of 1844, makes extensive use of personal correspondence from the 1840s and also employs compilations of voting statistics for those years.

Holt argues "that the Whig party was more robust and its issues more vital" than traditional interpretations suggest. Whig leaders tried several different strategies before they turned only in desperation to a presidential candidate who would say little or nothing about issues— military hero Zachary Taylor. It was only after they concluded that their initial plans to center their campaign either on economic issues or on questions of territorial expansion were doomed to fail that the Whig party turned to Taylor. Holt admits that many southern Whigs by the spring of 1847 pushed Taylor as a candidate who could "neutralize the slavery issue." However, he clearly demonstrates that most Whigs had other concerns.

Differences between North and South over slavery play a part in the essay by Stephen Maizlish, "The Meaning of Nativism and the Cri-

[4]Michael F. Holt, *The Political Crisis of the 1850s* (New York: John Wiley & Sons, 1978).

sis of the Union: The Know-Nothing Movement in the Antebellum North." Maizlish's essay, like that by Holt, concerns a briefer chronological period and a more limited topic than the essays by Alexander and Gienapp. Maizlish centers much of his narrative upon Ohio, using evidence drawn from newspapers, personal correspondence, published records of the Know-Nothing movement, and other such "literary" sources. But he sets his study in a broad historiographical perspective, noting that modern historians have maintained that the Know-Nothing movement contained stronger and more varied opposition to the new immigration of the 1840s and 1850s than some earlier historians had thought. However, that insight by modern historians should not obscure, Maizlish urges, the fact that Know-Nothingism arose in the political environment of the 1850s, an environment that included a strong North-South sectional component, which influenced the development of the Know-Nothing movement.

The political environment in the North was changing in the 1850s, and Maizlish, like Gienapp, describes a fundamental realignment of attitudes and of ideas underway. As part of that realignment, two attitudes became powerful in politics—opposition to immigration and opposition to the spread of slavery to the territories. Maizlish, citing events in Ohio as a case study, pictures a complex relationship between those two attitudes. For some northerners, the two attitudes were rivals and were mutually exclusive, so that a person held either one or the other. But other northerners subscribed to both attitudes simultaneously, more northerners, Maizlish suggests, than some current historians have indicated. Those members of the Know-Nothing movement who held both attitudes ultimately had to choose between the two when, in 1855 and again in 1856, southern members of the movement controlled the national conventions of the American party and prevented the passage of resolutions endorsing the Missouri Compromise. Faced with that situation, most northern members left the Know-Nothing movement and joined the Republican party. Opposition to the spread of slavery to the territories took precedence over opposition to immigration, and the Know-Nothing movement quickly collapsed. Slavery, Maizlish summarizes, "was not the only compelling political question facing America in the 1850s, but it was, nevertheless, the dominant issue of the day and the Know-Nothing movement was deeply affected by it. . . . The ideology, development, and demise of the . . . movement were inseparably intertwined with the slavery issue."

Balancing the essays by Maizlish and Gienapp, which focus on the northern United States and on northerners, the last essay concerns southern secessionists—"'The Surge of Republican Power': Partisan Antipathy, American Social Conflict, and the Coming of the Civil War," by Joel Silbey. Silbey's books on congressional voting behavior in the 1840s and 1850s, on the transformation of antebellum politics, and on the Democratic party, 1860–1868, have made him a well-known and highly respected interpreter of political developments in the mid-nineteenth-century United States. It is appropriate that his essay concludes the volume, for he touches on, and in some cases synthesizes, a number of themes expressed in one or another of the preceding essays.

Silbey seeks to bridge the gap between the findings of two groups of historians, the "new political historians" and the "most recent students of secession." The "new political historians," he writes, have demonstrated the importance of "ethnocultural conflict" in shaping behavior and in producing "the critical voter realignment of the mid-1850s," but few of them have sought to explain the coming of the Civil War. Conversely, "most recent students of secession" have cited sectional confrontation over issues, some of which pertained to slavery, but those historians "have rarely found much place in their explanations for the findings of the new political historians." Silbey notes that one historian, Ronald Formisano, has found that Republicans in Michigan in the 1850s did see a relationship between "ethnocultural matters and the expansion of slavery," integrating "attacks on Catholics with attacks on the slave power into a crusade for white freedom . . . [thereby uniting] Republicans behind an anti-slavery extension, anti-Democratic program." In an analogous manner, Silbey finds that southern secessionists united ethnocultural and slavery-sectional issues in their fears concerning Republicans.

Southern secessionists were primarily Democrats, Silbey maintains, and their fears about Republicans were heavily influenced by the partisan ideology of the Democratic party. With that ideology providing the lens of vision, the southern secessionists perceived, and feared, Republicans as cultural imperialists, crusaders who sought "to change and uplift people" in accord with New England standards, using the power of the state to enforce their mores and culture upon everyone.

In this view, the Republicans, "composed of Free Soilers, Abolitionists, Maine-Lawites, Free-Negroes and Spirit Rappers," sought "to
overthrow Democracy, Catholicism and Slavery." Republicans sought
to impose compulsory state-approved schools, "compulsory temperance," compulsory regulations to make Sunday "a day of sadness and
gloom," and compulsory "laws to bring the white man to the level of
the black." The southern secessionists, in Silbey's words, "saw no differences between conflicts over slavery-extension and conflicts originating in the coming of the immigrant and Catholic." Thus, with
"Lincoln, the interventionist Republican" on the verge of taking control of the federal government, the southern secessionists acted.

The evidence on which Silbey bases much of his description of the
fears held by secessionists is drawn from Democratic newspapers,
northern as well as southern. The use of northern Democratic papers
along with southern reflects Silbey's view that we "are so used to
seeing southern Democrats pulling away from northern Democrats in
the late 1850s that we are in danger of forgetting that despite . . . disagreements between them, both sectional Democratic factions shared
an integrated vision, a common ideology." Some readers may wonder
whether Silbey, in emphasizing this common ideology, has not down-
played factors which led northern Democrats and southern Democrats
to split from each other and run two separate candidates for president
in 1860. But if there are such questions about his interpretation in this
instance, they may have the happy effect of sending all of us back to
examine more closely the sources concerning southern secessionists.

From this summary of the essays by this latest group of historian-
climbers who have scaled the mid-nineteenth-century history peaks, it
is clear that not all the essays agree in all particulars. The most important disagreement concerns whether a fundamental realignment of political organizations and voting took place in the mid-1850s, away from
the earlier division on the basis of two political parties, Democrats versus Whigs, and toward a division on the basis of geography, North versus South. Alexander's essay greatly minimizes such a realignment,
while the essays by Gienapp, Maizlish, and Silbey picture the realignment as one of the central aspects of the 1850s. Other disagreements
between the various essays involve less fundamental issues, and that
lack of agreement on less fundamental issues can be seen as an advantage to the reader—providing the opportunity to observe the varied

ways in which different historians visualize their subjects, as well as the varied types of evidence they employ in doing so. Without seeking to minimize the differences between individual essays, however, one comes away impressed by the considerable areas of agreement.

One of those areas of agreement is that the political party system, with the accompanying ideologies and loyalties it generated or expressed, was a crucially important aspect of life in the 1840s and 1850s. Although Alexander's essay describes continuing loyalty to a political party as a more exclusive key to developments than do any of the other essays, the centrality of the political party system is a prominent theme explicit or implicit in all the essays. For historians investigating political life to find political parties important may seem no more than a truism, but what is suggested here is much more than a truism. For these essays suggest that political parties in the 1840s and the 1850s were the primary agencies through which many persons perceived reality and organized their ideas about the world in which they lived.

A second area of agreement, reflected explicitly or implicitly, is that ethnocultural issues formed a basic and fundamental ingredient in the political life of the 1840s and 1850s. These issues are described frequently in terms of hostility and conflict between different ethnocultural groups. That historians in the United States in the second half of the twentieth century are sensitive to ethnocultural issues and conflicts may seem an obvious example of the way the environment of historians is reflected in their perceptions of the past. Or, from another perspective, it may seem simply that evidence of ethnocultural conflict is so pervasive in the surviving sources from the 1840s and the 1850s that any conscientious historian would be impressed by it. In any case, the emphasis upon ethnocultural issues in many of the essays constitutes an important area of agreement in their description of the 1840s and the 1850s.

A third area of agreement is the fundamental importance of both ethnocultural conflicts and sectional North-South conflicts (centering particularly on slavery) in the 1840s, the 1850s, and the secession crisis which ended in civil war. That theme is especially prominent and explicit in the essays by Maizlish and Silbey, but it is also present to a lesser extent in the other essays. The description of the way in which both ethnocultural and sectional conflicts were present and were interrelated in the mid-nineteenth-century United States, *both* rather than one *or* the other, seems to be a fundamental contribution made by these essays, and it may turn out to be the most influential contribution.

As a final comment, it is worth noting that one perspective which has proved useful in the study of other aspects of the history of the United States does not receive any major attention in this volume. I refer to the perspective gained by comparing developments or situations or institutions or eras in the United States with their counterparts in other nations. The study of the institution of slavery in the United States, to name one example, has been enormously stimulated during the past two decades by the making of comparisons with slavery in other societies and comparisons with what happened after abolition to former slaves and their descendants in other societies. Might it not be fruitful to investigate in a similar fashion various aspects of the 1840s, the 1850s, the secession movement, and the coming of the Civil War? A few attempts in that direction have been made, but the major studies have not appeared. To undertake those major comparative studies no historians would be better qualified than the authors of the essays in this volume.

WILLIAM E. GIENAPP

"Politics Seem To Enter into Everything": Political Culture in the North, 1840–1860

DESPITE the sweltering August sun, the roads to Springfield were jammed. For several days, in response to a call by Republican leaders, people converged on the Illinois capital to honor Abraham Lincoln, the party's candidate for president and the town's most illustrious citizen. Advertisements for this grand ratification meeting, scheduled for August 8, 1860, had been circulated throughout the state, but the response surprised even the organizers. Participants came not only from central Illinois, but also from distant counties and even neighboring states. Rough-hewn farmers temporarily abandoned their wheat fields to join residents of countless small prairie towns in plodding over the rugged country roads to the capital; there they mingled with celebrants from the state's major cities, many of whom arrived on special trains totaling 180 cars that rolled into town on the morning of the rally. At least 50,000 men, women, and children gathered for the occasion.

It was not a day that those present would soon forget. In the morning a parade of wagons, floats, marching teams, equestrian groups, glee clubs, bands, and county and town delegations replete with cannons, flags, and banners filed by Lincoln's house. The procession stretched almost eight miles. That afternoon speakers from five separate platforms addressed the throng assembled at the state fairgrounds. Singing and cheering rent the air from morning until night. Darkness brought fireworks and a dazzling torchlight display by the Wide Awake clubs, followed by still more speeches. The activity did not subside until well after midnight, when the weary thousands dispersed to begin their journeys home. "The streets were all ablaze with light and enthusiasm," the local Republican newspaper excitedly proclaimed afterward. The day had been a "magnificent spectacle of triumph and joy."[1]

---

[1] *Illinois State Journal*, August 9, 1860; William Hawley Smith, "Old-Time Campaigning and the Story of a Lincoln Campaign Song," *Journal of the Illinois State Histori-*

Historians have long recognized that the American political system underwent fundamental change after 1820, when for the first time politics assumed a central role in American life. Previously deference to social elites and mass indifference characterized the nation's politics; despite suffrage laws sufficiently liberal to allow mass participation, few men were interested in politics, and fewer still actively participated in political affairs. Politics simply did not seem important to most Americans. This situation began to change in the wake of the psychological shock of the panic of 1819, and the subsequent election of Andrew Jackson, with his charismatic personality and controversial policies, further stimulated the transformation. By 1840 the revolution was complete. With the full establishment of the second party system, campaigns were characterized by appeals to the common man, mass meetings, parades, celebrations, and intense enthusiasm, while elections generated high voter participation. In structure and ideology, American politics had been democratized.[2]

This political revolution had important repercussions throughout the nineteenth century, as the new system of mass politics survived the disintegration of the Jacksonian party alignment. Perhaps at no time, however, did politics occupy a more central role in American life than during the period 1840–1860. These two decades witnessed not only the full maturation of the Jacksonian party system, but also its collapse in the 1850s in train with the country's first mass-based party realignment. The Civil War party system, in contrast to its predecessor, was decidedly sectional. The Republican party enjoyed no significant popular support in the South, while the Democratic party won a dis-

_____

cal Society, 13 (April, 1920), 23–32; Theodore Calvin Pease and James G. Randall, eds., The Diary of Orville Hickman Browning (2 vols.; Springfield: Illinois State Historical Library, 1925–33), 1:421–22.

In writing this essay, I have benefited from the criticisms and suggestions of a number of friends and colleagues, for which I am very grateful. Some of the calculations presented in this essay are based on data supplied by the Inter-University Consortium for Political and Social Research, Ann Arbor, Michigan. In addition, Paul Goodman generously shared statistical data for the New England states before 1861. Robert McBain aided with the calculations in Table 3, and Margaret Baker of the Survey Research Center, University of California, Berkeley, rendered invaluable assistance with the design and use of a number of computer programs. The Mabelle McLeod Lewis Foundation, Stanford, California, provided essential financial support.

[2] Richard P. McCormick, "New Perspectives on Jacksonian Politics," American Historical Review, 65 (January, 1960), 288–301; Chilton Williamson, American Suffrage: From Property to Democracy, 1760–1860 (Princeton: Princeton University Press, 1960).

proportionate share of its votes from below the Mason-Dixon Line. It is true, even in the face of this growing sectionalism, that politics in the North and the South shared much in common; in important ways, however, the political cultures of the two sections were strikingly different. Any full explanation of the ultimate breakdown of the democratic process in 1861 must take into account the nature of each section's political culture. This essay examines political culture in the North in the period 1840–1860 as a contribution to the larger analysis of American politics and the coming of the Civil War.

Popular interest in politics deeply impressed Alexis de Tocqueville when he visited America. "It is difficult to say what place is taken up in the life of an inhabitant of the United States by his concern for politics. To take a hand in the regulation of society and to discuss it is his biggest concern and, so to speak, the only pleasure an American knows," he wrote. "If an American were condemned to confine his activity to his own affairs, he would be robbed of one half of his existence; he would feel an immense void in the life which he is accustomed to lead, and his wretchedness would be unbearable." As was so often the case, Tocqueville perceptively discerned a fundamental aspect of American culture. Others made similar observations. In discussing politics during the decade before the Civil War, one widely traveled American commented that "political life to an American citizen has all the fanaticism of religion and all the fascination of gambling."[3] Despite such popular enthusiasm, some men infected by this political fever no doubt shared the lament of one officeholder who, in a moment of despondency, wished that he had nothing to do with politics or politicians. Nevertheless, he confessed that he found it "almost impossible to avoid an interest in the political affairs of the Nation."[4]

Women, too, evinced an interest in politics. Suffrage in the antebellum North was limited to adult males and in most states to adult white males, yet women attended political meetings, listened to speeches, participated in parades (where they were a popular feature

[3] Alexis de Tocqueville, *Democracy in America*, ed. Phillips Bradley (2 vols.; New York: Alfred A. Knopf, 1945), 1:250; Donn Piatt, *Memories of Men Who Saved the Union* (New York: Belford, Clarke & Co., 1877), 141.

[4] Benjamin Brown French, Journal, March 8, 1856, Benjamin Brown French Papers, Library of Congress.

on floats), and joined in party celebrations. To be sure, large numbers of females had no interest in politics or suppressed it in the face of criticism. Yet many others could not resist the attraction politics exerted, even while they sometimes expressed uneasiness over their political involvement. Thus the wife of a prominent California Republican noted in her diary: "I find myself deeply interested in politics this season, though Sister Mattie Cole thinks it sinful of me." Similarly, a former schoolmate of an Indiana congressman, confessing that she had become "that *unenviable* character, a *political woman,*" wrote that the present political crisis had "aroused every feeling of patriotism and justice of which my woman's heart is capable of feeling." Despite misgivings, she could not refrain from exerting her influence on behalf of what she conceived to be right principles.[5] Although they lacked the vote, women could still exercise some authority in politics by pressuring their husbands, brothers, and other menfolk of their families. "If Ladies cannot *vote,*" one woman confidently asserted, "they can at least influence others . . . we *have* influence." Emphasizing that women and children would be in attendance at a party meeting, one Indiana Republican urged that the speaker discuss Democratic support of polygamy. "If the women get down on" the Democrats, he predicted, "'their days are numbered.'"[6]

The best available indicator of the extent of popular interest in politics in pre–Civil War America, as well as the degree to which the political universe of the nineteenth century was unique, is voter turnout. Walter Dean Burnham, in comparing turnout in the nineteenth and twentieth centuries, calculates an average turnout of 75.1 percent in presidential elections for the period 1848–1872 and 65.2 percent for congressional elections in nonpresidential years 1850–1874. Figures for recent American history are a 60 percent turnout in presidential

[5]Catharine Coffin Phillips, *Cornelius Cole, California Pioneer and United States Senator* (San Francisco: John Henry Nash, 1929), 90; A. L. Ruter Deform to William H. English, October 6, 1855, William H. English Papers, Indiana Historical Society.

[6]M. B. Evans to Millard Fillmore, May 11, 1852, Millard Fillmore Papers, Buffalo and Erie County Historical Society; L. [?] F. Maxwell to Henry S. Lane, June 30, 1856, Henry S. Lane Papers, Indiana Historical Society. For examples of partisan appeals directed to women, see the Portland (Maine) *Eastern Argus,* September 7, 1855; Cleveland *True Democrat,* October 11, 1853, *Annals of Cleveland* (59 vols.; Cleveland: Works Progress Administration, 1937–38), 36: 517. For an example of women influencing men on political matters, see Jenny McCall to Lydia, August 12, 1855 [?], Typescript, Thomas Marshall Papers, Indiana Historical Society.

TABLE 1. Estimated Voter Turnout, Northern States, 1840–1860.

	1840S	1840P	1841	1842	1843	1844S	1844P	1845	1846	1847	1848S	1848P	1849
California	—	—	—	—	—	—	—	—	—	—	—	—	—
Connecticut	74.8	75.6	61.9	68.3	73.2	81.4	86.3	77.4	76.7	81.3	81.8	83.7	73.2
Illinois	—	86.0	59.6	69.4	70.8	70.3	77.5	—	64.3	—	60.0	72.1	—
Indiana	86.1	85.9	M	M	77.2	74.8*	85.6	73.7	67.1	73.1	70.5*	79.7	73.8
Iowa	—	—	—	—	—	—	—	—	76.0	78.7	78.4	72.0	64.8
Maine	80.3	81.9	74.1	60.3	40.9	63.6	68.1	50.5	55.4	49.0	58.3	64.4	53.1
Massachusetts	65.9	65.4	57.8	61.7	63.9	70.2	69.2	56.2	54.2	56.7	66.9	72.6	59.3
Michigan	71.0	85.6	66.8	M	59.7	79.5	79.4	52.9	35.8	55.2	74.8	73.8	55.3
New Hampshire	74.0	85.9	71.0	67.2	56.5	65.6	66.4	59.6	71.9	77.2	76.6	62.9	69.2
New Jersey	80.5	80.4	—	M	54.4	82.3	83.9	—	58.2	68.1	73.7	76.9	M
New York	91.8	91.8	74.8	79.6	69.6	92.4	92.1	62.6	73.9	57.8	80.3	79.1	69.6
Ohio	91.7	91.4	69.4	76.6	67.0	91.1	94.0	M	70.1	M	82.7	91.3	63.8
Pennsylvania	59.8	77.5	65.0	—	50.6	74.8	78.2	—	41.5	61.9	70.6	77.5	57.4
Rhode Island	76.6	80.0	46.7	60.9	75.7	26.3	55.5	68.3	62.7	48.6	38.6	43.4	32.7
Vermont	82.3	73.3	69.7	75.6	33.5	75.7	67.4	59.1	62.8	65.5	66.8	63.1	69.4
Wisconsin	—	—	—	—	—	—	—	—	—	—	58.0	66.5	45.3
Weighted mean turnout	79.3	83.4	68.0	72.8	62.0	79.8	82.4	62.0	61.5	62.0	72.9	77.1	63.3

	1850	1851	1852S	1852P	1853	1854	1855	1856S	1856P	1857	1858	1859	1860S	1860P
California	25.3	45.3	68.1	70.9	67.4	60.9	75.0	76.2	79.1	64.5	52.8	64.4	42.8	70.4
Connecticut	76.9	76.7	76.7	81.6	72.2	71.6	73.8	74.8	90.1	69.1	75.5	83.2	91.5	77.5
Illinois	55.7	32.8	65.4	67.1	—	48.8	56.7	74.8	75.4	—	70.1	—	83.4	84.4
Indiana	M	67.8	74.3	80.1	M	75.4	M	86.3	88.3	—	74.3	—	86.6	89.3
Iowa	62.7	42.6	63.4	70.3	38.3	74.3	59.8	72.9	91.1	66.9	76.0	80.5	86.2	86.9
Maine	57.0	—	64.8	56.7	56.9	61.0	73.7	79.8	72.4	63.3	73.2	65.6	78.4	63.8
Massachusetts	66.1	75.0	73.9	67.8	67.1	66.1	67.7	76.0	82.3	61.8	55.3	49.5	75.6	75.7
Michigan	51.9	39.2	75.0	74.6	53.9	63.5	—	83.9	84.0	56.4	71.9	67.1	82.4	82.4
New Hampshire	67.5	69.9	72.1	60.7	67.4	63.7	76.2	78.1	82.0	76.4	78.9	79.9	82.3	75.8
New Jersey	69.4	52.4	72.0	73.1	61.2	63.8	—	75.3	75.5	—	68.1	72.8	82.3	81.6
New York	72.6	66.1	85.0	84.5	59.1	73.4	66.9	88.8	89.1	64.1	77.5	69.8	91.3	91.5
Ohio	71.0	73.1	76.3	89.5	70.3	71.2	71.9	81.9	89.0	73.6	74.6	74.5	83.9	90.0
Pennsylvania	55.3	70.7	63.3	72.9	51.4	67.1	56.0	72.7	79.2	61.1	60.8	55.8	77.7	75.2
Rhode Island	16.6	47.7	63.6	60.3	66.8	53.5	43.3	57.2	65.9	31.5	37.1	39.6	72.7	62.4
Vermont	62.4	57.5	61.7	56.1	61.1	56.6	53.9	59.0	63.9	50.7	53.8	57.2	60.1	55.5
Wisconsin	52.6	47.7	62.1	62.4	45.6	45.4	52.6	78.9	80.8	55.2	68.0	66.8	78.0	78.1
Weighted mean turnout	62.5	62.9	72.4	75.3	59.7	66.1	64.2	79.2	82.8	63.8	69.3	66.3	81.3	82.0

NOTES: Minnesota (admitted 1858) and Oregon (admitted 1859) omitted; S = state election; P = presidential election; M = missing returns.
*Incomplete returns

elections 1948–1960 and 44.1 percent in congressional off-year elections 1950–1962.[7]

Burnham's figures lump several presidential elections together and combine the North and the South. Table 1 gives the estimated voter turnout for the 16 northern states for the period 1840–1860, including estimates for off-year elections.[8] Voter participation was strikingly high. The mean turnout for all elections was 70.3 percent. Turnout in presidential elections ranged from an estimated 75.3 percent in 1852 to 83.4 percent in the famous Log Cabin campaign of 1840, with an average of 80.5 percent.[9] The mean turnout in nonpresidential elections, though lower (67.3 percent), is still impressive. These high turnouts testify to mass interest in politics. Equally important is the relatively low drop-off from presidential to off-year elections. In our modern era characterized by widespread political apathy, presidential elections with their extensive media attention garner many more voters than do off-year elections. Although antebellum presidential elections generally did have a higher turnout than other elections, the drop-off was not nearly as sharp as is true today. Not only did northerners vote in greater numbers relative to the total eligible voting population, but this widespread interest extended beyond national campaigns to state and local politics. In fact, the average turnout in off-year elections in the North exceeded the modern turnout in presidential elections. A larger proportion of the antebellum electorate consisted of persistent voters, who turned out election after election, year after year. Casual, indifferent voters—those marginally involved men who appeared at the polls only in times of intense political excitement and then dropped out of the political system again—were significantly less prevalent in the pre–Civil War period.

Although turnouts were high during this period, variations over time were discernible. In the waning years of the second party system, as party organizations decayed and political chaos prevailed, turnout

[7] Walter Dean Burnham, "The Changing Shape of the American Political Universe," *American Political Science Review*, 59 (March, 1965), 7–28.

[8] See the Appendix for a discussion of how these figures were calculated.

[9] Nationally the highest turnout in a presidential election during the antebellum decades occurred in 1840, when an estimated 78.0 percent of the eligible electorate cast ballots. McCormick, "New Perspectives on Jacksonian Politics," 292, 296.

was somewhat lower. Beginning with realignment in 1854, turnout increased, and with the emergence of the new third party system it remained impressively high, climaxing with the crucial 1860 Lincoln election, when an estimated 82.0 percent of the eligible voters cast ballots. The mean turnout for these three periods was: 1848–1853 (end of the second party system), 67.8 percent; 1854–1856 (realignment), 72.5 percent; 1857–1860 (end of realignment and beginning of the third party system), 71.9 percent.

The realignment of the 1850s revitalized the political system: mass interest in politics, already substantial, increased in every northern state, and it grew stronger as the decade wore on. This increase may have reflected partially the competitiveness of the new party system, although by the end of the decade some states, such as Vermont, were already becoming solidly one-party states. Probably as important was simply the maturing of the new party system. As voters began to form stronger identities with their party, as the issues between the parties began to crystallize, as politicians adjusted to the new party system with its different conditions, and as the political crisis of the decade took on an ever-increasing momentum, the response of the electorate grew stronger.

Within this general pattern, voter turnout varied considerably from state to state. Table 2 gives the average turnout for each northern state during the period 1840–1860 and its rank (from highest to lowest turnout) relative to the other states. Turnout was lowest in Rhode Island, the only northern state that still retained a severely limited suffrage. There, restrictive voting requirements, corruption and intimidation, and a powerful antidemocratic tradition combined not only to disfranchise many adult males but also to lessen greatly public interest in politics. Ohio, in contrast, had the highest average turnout, followed closely by neighboring Indiana. In part Ohio's high turnout rate reflected the fact that politically it was an intensely competitive state, while beginning in 1851 Indiana allowed immigrants to vote before they became citizens, which helped swell that state's active electorate. Still, liberal suffrage laws cannot entirely explain the participation of Hoosier voters. Wisconsin, despite equally generous laws governing alien suffrage, had one of the lowest average turnouts of all the free states.

TABLE 2. Mean Voter Turnout, Northern States, 1840–1860.

State	Percentage Mean Turnout	Rank
California	62.7	13
Connecticut	77.3	3
Illinois	66.0	8
Indiana	78.5	2
Iowa	70.6	6
Maine	64.1	11
Massachusetts	65.9	9
Michigan	63.7	12
New Hampshire	71.7	5
New Jersey	69.3	7
New York	74.5	4
Ohio	79.2	1
Pennsylvania	65.4	10
Rhode Island	53.1	16
Vermont	62.0	14
Wisconsin	58.9	15
North	70.3	

No consistent pattern emerges from these figures: voter participation varied widely among the urban, industrial states and also among the rural, agricultural states; some states with few immigrants, such as New Hampshire, ranked relatively high in average turnout; others, such as neighboring Vermont, were low. The same was true of states with heavy immigrant populations: Ohio and New York, for example, ranked near the top, while California and Wisconsin occupied positions near the bottom. Nor was there any sectional pattern. Eastern and western states were scattered throughout the high, medium, and low categories of average turnout.

Turnout in these two decades was among the highest in American history. Historians and political scientists are cognizant of the strikingly different rates of voting in the nineteenth and twentieth centuries, but no general agreement prevails concerning the reasons for this difference. Several analysts, most notably Burnham, by focusing primarily on the closing decades of the previous century, point to the change in turnout after 1896 as evidence of a profound alteration in the

nature of American political culture.[10] Other scholars, relying principally on knowledge of the contemporary voters, deny that the nineteenth-century electorate was more politically involved and informed
than its modern counterpart.[11] Philip E. Converse, the leading proponent of this view, has specifically challenged the accuracy of turnout
figures calculated for the earlier century. He posits instead that the difference in the rate of voting in the two centuries arose not from greater
popular interest in politics or from a markedly different political culture in the years before 1900, but from two much more mundane factors: reform of the laws regulating voting during the Progressive era
and "the prevalence of voting fraud." Converse hypothesizes that consistently 5 to 10 percent of the votes counted in nineteenth-century
elections were fraudulent. Contending that Americans in these years
were more amused than angered by widespread ballot-box stuffing, he
argues that by the final decades of the century political corruption was
"blatant" and seemingly "rested on a surprising degree of public indul-
gence." Only after the turn of the century did this "atmosphere of in-
dulgence" give way to one of "moral indignation." Thus, according to
Converse's undocumented argument, nineteenth-century Americans
did not vote in significantly higher proportions than their contemporary descendants; they were simply more skillful at padding registration rolls, buying votes, engaging in repeat voting, and in various other
ingenious ways stuffing the ballot boxes.[12]

Because he is intent on rebutting Burnham's argument concerning

[10] Burnham, "Changing Shape of the American Political Universe"; Walter Dean
Burnham, *Critical Elections and the Mainsprings of American Politics* (New York: W. W.
Norton & Co., 1970); Walter Dean Burnham, "Theory and Voting Research: Some Re-
flections on Converse's 'Change in the American Electorate,'" *American Political Science Review*, 68 (September, 1974), 1002–23; Richard Jensen, *The Winning of the Midwest* (Chicago: University of Chicago Press, 1971); Paul Kleppner, *The Third Electoral
System, 1853–1892* (Chapel Hill: University of North Carolina Press, 1979).

[11] Philip E. Converse, "Change in the American Electorate," Angus Campbell and
Philip E. Converse, eds., *The Human Meaning of Social Change* (New York: Russell
Sage Foundation, 1972), 263–301; Philip E. Converse, "Comment on Burnham's 'Theory and Voting Research,'" *American Political Science Review*, 68 (September, 1974),
1024–27; and Jerrold G. Rusk, "The American Electoral Universe: Speculation and Evidence," *ibid.*, 1028–49.

[12] Converse, "Change in the American Electorate," 282, 284, and *passim*; Converse,
"Comment on Burnham's 'Theory and Voting Research,'" 1024–25. Converse's estimate
of the extent of fraudulent voting represents a considerable retreat from his earlier suggestion that, by the turn of the century, the figure was anywhere from 30 to 75 percent.

the changing nature of the American political universe, Converse focuses his attention exclusively on the era after 1870. The antebellum period, however, is equally critical to his thesis. His denial of a more politically active electorate requires that the projected rate of illegal voting show no significant geographic or temporal variation. The high figures contained in Table 1 are not the product of a few counties reporting nearly 100 percent turnouts. Instead, one observes turnouts substantially higher than those of the present century in virtually all northern counties during these two decades. Consequently, for Converse's thesis to be valid, the turnouts in virtually *every* county for *every* election must reflect substantial fraud. If systematic, pervasive electoral dishonesty cannot account for these high turnouts, then Converse's insistence that the American political universe has remained largely immutable is untenable. It is therefore important to examine the validity of his hypothesis for the last decades before the Civil War.

Converse's first causal factor—the reform of voting laws in the Progressive era, which he points to as deflating twentieth-century turnouts—was of limited importance in the antebellum period. Registration of voters, though not unknown before 1861, was not common.[13] The assumption, however, that had requirements existed they would have severely deflated antebellum voting rates is open to serious question. The New England states, which enacted registration laws earlier, ranged widely in their rates of participation, with Connecticut virtually at the top and Vermont essentially at the bottom (Rhode Island's restricted suffrage makes its experience less relevant). Voting in Portland, Maine, provides additional evidence that registration did not seriously restrict turnout. In the 1850s Portland, like several other northern cities, was subject to deliberately cumbersome registration requirements imposed by the rural-dominated state legislature in order to limit immigrant voting. Registration requirements, however, proved no barrier to polling a full vote when important, deeply felt issues were at stake. Turnout dramatically rose after 1850 with the injection of the liquor issue into the city's politics, and the 1852 municipal contest produced the heaviest vote yet polled, despite the fact that the balloting took place in a driving snowstorm. The tally three years later

---

[13] Joseph P. Harris, *Registration of Voters in the United States* (Washington, D.C.: Brookings Institution, 1929), 65–89.

in another bitterly contested mayoral election eclipsed earlier turnouts, as both sides rounded up every available vote, including, according to one reporter, "the lame, the halt and the blind."[14]

New York furnishes the best test of the impact of registration requirements on turnout. An 1840 state registration law for cities was largely ignored; in 1859, the legislature passed a new statute that tightened registration requirements and, more importantly, extended them to every county. Yet statewide turnout in the 1860 presidential election actually increased compared with 1856; turnout declined following implementation of the law in only 9 of the state's 60 counties. Increases occurred in all regions of the state and in both urban and rural counties. Indeed, the 1860 turnout was the highest of any election in the state up to that time. Whatever their impact on today's apathetic voters, registration requirements apparently worked little hardship on the committed and involved mid-century electorate.

The other part of Converse's thesis—systematic voting fraud—is more relevant to antebellum elections. Without question, some fraudulent voting did occur. A few cases are well documented. One notorious example was the 1856 Pennsylvania state election, when illegal voting in Philadelphia enabled the Democrats to triumph over a joint Republican-American ticket. Contemporary observers immediately raised the cry of fraud, and subsequent testimony before a congressional investigating commmittee established that as many as 4,000 illegal votes were polled in the metropolis.[15] Nevertheless, this figure, which represents the maximum possible fraud in the city, constituted less than 1 percent of the total vote cast in the state. If sizable fraud occurred in other Pennsylvania counties, it escaped the notice of *all* observers at the time; considering the immediate outcry over the Philadelphia totals, as well as the close scrutiny of the statewide results by political commentators of all persuasions (since all agreed that the Pennsylvania contest would determine the outcome of the national election), the allegation that other counties' totals reflect similar fraud is simply not credible.

A more congenial example for Converse's purposes is Indiana,

[14] Portland *Transcript*, April 10, 1852, April 7, 1855.
[15] Francis P. Blair to Montgomery Blair, Friday [October 17?, 1856], Blair Family Papers, Library of Congress; New York *Evening Post*, October 8, 22, November 6, 1856;

where illegal voting swelled the state's record turnouts. The documentary evidence is clear that Republicans, angered by Democratic achievements in this field of endeavor, decided in 1856 to poll as many illegal votes as possible until the opposition agreed to electoral reform.[16] Several additional points, however, should be noted. First, the possibility of illegal voting was much higher in the October state election than in presidential elections. Any voter colonized from another state (the most common complaint) in November would necessarily deflate the turnout in his home state. Second, even in Indiana, which provided the most extreme example, the extent of fraud almost certainly did not reach Converse's stipulated level. The most credible accusations of illegal voting followed the state election in October, 1856. Careful observers placed the number of fraudulent votes at less than 5,000, or approximately 2.2 percent of the total vote cast, which even making generous allowance for error is well below Converse's minimum figure.[17] That other elections in Indiana during these years did not precipitate similar vociferous protests suggests that the extent of illegal voting in 1856 was unusual. Even with this smattering of rural corruption deducted, the state's turnout in the antebellum period still dramatically exceeded that of the present era.

The 1856 elections in Pennsylvania and Indiana furnish the strongest evidence available from these decades to bolster Converse's hypothesis. That neither example meets even his minimum level of illegal voting illustrates how untenable his interpretation is. Illegal voting in these decades was neither widespread nor significant. This is hardly surprising in view of the popular values of the period. Whatever the situation by the end of the century, Converse's assertion that the popular attitude toward illegal voting was one of amusement finds little sup-

Pittsburgh *Gazette*, October 18, 20, 21, 1856; John W. Forney to James Buchanan, October 3, 1856, William Hirst to Buchanan, October 12, 16, 1856, James Buchanan Papers Historical Society of Pennsylvania.

[16] Dr. Patrick Henry Jameson, Memoirs, Typescript, Ch. 6, Indiana Historical Society; Calvin Fletcher, Diary, September 15, 24, 25, 28, October 16, 25, 1856, Indiana Historical Society.

[17] Samuel W. Parker to Ignatius Brown, October 22, 1856, quoted in Roger H. Van Bolt, "The Rise of the Republican Party in Indiana, 1855–1856," *Indiana Magazine of History*, 51 (September, 1955), 218; Indianapolis *Journal*, October 20, 1856, quoted in the Cincinnati *Commercial*, October 22, 1856; Charles James to Edwin D. Morgan, October 27, 1856, Edwin D. Morgan Papers, New York State Library.

port in the antebellum sources. The mere hint of such tactics generated strong protests in the newspapers and in private correspondence. Truth and honesty were, to say the least, more deeply respected and upheld in the years before the Civil War than in recent times. Even a casual reading of newspapers before 1861 amply reveals that northern public opinion did not condone, implicitly or explicitly, electoral dishonesty. The dispute over the Pennsylvania election of 1838, which gained the colorful though inaccurate title of the Buckshot War, demonstrated the public's commitment to procedural norms. Similarly, protests in the mid-1850s against the voting frauds perpetrated by Missourians in the Kansas territorial elections revealed how deeply violations of the principles of republican government were resented.[18]

Most complaints of fraudulent voting in the North before the Civil War focused on immigrants in the large cities. Mass naturalizations shortly before an election were standard, as each party herded would-be new voters, a number of whom did not meet the legal residency requirements, before politically sympathetic judges. Discontent over such tactics was not confined to native-born voters. In disgust one Irishman described New York City as "a sort of university for educating the rising generation in the endless variety of means of cheating the public out of their votes and places of Emolument."[19] Still, assertions that illegal voting flourished in the cities are greatly exaggerated. The idea of widespread ballot-box stuffing in cities, principally by immigrants (especially the Irish), is one of the most persistent misconceptions concerning antebellum political culture.

After correcting for the year effect, an analysis of turnout in New York shows that urban counties consistently ranked near the bottom.[20] The four counties composing metropolitan New York all were in the bottom ten, averaging more than 12 percent below the state's median turnout (Table 3). Another significant urban area, Erie County (Buf-

[18]Charles M. Snyder, *The Jacksonian Heritage: Pennsylvania Politics, 1833–1848* (Harrisburg: Pennsylvania Historical and Museum Commission, 1958), 131–35; New York *Tribune*, December 11, 12, 22, 25, 1854, April 17, 18, 20, 23, 27, 1855.

[19]Richard O'Gorman to William Smith O'Brien, January 1, 1859, December 12, 1852; Michael Doheny to O'Brien, August 20, 1858. I am indebted to Kerby A. Miller for copies of these letters.

[20]The technique is described in John L. McCarthy and John W. Tukey, "Exploratory Analysis of Aggregate Voting Behavior: Presidential Elections in New Hampshire, 1896–1972," *Social Science History*, 2 (Spring, 1978), 292–331.

TABLE 3. Turnout in New York Counties with More Than One-Fourth
Naturalized Voters, 1848–1860.

County	Percentage Naturalized Voters	Percentage Mean Turnout	Percentage County Effect	Rank
New York	48	69.6	−6.6	52
Kings	44	64.5	−11.7	57
Erie	43	73.3	−2.9	43
Richmond	36	60.3	−15.9	59
Albany	33	80.4	4.2	10
Clinton	30	76.5	0.3	28
Monroe	27	73.7	−2.5	38
Oneida	27	77.1	0.9	20
State Mean	21	76.2		
N = 60				

falo), ranked forty-third, and, moreover, the city of Buffalo usually had a lower turnout than the surrounding country townships. The only major urban center with a high average turnout was Albany County, which ranked tenth. Of the state's eight counties where one-fourth or more of the voters were foreign born, only three had average turnouts above the statewide median.

Comparison of the rates of participation of native-born and naturalized voters in New York elections between 1850 and 1860 reveals why turnout was lower in urban areas. The difference in the proportion of each group that cast ballots was somewhat larger in rural townships than city wards, but in both turnout was markedly higher among voters born in the United States. This relationship pertained in almost every election, although the widest differences occurred in nonpresidential elections (Table 4). Because urban areas generally contained proportionately more naturalized voters, turnout in the state's cities consistently lagged behind that of the countryside. In Iowa as well, native-born voters displayed a greater tendency to vote than naturalized voters (Table 5).[21] As a group, foreign-born citizens were slower to exercise

[21] New York and Iowa were the only northern states to distinguish between native-born and naturalized citizens when enumerating voters. Because naturalized voters were

TABLE 4. Estimated Percentages of Native-Born and Naturalized Voters Casting Ballots: New York, 1850–1860.

	Wards (87)		Townships (273)		Counties (60)	
	Native	Naturalized	Native	Naturalized	Native	Naturalized
1850	72%	42%	77%	57%	75%	67%
1851	—	—	—	—	71	57
1852	88	65	88	71	91	82
1853	62	50	58	46	66	56
1854	79	66	74	61	83	59
1855	61	71	66	62	81	31
1856	85	88	89	78	91	82
1857	63	62	62	55	66	56
1858	70	73	77	74	83	58
1859	—	—	—	—	81	30
1860	90	84	91	86	91	82
Mean	74	67	76	66	80	60

TABLE 5. Estimated Percentages of Native-Born and Naturalized Voters Casting Ballots: Iowa, 1854–1860.

	Counties	
	Native	Naturalized
1854	73%	84%
1856S	77	40
1856P	92	75
1857	72	33
1858	75	82
1859	81	84
1860	89	58
Mean	80	65
N = 64		

NOTE: S = state election; P = presidential election.

TABLE 6. Pearson Product Moment Correlations:
Percentage of Aliens and Turnout.

| | New York | | | Iowa |
	Wards	Towns	Counties	Counties
1848P	−.09	−.06	−.36	
1849			−.16	
1850	−.35*	−.23*	−.31	
1851			−.05	
1852P	−.17	−.26*	−.24	.28
1853	−.31†	−.18*	−.24	
1854	−.33*	−.27*	−.33	.06
1855	−.21‡	−.11‡	−.46	
1856S				−.29
1856P	.00	−.25*	−.24	−.08
1857	−.27†	−.11‡	−.24	.01
1858	−.16	−.14†	−.33	.06
1859			−.46	−.04
1860	−.10	−.09	−.24	−.31
N	87	273	60	64

NOTES: P = presidential election; S = state election.
*Significant at the .001 level
†Significant at the .01 level
‡Significant at the .05 level

their political privileges than were the native born. The patterns of turnout in New York and Iowa suggest in addition that factors unique to each state's political system were important in mobilizing foreign-born voters.

Contemporaries attributed illegal voting primarily to the foreign

tallied separately in the 1855 New York state census but not in 1845, it seems unwise to extend these estimates back beyond 1850. Similarly, the rapid growth of Iowa's population between 1850 and 1855 makes estimates based on the 1856 state census figures risky for the years before 1854. For an explanation of the technique of ecological regression from which these estimates are derived, see E. Terrence Jones, "Ecological Inference and Electoral Analysis," *Journal of Interdisciplinary History*, 2 (Winter, 1972), 249–62; J. Morgan Kousser, "Ecological Regression and the Analysis of Past Politics," *ibid.*, 4 (Autumn, 1973), 237–62; and W. Phillips Shively, "'Ecological' Inference: The Use of Aggregate Data to Study Individuals," *American Political Science Review*, 63 (December, 1969), 1183–96.

born. Illegal immigrant voting was of two quite different varieties: receiving naturalization papers without meeting the five-year residency requirement or voting while unnaturalized or underage; and multiple voting. The most common fraud, premature naturalization, would not swell the turnout figures for New York or Iowa, since both native-born and naturalized voters (whether "legitimate" or not) were included in the census of voters. Thus only the other types of fraud could increase turnout. The absence of a positive relationship between the proportion of aliens and turnout in these two states is consistent with the thesis that illegal immigrant voting, at least of the latter kind, was not widespread (Table 6). The same situation prevailed in Ohio, Illinois, and Pennsylvania, where the presence of large numbers of immigrants also reduced rather than increased turnout (Table 7). The conclusion seems inescapable: complaints of illegal voting, both urban and rural, greatly exaggerated the amount of electoral fraud in this period.

Whatever higher turnouts indicate about the nature of northern political culture before the Civil War, no persuasive reasons exist to question the general reliability of these figures. Hypotheses that in-

TABLE 7. Pearson Product Moment Correlations: Turnout and Percentage of Foreign-born, 1848–1860.

	Ohio	Pennyslvania	Illinois
1848S	−.28	−.69	
1848P	−.23	−.70	.03
1850	−.33	−.57	−.38
1852S	−.37	−.61	
1852P	−.54	−.64	−.33
1853	−.35	−.41	
1854	−.33	−.54	−.38
1855	−.30	−.47	−.25
1856S	−.11	−.46	
1856P	−.63	−.61	−.51
1857	−.41	−.60	
1858	−.33	−.29	−.22
1860S	−.35	−.60	
1860P	−.49	−.59	−.61
N (counties)	88	63	99

NOTE: S = state election; P = presidential election.

voke massive, systematic fraud to account for wider political participation before 1861 are without factual basis. We must look elsewhere for the origins of mass political involvement in the North before the Civil War.

One important reason for mass interest in politics was the party system's social function as popular entertainment. Because entertainment was relatively limited in the antebellum period, political meetings were designed to be—and the audience expected them to be—entertaining as well as informative. Men in all parties invested great emotion in a campaign. They celebrated victories with an exuberance today more typically reserved for sporting events. Some of the more zealous risked more than emotions: betting on the outcomes of elections was common, and normally after the votes were counted large sums of money changed hands. Even contemporary sports contests were subject to political intrusions. At the conclusion of a ballgame in the summer of 1856 between Ellington and Frewsburgh, New York, the Ellington team gave three tremendous cheers for John C. Frémont, the Republican presidential candidate, before leaving the field.[22] Parades, political clubs, bands and glee clubs, marching associations, pole raisings, bonfires and mass rallies, barbeques and picnics, debates and stump speaking were all intended both to entertain and to generate interest and enthusiasm not only among the party faithful, but also among the less-committed observers. One Whig congressman acknowledged that it was a hardship for many voters to attend rallies, but added that "the fun, the joy, the excitement, the vim and go of it all, repaid them for the loss of time and the necessary expenditures of money and energy it required."[23]

To the modern observer, the numbers involved in these demonstrations seem incredible. Over a quarter of a million persons witnessed a Republican parade in New York City during the 1860 campaign. In Philadelphia in 1856 Charles Francis Adams spoke to a mass meeting that was larger than half the eligible voters of that city. Relative to the population, far more Americans attended political meetings

---

[22] Jamestown (N.Y.) *Journal*, July 18, 1856. Perhaps the Ellington team needed something to cheer about, since they had lost both games.

[23] "The Humors of Early Politics," MS, Typescript, Benjamin S. Parker Papers, Indiana State Library. Also see Albert J. White to Thomas Ewing, October 12, 1852, Ewing Family Papers, Library of Congress.

in the antebellum period than do today. From 1840 on, every presidential campaign produced enormous rallies that attracted participants from a wide geographic area. Local meetings were even more frequent. According to one 1856 campaign reporter in Philadelphia, there were "ward meetings and mass meetings and committee meetings every day and every night" and seemingly "at every hour in the day and night."[24]

The Whigs' revolutionary Log Cabin campaign of 1840 popularized party songs as a new ingredient of American politics. Glee clubs singing a repertoire of partisan tunes quickly became standard features of political contests, especially those for the presidency. Several party songsters were published during these two decades, and newspapers gave additional circulation to the most popular songs.[25] George W. Clark, the author of a number of political melodies, stressed their value in rousing popular excitement. Clark had an interest in promoting them, but another man, after attending a political club meeting, reported that he had "a capital social time—sung lots of campaign songs."[26] Partisan songs were not always devoid of content. Many contained references to party symbols, such as hard cider in 1840, or invoked party code words, as for example the numerous references to freedom in Republican songs. Even if the lyrics were merely delightful nonsense, as they often were, these tunes fulfilled their main purpose, which was to provide entertainment and generate enthusiasm while lampooning the opposition. "Nobody cared how sorry the doggerel might be," one western politician recalled, "if it contained a hit at the

[24] Allan Nevins, *The Emergence of Lincoln* (2 vols.; New York: Charles Scribner's Sons, 1950), 2:305; Charles Francis Adams, Diary, October 9, 1856, Adams Family Papers, Massachusetts Historical Society; Philadelphia correspondence, *National Intelligencer*, October 11, 1856.

[25] Examples include: *Whig Songs for 1844* (New York: New York Tribune, 1844); E. D. Howard and J. H. Clare, *The Clarion of Freedom: A Collection of Free Soil Songs* (Cleveland: Smead & Cowles, 1848); *Scott and Graham Melodies* (New York: Huestis & Cozans, 1852); *Fillmore and Donelson Songs for the Campaign* (New York: Robert M. DeWitt, 1856); *The Fremont Songster* (New York: H. S. Riggs & Co., 1856); *The Wide Awake Vocalist; or, Railsplitters' Song Book* (New York: E. A. Daggett, 1860).

[26] George W. Clark to George W. Cheever, November 25, 1856, George W. Cheever Papers, American Antiquarian Society; Walter Van Tilburg Clark, ed., *The Journals of Alfred Doten, 1849–1903* (3 vols.; Reno: University of Nevada Press, 1973), 1:306, 308. Also see Pease and Randall, eds., *Diary of Orville Hickman Browning*, 1:74; William Foster to John H. George, August 5, 1852, John H. George Papers, New Hampshire Historical Society.

opposite party, its candidates or some one of its leaders, or a rattling chorus." Thus in 1844 Whigs sang to the tune of "Old Dan Tucker": "Out of the way, you're all unlucky / Polk can't come in with old Kentucky / With a ring dang da and a ring dang daddy." When news arrived in Springfield on election night, 1860, that Lincoln had been elected, Republicans gathered in the town square spontaneously struck up the chorus of "Ain't you glad you joined the Republicans?"; it was one of the most popular songs of the just-completed campaign. A few party leaders viewed these songs with some embarrassment. Years later one Illinois office holder included among the "horrible inflictions" of antebellum politics "campaign glee clubs—male and female—singing ridiculous party ditties through their noses." Be that as it may, beginning in 1840, whatever the quality of the lyrics and singing, music played an integral part in mass-oriented presidential contests.[27]

In the western states, where a less-decorous form of campaigning prevailed, political barbeques were a popular way of combining politics and pleasure. One participant described such an event in California during the 1856 campaign. On the day preceding the meeting, men dug a trench six feet wide, forty to sixty feet long, and four feet deep to roast a whole ox, sheep, pigs, and quarters of beef. As the meat roasted all night, the organizers prepared provisions for thousands of people.

> Bread was brought on by the cart load. Vegetables in great variety were prepared & every thing else, that was necessary to appease the appetite of ravenous politicians, was provided. After stump speakers harangued a few hours & crowds had listened till they were "right smart" hungry, dinner is announced. Then hurrah for a rush! Away they scamper for the table. Then comes the battle of knives & forks. Beef disappears! Potatoes follow! Venison grows scarce! The hungry appease their hunger! Every thing takes [tastes?] good, first rate. The boys amuse themselves by throwing what is left at each other. . . . After dinner they again resort to the speaker's stand & listen till dark, when hoarse and weary they go home, every body satisfied that the success of his party is sure & that the Union is safe.[28]

Rural life was hard and monotonous in antebellum America. Political events provided a welcome respite from drudgery and social isolation,

[27]"The Humors of Early Politics," Benjamin S. Parker Papers; Thomas J. McCormack, ed., *Memoirs of Gustave Koerner, 1809–1896* (2 vols.; Cedar Rapids: Torch Press, 1909), 1:598.

[28]Francis E. Prevaux to his parents, November 4, 1856, Francis E. Prevaux Papers,

a chance for men to let off steam without feeling that their time had been spent frivolously.

Whether such events were conducive to a careful discussion of the issues is problematic. Campaign hoopla generated popular interest, but at times this pageantry took precedence over the dissemination of political information. Consequently, some observers sharply criticized these practices. One confessed his astonishment at "these political displays, processions and the like, gotten up as they are for the express purpose of entraping the floating weekminded vacillating class." The prominent clergyman Edward Everett Hale complained of the Republicans' use in the 1856 campaign of a mammoth tent, complete with a traveling blacksmith orator and a glee club, to attract public attention. "This is putting politics on just the level of Circus Riding," he wrote in disgust.[29] The actions of Preston King, a shrewd politician with a firm grasp of mass sentiment, provided a better comment on the nature of antebellum politics. While Hale protested, King was accompanying the tent and glee club throughout his home county, delivering political speeches.

Several other factors sustained mass political participation. One was mere force of habit.[30] Once they developed an abiding interest in politics, men frequently maintained it throughout their lives. At the same time, they transmitted this commitment to their sons. Also important was the sense of association, the sheer excitement of waging a vigorous campaign, and the genuine enjoyment of victory after a hard battle. One foreign traveler commented (with some amazement) that American elections "struck me as a sort of political game or race; and the spirit which impels these gamblers and wrestlers on this scene of action, is often little better than that of the ordinary gambling-houses." In discussing the loyalty of men to their party, one newspaper perceptively emphasized "the sympathy engendered by association—of sharing alike the joys of success and the regrets of defeat." The presence of

---

Bancroft Library, University of California, Berkeley. Also see Clark, ed., *Journals of Alfred Doten*, 1:309; and William Eldon Baringer, "Campaign Technique in Illinois—1860," *Transactions of the Illinois State Historical Society* (1932), 253, 265.

[29] John McCrackan to Lottie, October 29, 1852, John McCrackan Papers, Bancroft Library, University of California, Berkeley; Edward Everett Hale, Journal, August 6, 13, 1856, Edward Everett Hale Papers, New York State Library.

[30] John Weidman to William Bigler, October 3, 1852, William Bigler Papers, Historical Society of Pennsylvania.

a strong opposition further stimulated popular interest.[31] In fact, when elections ceased to be competitive, party unity frequently deteriorated into factional squabbling while voter turnout plummeted.[32] Elections in this period tended to be close and bitterly fought, thereby heightening voters' involvement.

Frequency of elections also served to maintain popular interest. Often state elections did not coincide with national contests, and balloting for city, county, and township offices took place at still another time. Noting that there had been six separate elections in one year, a New Haven lawyer understandably complained that there were "vastly too many elections" in the city. "Frequent elections keep us in hot water," Edward Everett, the famous Massachusetts conservative, admitted, yet he saw benefits as well: "Our eternal elections are a safety valve, & stand us instead of an occasional revolution."[33] As is true today, mass interest was normally highest in presidential campaigns but sometimes voter participation in particularly hard-fought state or local elections exceeded that of even presidential contests. Whatever a state's political calendar, frequent elections gave prominence to political activity throughout much of the year.

The infusion of religion into politics, a phenomenon that began in the 1820s and became even more pronounced after 1840, also stirred intense mass interest. From its inception the Whig party appealed to the evangelical segments of society, and the Republican party continued this tradition.[34] The revivals that swept the North in the 1820s

---

[31] Fredrika Bremer, *The Homes of the New World*, trans. Mary Howitt (2 vols.; New York: Harper & Brothers, 1853), 2:410–11; Jamestown *Journal*, February 13, 1857.

[32] John Slidell to James Buchanan, October 18, 1854, Buchanan Papers; Rutherford B. Hayes to Sardis Birchard, November 3, 1852, Charles R. Williams, ed., *Diary and Letters of Rutherford Birchard Hayes* (5 vols.; Columbus: Ohio State Archaeological and Historical Society, 1922–26), 1:429.

[33] Joseph Sheldon, Jr., to Alexander H. Holley, April 14, 1857, quoted in Robert D. Parmet, "The Know-Nothings in Connecticut" (Ph.D. dissertation, Columbia University, 1966), 31; Edward Everett to Sir Henry Holland, June 25, 1854, Copy, Edward Everett Papers, Massachusetts Historical Society.

[34] Bertram Wyatt-Brown, "Prelude to Abolitionism: Sabbatarian Politics and the Rise of the Second Party System," *Journal of American History*, 58 (September, 1971), 316–41; Kleppner, *Third Electoral System*; John L. Hammond, *The Politics of Benevolence: Revival Religion and American Voting Behavior* (Norwood, N.J.: Ablex Publishing Corp., 1979). A local study which skillfully examines the connection between religion and politics is Paul E. Johnson, *A Shopkeeper's Millenium: Society and Revivals in Rochester, New York, 1815–1837* (New York: Hill & Wang, 1978).

and 1830s spawned several reform movements, the most significant of which—nativism, temperance, and antislavery—were increasingly important in northern politics after 1840. In the 1850s a growing number of Protestant clergymen, especially from the evangelical denominations, were pronounced partisans. "Correct political action is religion in practice," wrote one minister in defense of such activity. The New York *Times* decried the contention that religion had no place in politics and argued that if "a man's religion . . . is worth anything, he should take [it] with him to the polls as punctually as to church."[35] Many Americans, strenuously objecting to what they termed "Bible politics," indignantly condemned ministers who strayed from their strict religious duties. As a result, the injection of religious and moral questions into partisan conflict brought large numbers of both supporters and opponents to the polls. Equally important, revivalistic religion gave a different tone and texture to political culture. Agitation of moral questions that deeply divided the community created a strong sense of earnestness among the electorate. The crusading zeal that characterized politics in this period made the antebellum political universe quite distinct from that of the twentieth century.

The act of voting had an ideological component as well. Since the Revolution, American parties had stressed fear of internal conspiracies to overthrow republican government, which all Americans believed particularly vulnerable to subversion. Both the Jacksonian party system, which coalesced around the dual threats of the monstrous Second Bank of the United States and Jackson's frequent use of the veto, and the Civil War party system, which focused in part on the issue of majority rule and minority rights, adapted the political heritage of the Revolution to the changing conditions of American life.[36] Party conflict before the Civil War strengthened the notion that voting was a citizen's duty, that every man must vote in order to protect republicanism. Thus a nonpartisan Maine paper intoned on the eve of one election: "It is the positive duty of every citizen of a Republic to vote . . . when people lose their interest in elections, freedom cannot be preserved."

[35] John G. Fee to Gerrit Smith, January 4, 1856, Gerrit Smith Papers, Syracuse University; New York *Times*, June 22, 1854.

[36] Michael F. Holt, *The Political Crisis of the 1850s* (New York: John Wiley & Sons, 1978); Rush Welter, *The Mind of America, 1820–1860* (New York: Columbia University Press, 1975), 3–45, 165–218.

In much the same vein an Indiana voter attributed his increased partisanship to his belief that "the institutions of our Country are in more danger" than ever before.[37] This generation of Americans embraced a sense of mission that they traced back to the founding fathers: to defend, protect, and extend the creed of republicanism, which Lincoln concisely defined as government of, by, and for the people.

Partisan differences over how to defend republicanism did not extend to the legitimacy of republicanism itself. By 1840, the tide of political democracy had swept all before it. The Whig party, which initially betrayed uncertainty about the emerging democratic ethos, quickly adjusted to the new realities of American politics. Any member of the elite unwilling to make this transition either muffled his dissent or retired from public life.[38] As Everett insisted, when it came to upholding popular government, "we are all democrats." An Ohio paper agreed that both parties fully endorsed democratic principles. "No party . . . dared to go before the people upon any other avowed object." Instead, the struggle between the two parties was over how best to promote these principles.[39] Another facet of the democratic consensus was popular hatred of aristocracy. Northern politicians were careful when among the voters to avoid the image of one who spent "too much time at the 'toilet' to suit . . . agrarian & leveling notions." Aristocratic pretensions were politically fatal. "If there is anything in this country fixed," explained a Bostonian before the Civil War, "it is the prejudice against aught which has the appearance even of aristocracy."[40]

The role of political conflict in American society also promoted popular involvement. Mass interest was not the product of an active state intervening in people's daily lives, for government occupied a

[37] Portland (Maine) *Transcript*, November 1, 1856; Thomas A. Hendricks to Allen Hamilton, March 31, 1856, Allen Hamilton Papers, Indiana State Library; Cincinnati *Gazette*, September 29, 1852.

[38] John G. Atterbury to Julia Allen, October 5, 1839, quoted in Alexandra McCoy, "Political Affiliations of American Economic Elites: Wayne County, Michigan, 1844–1860, as a Test Case" (Ph.D. dissertation, Wayne State University, 1965), 203.

[39] Everett to Abbot Lawrence, January 6, 1852, Copy, Everett Papers; *Ohio State Journal*, May 18, 1854.

[40] Godlove S. Orth to Schuyler Colfax, Wednesday morning [Fall, 1845], Herman Schauinger, ed., "The Letters of Godlove S. Orth, Hoosier Whig," *Indiana Magazine of History*, 39 (December, 1943), 377; John M. Forbes to J. Hamilton Cowper, December 4, 1856, Sarah Forbes Hughes, ed., *Letters and Recollections of John Murray Forbes* (2 vols.; Boston: Houghton, Mifflin, 1899), 1:156–57.

much more limited sphere in the nineteenth century. "With their eyes and ears shut," one editor asserted with much justice, "half the population of an inland town would never know the existence of a national government, a State government, a Congress or a legislature; much less would they know of their proceedings. Nothing happening to themselves, or affecting their present condition, would inform them."[41] Most people, however, kept their eyes and ears open. Some government activity, of course, such as taxes and temperance legislation, did forcefully touch citizens' daily lives. But the bulk of government action did not. Much of the political conflict of the decade was more symbolic in nature: it affirmed or denied deeply rooted values among competing groups in a fragmented society, thereby serving a vital psychological function more than altering a person's daily existence. Without a privileged aristocracy or an established church, American society lacked many of the traditional sources of authority other societies enjoyed. Unlike more stratified and stable societies, it did not assign certain values and patterns of behavior to definite groups. America's ethnic, religious, and cultural diversity generated additional conflict. With the rise of mass parties, conflicts within society quickly permeated politics as groups sought symbolic and sometimes specific endorsement of their values and affirmation of their self-worth.

For a number of reasons, then, antebellum politics raised issues which Americans perceived as vital. Whether the voter's response to these issues was sophisticated or simple, he believed important considerations were at stake. One of the impressive achievements of politicians in the 1850s, following the collapse of the Jacksonian party system, was their success in maintaining among the mass electorate a high interest in and commitment to the political system. "Politics seem to enter into everything," one nonpartisan paper complained in frustration, "and very little attention is now paid to anything unless it be mixed up in some way with the political movements of the day."[42]

[41] Charles Hale, *"Our Houses are Our Castles": A Review of the Proceedings of the Nunnery Committee* (Boston: Daily Advertiser, 1856), 21. Also see M. Y. Tilden to Samuel J. Tilden, September 25, [1855], Samuel J. Tilden Papers, New York Public Library.

[42] Urbana *Clarion*, September 1, 1860, quoted in Baringer, "Campaign Technique in Illinois," 266. One Indiana agricultural society announced in 1854 that it was discontinuing its public speakers series "on account of frequent meetings for political speech mak-

Intense popular interest in politics produced a demand for gifted and entertaining speakers. Audiences were willing—and able—to sit through speeches lasting three hours or more without losing interest. Popular oratory flourished in this period, and the capable stump speaker was a great asset to his party. Despite his elitist bias, a New York City resident provided striking testimony of the power of an effective stump speech: "It was not exactly like Demosthenes or the *Areopagitica*, being made up of slang, funny stories, and an occasional modulation into a high flight of Bowery theatre declamation, indignation, and 'pathos and bathos delightful to see.' But it was immensely effective, [the speaker] kept his audience in an uproar of cheers and genuine laughter. . . . I was sick and sore with laughing when he finished." As befit the tumultuous nature of a less-established society, campaign speaking in the West was even less refined.[43]

Stumping the state by candidates (except for president) was not only accepted but expected. Joint appearances of opposing party speakers, even rival candidates, as in the famous Lincoln-Douglas debates of 1858, were common. A good speaking voice, an attractive personality, and an easy rapport with the masses doubtlessly improved a candidate's chances, but the importance of such qualities can be easily overstated. Not only was much campaigning done by party surrogates, but antebellum voters, with stronger party loyalties and less exposure to a candidate, were not as strongly influenced by the candidate's personality as they are today. Not all leaders approved of this strenuous style of electioneering. Everett, a thoughtful commentator, deplored stumping as "one of the downward tendencies" of the age. This practice not only rendered campaigns "much more laborious," but it tended to put the active duty "more and more into the hands of the young & able-bodied," as well as men he loathingly termed mere "adventurers."[44] But the public, its political appetite whetted, demanded such activity.

---

ing," which rendered it "impossible to get sufficient numbers of farmers together." Roger H. Van Bolt, "Fusion out of Confusion, 1854," *Indiana Magazine of History*, 49 (December, 1953), 386.

[43] Allan Nevins and Milton Halsey Thomas, eds., *Diary of George Templeton Strong* (4 vols.; New York: Macmillan Company, 1952), 2:301; Roger H. Van Bolt, "The Hoosier Politician of the 1840's," *Indiana Magazine of History*, 48 (March, 1952), 23; Richard Hinton, Journal, July 11, [1856], Richard Hinton Papers, Kansas State Historical Society.

[44] Edward Everett, Diary, October 20, 1853, Everett Papers.

Stump speeches and mass meetings were not the only sources of information or even the most important ones to the voter. In the countless small towns which dotted the northern landscape, the general store and the tavern, where village statesmen held forth, served as prominent centers of political discussion. Lecture series, debating clubs, and lyceums, even when avowedly nonpolitical, frequently disseminated such information. County court days and militia musters were invariably occasions for political discussions. But throughout the year the most important source of political information was the newspaper. These ranged from the large, eight-page dailies in New York City, with their vast financial resources, large staffs of correspondents, and daily telegraphic dispatches, to the more typically languid four-page country weeklies, one or at most two pages of which were devoted to news, much of it stale and dated. Yet both types exercised a powerful influence on public opinion. Some party leaders, noting that audiences were largely composed of a party's supporters, questioned the utility of speeches in converting opponents. Newspapers, in contrast, reached diverse groups and consequently changed opinions. For this reason, an experienced Massachusetts politician insisted that "by far the most potent agency in politics is the press."[45]

Virtually all newspapers in this period were frankly partisan. Openly avowing the cause of one party, sometimes even of a particular leader, newspapers transmitted the party creed to the reader. After a lifetime in journalism, one prominent editor aptly characterized newspapers before the Civil War as "literally drenched with eternal politics." Editors unabashedly shaped the news and their editorial comment to partisan purposes. They sought to convert the doubters, recover the wavering, and hold the committed. "The power of the press," one journalist candidly explained, "consists not in its logic or eloquence, but in its ability to manufacture facts, or to give coloring to facts that have occurred."[46] The press's influence derived from the fact that newspapers were the most convenient and accessible sources of political information, and also from the fact that many readers, consciously or unconsciously, took their positions on public issues from the newspaper

---

[45]Julius Rockwell to Seth Webb, Jr. (Confidential), April 7, 1856, Norcross Collection, Massachusetts Historical Society; Rev. G. M. Perkins to Joseph Hawley, September 14, 1852, Joseph Hawley Papers, Library of Congress.

[46]John W. Forney, *Anecdotes of Public Men* (2 vols.; New York: Harper & Brothers, 1873–81), 1:383; Cincinnati *Catholic Telegraph*, February 11, 1854.

they read. Because of the necessity of having a channel of communication with the public, party divisions frequently led to the formation of additional newspapers or the purchase of existing ones. Thus, following the split in the New York Democratic party in the late 1840s, one side founded the Albany *Atlas* to do battle against the *Argus*, the party's longtime organ, which was controlled by the rival faction. In the next decade, a similar division in the American party led one group to buy control of the Albany *Statesman* in order to combat the heresies of the renegade *Register*.

The partisan role of newspapers made editors a major force in politics. Congressman Schuyler Colfax, who was also a journalist, described an editor as "the power that makes Administrations, breaks down & builds up parties, controls or directs public opinion, & in the foreground of the fight, receives all the arrows of the enemy." Colfax exaggerated, but editors did wield substantial political power.[47] Some, like Thurlow Weed, combined journalistic ability with the powers of personal persuasion and a talent for organization to become, without the trappings of public office, the real leaders of a party. Others, like Henry J. Raymond of the New York *Times*, combined journalism with a successful quest for public office. In contrast, still others, most notably Horace Greeley of the New York *Tribune*, were bitterly disappointed in their political ambitions. Even so, Greeley continued to exercise considerable influence on public opinion, particularly through the weekly edition of his paper, which had a vast circulation throughout the North; one observer claimed that many of its readers rated it "next to the Bible" as a source of guidance.[48] No wonder one exasperated politician finally complained of "that rabid arrogance which characterizes all small editors who have learned from the twaddle about 'the Press,' to regard themselves as divinely-appointed potentates."[49]

Mass politics also thrust into prominence the professional politician. Although every campaign contained enthusiastic volunteers, and some, like the 1856 Republican national campaign, were plagued by

---

[47] Schuyler Colfax to Francis Stebbins, April 29, 1856, Francis Stebbins Papers, Michigan Historical Collection, University of Michigan; Mrs. William S. Robinson, "Warrington" Pen Portraits (Boston: Lee & Shepard, 1877), 54.

[48] Charles B. Johnson, *Illinois in the Fifties* (Champaign: Flanigan-Pearson Company, 1918), 120, 157; Jeter Allen Isely, *Horace Greeley and the Republican Party, 1853–1861* (Princeton: Princeton University Press, 1947), 5.

[49] J. S. McConnell to John M. Palmer, January 1, 1855, John M. Palmer Papers, Illinois State Historical Library.

them, professional politicians largely controlled the political system. The rise of such a class—men who sought to spend a lifetime in public office and often depended financially on political rewards—had begun before 1840. The pre–Civil War decades witnessed an intensification of this trend, as the federal patronage continued to increase more rapidly than the population as a whole. Burgeoning state patronage provided numerous additional opportunities.[50]

As the prominence of professional politicians increased, many Americans developed a healthy skepticism of their purposes and a strong distrust of their principles. Thus an Indiana man who dabbled in politics contemptuously spoke of "the vile tribe of politicians-by-trade—a tribe I loathe and despise, more and more as I see more and more of their hollowness & rascality."[51] Contemporaries expressed disgust at politicians' lack of principles—at their sacrifice of everything for personal and often financial gain. Such hostility was especially common among social elites, who in the earlier, more sedate era of deference politics would have been the country's natural political leaders. They now found themselves without influence and following, or else compelled to compete in the rough-and-tumble world of politics where they had to resort to distasteful expedients.[52] A Philadelphia conservative, who later served as minister to Constantinople, complained of "the mere chicanery of politics," which made the pursuit of office "attended by a degradation of character & sacrifice of principle startling enough to drive every man of taste & feeling into deeper shades of private life." The prominent educator Francis Wayland justified his desire to remain free from politicians with the pithy comment, "No one knows what they will be next year by what they are this year."[53]

---

[50] Between 1830 and 1860 the number of federal employees increased 3.2 times, whereas the population grew 2.4 times. Inclusion of state government workers would make the difference more striking. Because in the 1830s and beyond many northern states undertook extensive public works projects, most notably canals, the number of such employees dramatically expanded. United States Bureau of the Census, *The Statistical History of the United States from Colonial Times to the Present* (New York: Basic Books, 1976), 8, 1103.

[51] A. S. Roache to John G. Davis, September 7, 1855, John G. Davis Papers, Indiana Historical Society.

[52] Charles Francis Adams, Diary, October 17, 1856, Adams Family Papers; Joseph M. Churchill to Francis W. Bird, September 13, 1856, Francis W. Bird Papers, Harvard University; Samuel Shapiro, *Richard Henry Dana, Jr., 1815–1882* (East Lansing: Michigan State University Press, 1951), 75.

[53] Edward Joy Morris to John M. Clayton, February 21, 1855, John M. Clayton Pa-

These complaints should not be taken at face value. Antiparty and antipolitician sentiments have been commonplace throughout American history, although as Michael Holt notes, they are felt more deeply at some times than at others. Several observations about these expressions in the 1840s and 1850s are in order. Most important, perhaps, is the fact that they generally did not lead to lasting cynicism about the political system or to widespread apathy. Rather than concluding that the system was hopeless, that change could never be achieved, Americans, with their faith in progress and human perfectibility, concluded instead that the problem lay with the leaders; the remedy was to elect new men to office. The Know-Nothing party most spectacularly capitalized on this popular disgust with politicians in the 1850s, but the new Republican party also voiced (though less fervently) this same appeal.[54] Expressions of cynicism during this period for the most part lacked conviction. A disgruntled New York Democrat, to take one example, dismissed all politicians as "scamps" and politics as solely "a game to cheat somebody" in which "all talk about principle is twaddle." Yet he continued to participate zealously in politics, cared deeply about the outcome of elections, and eventually became a local party boss.[55] Despite setbacks, northerners' faith in the efficacy of politics remained unshaken. Attacks on politicians were much more common at the end of the second party system, before realignment began, when partisan divisions seemingly reflected no great principles. As soon as new issues arose and realignment commenced, these complaints all but ceased as men again found purpose in politics and enthusiastically entered the battle.[56]

A feeling of uneasiness about politics accompanied by a strange, ir-

---

pers, Library of Congress; Francis and H. L. Wayland, *A Memoir of the Life and Labors of Francis Wayland* (2 vols.; New York: Seldon & Company, 1867), 1:405. Veteran politicians accepted sharp tactics as a necessary part of politics. Weed, for example, acknowledged that "we are compelled to do things that will not bear the blaze of light." Weed to Hamilton Fish, November 13, 1853, Hamilton Fish Papers, Library of Congress.

[54] Michael F. Holt, "The Politics of Impatience: The Origins of Know Nothingism," *Journal of American History*, 60 (September, 1973), 315–22.

[55] Ansel J. McCall to James Chamberlain, September 17, 1854, McCall Family Papers, Cornell University.

[56] Although not identical, antipolitician statements were the most common manifestation of antiparty attitudes. For the erosion of these attitudes, see Holt, *Political Crisis of the 1850s*, 163–76; Joel H. Silbey, *A Respectable Minority: The Democratic Party in the Civil War Era* (New York: W. W. Norton & Co., 1977), 29n.

resistible attraction to it was well illustrated by Henry L. Dawes of Massachusetts. A young man in the 1850s at the beginning of a long public career, Dawes was already a prominent party leader in his county. When he was elected a Whig National Convention delegate in 1852, he privately recorded his doubts about political life: "Politics are a quagmire—whoever attempts to travel it will find that the farther he goes the deeper will he sink—nor can he stand still, for everything around and beneath him shakes." At the same time, he recognized the attraction politics exerted on him. "Like the appetite for strong drink so is the hunger after the excitement and turmoil of politics." At home or in the office it had no attraction, "but the moment I come within the Circle of the excitement or sound of it I yield to the temptation and throw myself into the whirlpool. . . . Thus have been paralyzed all my efforts to break away from its spell."[57]

In analyzing the Jacksonian party system, some historians have detected a greater antiparty sentiment among Whigs than Democrats. They argue that the party of Jackson more quickly and easily adapted to mass politics and the new structure of party organization; Whigs, with a different sense of community and stronger links to local elites, found the adjustment more difficult—indeed, were never able fully to make the transition.[58] This argument has merit. Despite their success in 1840, Whigs in general did have a more difficult time mobilizing a full vote, and they accepted the idea of party discipline less easily than did Democrats. But the important point is that this pervasive sense of antipartyism along with its accompanying though muted elitism died with the Whig party. Only lingering echoes of this tradition remained after the war.[59] It was not transmitted to the new anti-Democratic par-

[57] Henry L. Dawes, Diary, June 4, 5, [1852], Henry L. Dawes Papers, Library of Congress.

[58] Ronald P. Formisano, "Political Character, Antipartyism, and the Second Party System," *American Quarterly*, 21 (Winter, 1969), 683–709; Lynn L. Marshall, "The Strange Stillbirth of the Whig Party," *American Historical Review*, 72 (January, 1967), 445–68. For examples of these differing attitudes, see Edward Kent to Israel Washburn, Jr., June 22, 1852, Israel Washburn, Jr., Papers, Norlands Library; Roland Howard to O. O. Howard, November 1, 1852, O. O. Howard Papers, Bowdoin College; John Harper to John A. Harper, October 13, 1856, Harper Family Papers, Historical Society of Western Pennsylvania; Benjamin H. Brewster to Edmund Burke, November 1, 1852, Edmund Burke Papers, Library of Congress; *Illinois State Journal*, November 6, 1854.

[59] For a contrary argument, see Kleppner, *Third Electoral System*, 70–86, 293–96, 331–34.

ties which formed in the 1850s. The Know-Nothings, for example, were more tightly organized and disciplined than the Democrats, with a carefully structured hierarchy of councils from the local to the national level. Nor did Republicans, whose party apparatus was not as tightly structured, manifest hostility to party organization. From its founding, the goal of the Republican National Committee was to establish an effective and reliable organization from the national down to the local level. Rank-and-file Republicans and local leaders complained, not about the party's growing centralization, but that its organization was inefficient.

By the final decade before the Civil War, men who participated in politics—and this included the vast majority of all eligible voters—accepted the necessity of parties and party organization and looked to politics as a means to accomplish desired goals. Although many men labored in reform movements that did not explicitly work within the political system, few endorsed William Lloyd Garrison's rejection of political action as sinful and corrupting. More often than not, even nonpolitical reform movements eventually turned to political action. The temperance movement, for example, which at its inception relied exclusively on moral suasion, had by the 1850s become intensely political. In state after state, supporters sought to enact stiff prohibition laws modeled after Maine's pathbreaking 1851 statute.[60] Mass interest in politics was too strong, and the possibilities for immediate, sweeping reform too tempting, for many Americans to adhere long to a nonpolitical course of action.

Popular enthusiasm also fostered several unseemly features of American politics. Free drinks were an important component of urban elections. In one hotly contested election in Chicago, Democrats used wagons with whiskey barrels and temporary seats to bring voters to the polls. In many cities, political gangs and rowdies sought to intimidate opposition voters. Occasionally election riots occurred. One of the worst in any northern city in these decades took place in Cincinnati, where in April, 1855, native and immigrant voters clashed after a

[60] Frederick N. Dow, ed., *The Reminiscences of Neal Dow* (Portland, Maine: Evening Express Publishing Company, 1898), 118–569; Frank L. Byrne, *Prophet of Prohibition: Neal Dow and His Crusade* (Madison: State Historical Society of Wisconsin, 1961), 35–69, 76–77.

deeply divisive campaign. Rioting continued in the city for several days after the election, and several men lost their lives.[61]

Voting in the rural areas, though less tumultuous perhaps, was not necessarily more decorous. Because an election was one of the few events which brought virtually all the men from the surrounding countryside into the village, it was very much a social occasion. While the balloting progressed, a holidaylike atmosphere frequently prevailed and, as in cities, whiskey was ever present. Encountering many of his acquaintances at the polls on election day, one California voter reported that everyone stood treat for drinks. Estimating that they each imbibed as many as twenty-five drinks in an hour and a half, he admitted that "as a matter . . . of course, many of us got pretty essentially tight." Gathering some additional bottles of stimulants, they eventually staggered off for dancing and horse racing.[62] Party organization was also equally critical in the countryside, where close elections produced strenuous efforts to secure every available vote. One antislavery man described the activity of future president Franklin Pierce in a particularly bitter New Hampshire election. Hell itself "could not have belched up so miserable, so degraded a group of drunken vagabonds" as those Pierce rounded up and brought to the polls. "It is notorious that Pierce scoured round among these underground drunken holes and led men to the Ballot Box so drunk they could not stand without his aid. In this way he worked . . . as if life or death depended upon the result."[63] Antebellum America was a boisterous, turbulent society, and politics mirrored society.

So, too, did party organization. A fundamental characteristic of political parties before the Civil War was their decentralization. In another context Thomas Cochran has criticized what he terms the "presidential synthesis" of United States history. More interested in national issues and political developments than in state and local politics, historians have concentrated excessively on presidential elections in analyz-

---

[61] George Baldwin to Roger S. Baldwin, March 5, 1856, Baldwin Family Papers, Yale University; Cincinnati *Gazette*, April 3–6, 1855.

[62] Johnson, *Illinois in the Fifties*, 142–43; Clark, ed., *Journals of Alfred Doten*, 1:191; Horace Greeley, *Recollections of a Busy Life* (New York: J. B. Ford & Company, 1868), 100.

[63] James Peverly to John P. Hale, March 15, 1846, quoted in Lucy M. Lowden, "'Black as Ink–Bitter as Hell': John P. Hale's Mutiny in New Hampshire," *Historical New Hampshire*, 27 (Spring, 1972), 42-43.

ing American politics. Such history, with its rhythm of four-year cycles, seriously distorts the reality of politics before the Civil War.[64] In particular, it exaggerates the national cohesion and unity of parties at the expense of state and local variations and mutations.

In reality, national parties were a loose coalition of state parties, each of which jealously guarded its prerogatives. National committees sought to give some direction to presidential campaigns and, more particularly, raised and channeled campaign funds to doubtful states that needed assistance, but no national committee could dictate acceptance of its directives. Each state committee felt free to run the campaign within its borders as it thought best, and thus each functioned more or less independently of the others. The American party's rigid pyramidal structure from local councils to the Grand Council, which was designed to ensure national unity, failed miserably. When a series of divisive issues split the national council in 1855, each state organization charted its own course, as the national leadership proved utterly unable to enforce adherence to the platform. In New York, for example, the state convention repudiated the national platform and adopted its own version for the state campaign that year, much to the dismay of members who envisioned the party as a truly national alternative to the Republicans and Democrats. To compound this division, several county conventions adopted different platforms on which the party conducted its local campaigns.[65]

After the war, in order to avoid such problems, the Republican National Committee brought a degree of centralization to party structure previously lacking in American politics. In the 1850s, however, the party remained a loose confederation of state organizations. Only in Pennsylvania, where in 1856 the party was badly rent by factionalism and completely lacked funds, did the national committee, with its power over party finances, take control of the presidential campaign, first informally and then more formally. But such central direction was

[64]Thomas C. Cochran, "The 'Presidential Synthesis' in American History," *American Historical Review*, 53 (July, 1948), 748–59; Joel H. Silbey, "The Civil War Synthesis in American Political History," *Civil War History*, 10 (June, 1964), 130–40.

[65]New York *Tribune*, August 30, 31, 1855; Jamestown *Journal*, June 22, 1855; Kenneth Rayner to Daniel Ullmann, May 8, August 21, 1855, June 2, 1856, Daniel Ullmann Papers, New-York Historical Society; Mark L. Berger, *The Revolution in the New York Party System, 1840–1860* (Port Washington, N.Y.: Kennikat Press, 1973), 75–77.

temporary and very unusual. Decentralization also extended, though less dramatically, to the state parties, as county committees conducted local campaigns to suit best their needs. One student of state politics in the 1850s accurately describes parties as "a conglomeration of party units which functioned at several different levels, very frequently at cross purposes to one another."[66]

The lack of centralized party control at once encouraged local factionalism and bolts, while simultaneously it strengthened voter allegiance to the party by allowing politicians to tailor their appeal to local concerns. Within this context, party leaders enjoyed a certain amount of leeway in directing public affairs, manipulating issues, and shaping public opinion. Consistency has rarely been valued over success in American politics, and the antebellum period was no exception. Parties adapted campaigns to particular regions and showed no embarrassment over contradictory assertions. In Pennsylvania both parties traditionally affirmed support for the tariff, regardless of their national creed. Confronted with divisions between the North and the South over sectional issues, Whigs shamelessly ran a Janus-faced campaign in 1848. Congressman Washington Hunt outlined the party's strategy when, in discussing the Wilmot Proviso, he shrewdly (if somewhat cynically) advised: "Our Southern brethren are fractious and they sometimes threaten to draw Mason & Dixon's line between us. I tell them they may have their way south of it, & we must manage things for ourselves on the north side."[67]

The Jacksonian party system derived considerable strength from the capability of parties to emphasize national, state, or local issues as their situation dictated. Thus parties could safely divide on issues at one level while avoiding or minimizing troublesome issues on another level. Limits to such diversity, of course, existed. No state or local party, especially over an extended period of time, could repudiate fundamental party principles and preserve party harmony. When divi-

[66] Richard R. Wescott, "A History of Maine Politics, 1840–1856: The Formation of the Republican Party" (Ph.D. dissertation, University of Maine, 1966), 14–15.

[67] Washington Hunt to Thurlow Weed, March 19, 1848, Thurlow Weed Papers, University of Rochester. For a similar response by a Know-Nothing leader to a different problem, see James R. Thompson to Daniel Ullmann, August 14, 1855, Ullmann Papers. Also see Edwin D. Morgan to Henry Carey, October 2, 1856, Henry C. Carey Papers, Historical Society of Pennsylvania.

sions became too deep, such as in the Democratic party in the late 1850s, the disruption of the national party—at least temporarily—was the consequence. Still, the extent of these local variations remains impressive. By 1850, for example, western Democratic organizations had repudiated the party's traditional position on internal improvements, yet the party retained national unity in presidential campaigns. Michael Holt has demonstrated that such flexibility was crucial to the second party system and that the eventual loss of adaptability undermined both major parties, especially the Whigs.[68]

As the 1850s wore on, the coercion of national events limited the flexibility available to politicians. The Republican party's handling of the issue of nativism is a case in point. The issue produced deep divisions in the party. While national leaders groped for a reasonably satisfactory solution, each state party developed its own position on the question. In some states, such as Pennsylvania, the Republicans made an open alliance with the Know-Nothings. In New York, on the other hand, the party rejected such a course and denounced nativism. In still other states, Republican leaders sought a middle ground. In Ohio, for example, they rejected any alliance with a separate nativist party, yet actively sought nativist support under the soothing rubric of "fusion."

The significance of state and local issues in antebellum politics should not be minimized. The dramatic nature of national issues in this decade, along with the looming specter of civil war, inevitably tends to overshadow state and local concerns and thus to distort the political reality of the period. Some men, certainly, were primarily concerned with national issues and were willing to sacrifice state and local interests for national purposes. A good example was Edwin D. Morgan, the national chairman of the Republican party, who viewed presidential and congressional elections as overriding all other races. Other politicians, however, provided ample testimony concerning the importance of state and local contests. The state election was "quite as important" as the national election, one Massachusetts Whig declared in 1852, for "the [state] Constitution, the Supreme Court, & every thing else that gives us stability & character are at stake." Although he expressed hope of winning the presidential election in 1856, James G. Blaine, then a rising young Republican editor in Maine, nevertheless pro-

[68] Holt, *Political Crisis of the 1850s*, 1–138.

claimed: "We must take such a course as will save our state & our districts. We must not prove worse than heathen[s] by neglecting to provide for our own households."[69] Obviously, politicians would prefer to carry all elections, national, state, and local. But party leaders, even national party leaders, were above all tied to state organizations, and carrying one's state, especially the governorship and legislature, thereby gaining control of the state patronage, was their primary consideration.[70]

Politicians were willing to make certain concessions for national unity and success, but they were understandably unwilling to sacrifice their own bases of power for such ends. At the Charleston convention in 1860, when southern Democrats demanded more than their northern allies could concede and politically survive, George Pugh, a prominent northern Democrat, angrily retorted, "Gentlemen of the South, you mistake us—you mistake us—we will not do it." Similarly, northern delegates to the 1855 American National Council, exclaiming that the party could not carry a single township in the free states on the platform adopted by the council, bolted rather than be saddled with such an unbearable burden.[71]

Elections between 1840 and 1860 manifested great popular enthusiasm, but organization was essential for victory. Few contests have matched the unsuccessful Frémont campaign in crusading fervor; yet, as one Republican reflected afterward, "We were a sort of mob, unorganized, contending with a well drilled and bold enemy . . . no enthusiasm or earnestness can stand against cold blooded and efficient drill."

[69] Edwin D. Morgan to David Ripley, September 12, 1856, Copy, Edwin D. Morgan Papers; R. A. Chapman to John H. Clifford, August 20, 1852, John H. Clifford Papers, Massachusetts Historical Society; James G. Blaine to Israel Washburn, Jr., February 22, 1856, Washburn Papers.

[70] Martin Van Buren to Bedford Brown, September 17, 1852, "Correspondence of Bedford Brown," *Historical Society of Trinity College Historical Papers*, 6 (1906), 85; Milton Harmon to Benedict Lewis, August 28, 1852, Ullmann Papers. Holt makes the same point in *Political Crisis of the 1850s*. Also see Mildred Stoler, "The Democratic Element in the New Republican Party in Indiana," *Indiana Magazine of History*, 36 (September, 1940), 198. For an excellent analysis of how state considerations influenced the Van Burenites during the controversy over the expansion of slavery in the 1840s, see Eric Foner, "The Wilmot Proviso Revisited," *Journal of American History*, 56 (September, 1969), 262–79.

[71] Robert W. Johannsen, *Stephen A. Douglas* (New York: Oxford University Press, 1973), 754; Henry Wilson, *History of the Rise and Fall of the Slave Power in America* (3 vols.; Boston: Houghton, Mifflin & Company, 1872–77), 2:423–32.

Party success required tedious and usually not very glamorous work, which only the most committed were willing to perform.[72] Canvassing the precinct, organizing rallies, putting up posters and banners, distributing election tickets, bringing voters to the polls, and poll watching—these activities were critical to mustering a party's full strength in an election.[73] To party workers, the emotional satisfaction when victorious, the receipt of party honors and recognition, and for some the reward of a public job or contract made the hard and sometimes unappealing work seem worthwhile. By the time of the next election, these same men could usually be found once again in the party harness hard at work.

In order to wield power, party leaders obviously needed the support of their constituents. "Arguments will avail nothing," one representative explained during the fight in Congress over the Kansas-Nebraska bill. The only hope to defeat the bill was to satisfy its supporters "that their constituents will be *after them.*" Or, as Salmon P. Chase expressed it, adverse election results, rather than petitions, "are *memorials* which some politicians will be likely to hold in lasting remembrance."[74]

The complex relationship between political leaders and voters is difficult to unravel. Certainly the concerns of politicians were not always identical with those of the mass electorate. Patronage is a good example. Squabbles among rival leaders over patronage permeated politics, yet rarely did the regular voters show great concern over the distribution of offices. "Ordinarily the people do not give themselves a moments concern about who holds the offices," one politician frankly conceded. "It is usually a thing that only concerns the individual and his particular friends."[75]

[72] Charles W. Elliott to Robert Carter, February 6, 1859, Robert Carter Papers, Harvard University; Nevins and Thomas, eds., *Diary of George Templeton Strong*, 2:306; Dr. Patrick Henry Jameson, Memoirs, chapter 6.

[73] Weed, a master political operator whose power rested on his organizational skills, contended that "a perfect Poll List in each town and ward, is worth more than twenty speeches." Richard L. Watson, Jr., "Thurlow Weed, Political Leader, 1848–1855" (Ph.D. dissertation, Yale University, 1939), 36–37, 111.

[74] Edwin B. Morgan to his mother, February 12, 1854, Edwin Barber Morgan Papers, Wells College; Salmon P. Chase to [Theodore Parker?], April 5, 1854, Copy, Salmon P. Chase Papers, Historical Society of Pennsylvania.

[75] James B. Bowlin to James Buchanan, January 16, 1854, *Private*, Buchanan Papers. Also see Hamilton Fish to Lewis Kingsley, December 30, 1852, Copy, Fish Papers; A. L.

On issues of greater public concern, politicians both reflected and molded the views of the electorate. Careful politicians always kept their ears closely attuned to public opinion. At times, with an eye to success, they simply followed public sentiment. Wily manipulators such as Henry Wilson and Simon Cameron quickly scampered into the suddenly resurgent nativist movement in the mid-1850s, only to desert it promptly when more favorable opportunities beckoned. Similarly, as the temperance movement began to gather momentum in Ohio, Lewis D. Campbell, a prominent Whig congressman, took up the cause with more alacrity than sincerity. "I am not exactly a Maine Law man," he bluntly told a party colleague, "but I say, Heaven send us any thing that will help break down" the Democratic party.[76] Yet politicians also sought to mold public opinion to their own ends and purposes. Stephen A. Douglas' bold effort to reconcile Democratic voters to his doctrine of popular sovereignty is a case in point. Nevertheless, successful politicians could not disregard with impunity the views of the rank and file. When, after almost a decade of agitation the Van Burenites abruptly jettisoned the free-soil issue, as one Democrat observed, "multitudes of those who followed at the beginning marched right on in defiance of former leaders."[77]

The average antebellum voter unfortunately has left little direct evidence concerning his political beliefs. Here research on the modern electorate, which points to the importance of party identity in determining voting behavior, is particularly relevant.[78] Party identification played an even more important role in the nineteenth century.[79] As one senator noted, in the Civil War era "party zeal ran higher than it has since."[80] Then, as today, voters commonly identified with a party

---

Roache to John G. Davis, December 23, 1853, Davis Papers. For a different interpretation, see David E. Meerse, "The Northern Democratic Party and the Congressional Elections of 1858," *Civil War History*, 19 (June, 1973), 119–37.

[76] Lewis D. Campbell to Benjamin F. Wade, August 16, 1853, Benjamin F. Wade Papers, Library of Congress.

[77] Samuel Beardsley to Buchanan, November 7, 1856, Buchanan Papers.

[78] Most notably Angus Campbell, Philip E. Converse, Warren E. Miller, and Donald E. Stokes, *The American Voter* (New York: John Wiley & Sons, 1960); and by the same authors, *Elections and the Political Order* (New York: John Wiley & Sons, 1966).

[79] See the excellent discussion in Silbey, *A Respectable Minority*, 3–29.

[80] Cornelius Cole, *Memoirs of Cornelius Cole* (New York: McLoughlin Brothers,

and clung to it even as new crises arose, issues changed, and new personalities emerged on the political scene.[81] For many antebellum Americans a party identity, once formed, proved a lifelong commitment. A graphic illustration of this tenacious party allegiance was the remark of one semiliterate Pennsylvania Democrat that he had never been a Federalist, an Anti-Mason, or a Whig, for "it all Amounts to one thing . . . I got a dislike agains[t] that party when I was young[.] I am now about 56 years old [and] have always Suported a dimocrat Party."[82] An English clergyman, who was traveling in the United States during a presidential campaign, was surprised by the strength of Americans' attachment to parties. "Unflinching adherence to party is principle with them," he commented, "and to forsake a party is regarded as an act of the greatest dishonour."[83]

As is the case in the modern era, party identities of many antebellum voters stemmed from parental or family influence. "My political principles . . . have come to me by inheritance," one man frankly admitted. An Illinois resident asserted that, had he been old enough, he certainly would have voted for prohibition in the 1855 state referendum, "as all my uncles did and as I felt sure my father would have done had he been alive."[84] Family divisions over politics, though not common, sometimes occurred. Reporting in 1856 that two of his sons supported John C. Frémont, two supported James Buchanan, and one abstained, a father mused: "It is said a house divided against itself cannot stand[.] if so mine is likely to tumble down."[85]

1908), 109. In a campaign speech delivered in 1858, the widely respected Senator William Pitt Fessenden of Maine proclaimed (no doubt partly for effect): "I would vote for a dog if he were the candidate of my party." Charles A. Jellison, *Fessenden of Maine: Civil War Senator* (Syracuse: Syracuse University Press, 1962), 111.

[81] Thomas B. Alexander, "The Dimensions of Voter Partisan Constancy in Presidential Elections from 1840 to 1860," in this volume, estimates that in the North the Democrats retained 96 percent and the Whigs 74 percent of their 1840 supporters in the 1852 election. In his essay, Alexander provides considerable evidence of the enduring strength of Jacksonian party loyalties.

[82] Richard Woolverton to William Bigler, April 3, 1854, Bigler Papers.

[83] Frederick J. Jobson, *America and American Methodism* (New York: Virtue, Emmins, 1857), 116–17. The Cincinnati *Gazette*, August 21, 1854, averred that "there are few stronger feelings in the American heart than that of party fealty."

[84] William Slade, Jr., to William H. Seward, October 19, 1855, William H. Seward Papers, University of Rochester; Johnson, *Illinois in the Fifties*, 144–45; George Haven Putnam, *Memories of My Youth, 1844–1865* (New York: G. P. Putnam's Sons, 1914), 55.

[85] Alexander Johnson to Allen Hamilton, November 12, 1856, Hamilton Papers; A. Holbrook, Jr., to James Buchanan, October 13, 1856, Buchanan Papers.

TABLE 8. Estimated Party Voting By Age Group.

PENNSYLVANIA (Supreme Court Justice, 1854)

Male Age, 1850	Whig	Democrat	Know-Nothing	Not Voting	Percentage of Electorate
21–29	.4	−10	12	33	35
30–39	−19	11	4	31	27
40+	32	28	6	−28	38
Percentage of Electorate	13	30	22	35	

N = 63 counties

NEW YORK (Governor, 1854)

Male Age, 1855	Whig	Democrat		Know-Nothing	Not Voting	Percentage of Electorate
		Soft	Hard			
21–24	3	−9	3	11	8	15
25–29	−3	9	−1	7	8	18
30–39	−3	25	2	0	5	29
40+	24	1	2	4	7	37
Percentage of Electorate	20	26	5	21	27	

N = 351 townships and wards

NOTE: Negative entries result when subgroup voting behavior is not uniform across spatial units. For interpretive purposes they can be considered essentially zero.

Antebellum party loyalties, like those of present-day voters, apparently grew stronger with age. The Know-Nothing revolt in the mid-1850s strikingly illustrates this phenomenon. It appears that contemporary observers were justified in their belief that Know-Nothingism was particularly strong among young men (Table 8).[86] In Pennsylvania, for example, males between the ages of 21 and 30 were more than twice as likely to vote Know-Nothing as those over 30. In New York this relationship was even more clear-cut: not only did the Know-Nothings secure considerably greater support from males under 30, but the proportion casting nativist ballots was twice as large for those

[86] Richard Morgan to Edwin B. Morgan, February 10, 1856, Edwin Barber Morgan Papers; Nevins and Thomas, eds., Diary of George Templeton Strong, 2:197; Springfield Republican, November 27, 1854.

under 25 as for those between 25 and 30. Probably the best explanation of the order's attractiveness to young voters is, not its emphasis on reform or its novelty and mystery, but the weaker party identities of young voters. The act of repeatedly voting for a party strengthened the emotional tie between a voter and his party. As a group, younger voters, not having participated in the electoral process for very long, presumably had weaker party identities and thus found it much easier to join a new party. For older voters, even those unhappy with their party, repudiation of their past affiliation involved a great psychological loss. Observers also emphasized that the Republican party was particularly strong among young and new voters, and the same psychological phenomenon seems to be operative.[87] The Republican party's rise to power depended in part on its preponderant strength among younger voters. Just as was the case in the New Deal realignment of the 1930s, young voters in the 1850s apparently gravitated in disproportionate numbers to one party, thereby producing a significant shift in party strength.[88]

Political analysts widely commented on the importance of party identities in governing political behavior before the Civil War. "When men have formed the habit of acting together & have got their party into power," one New York Republican observed, "its policy will be shaped by the majority of the party and the minority however reluctant will continue to act for a long time & till they are led far away from their own purposes rather than seek a new alliance." For proof, he pointed to the free-soil Democrats who finally joined the Republican party. "They feel no differently now than they did at the time of the annexation of Texas, yet it required twelve years following of the south through the bogs before they could make up their minds to quit the fellowship" of the Democratic party.[89] Focusing on another aspect

---

[87] Charles Francis Adams, Diary, November 3, 1856, Adams Family Papers; William Cullen Bryant to John Bryant, October 14, 1856, in Parke Goodwin, *Life of William Cullen Bryant* (2 vols.; New York: D. Appleton & Co., 1883), 2:91–93; New York *Herald*, June 27, 1856; Portland *Daily Advertiser*, September 22, 1856, quoted in Wescott, "History of Maine Politics," 315.

[88] Paul Allen Beck, "A Socialization Theory of Partisan Realignment," Richard G. Niemi, ed., *The Politics of Future Citizens* (San Francisco: Jossey-Bass, 1974), 199–219.

[89] E. Peshire Smith to Henry C. Carey, November 21, 1856, October 30, 1855, Carey Papers; Horace Greeley to Schuyler Colfax, June 28, 1854, Greeley-Colfax Papers, New York Public Library.

of this phenomenon, the Connecticut Jacksonian Democrat Gideon Welles denounced those he termed "mere party disciplinarians" found in every party. "With them organization is everything, and principles of little account. If a majority of the organization were suddenly to reverse its position on any important principle, they would become transformed without hesitation."[90] Welles did not claim to be speaking of every party member, or even the majority, but this group was not numerically insignificant.

Changing one's party was almost always a difficult and uncomfortable decision. One Whig who switched to the Democratic party commented, "To change one's party relations under any circumstances requires some courage," and at times it "subject[s] one's fortitude to severe tests." Such decisions, which disrupted old friendships and associations, understandably produced deep feelings. Even as hardened a politico as Thurlow Weed despaired over the estrangement of so many old friends from "the arbitrary and perverse way the political world severs social as well as political ties." Welles suffered a similar sense of loss as he drifted away from his lifelong party connection into the Republican fold. He found his daily visit to the office of his old paper, the Democratic Hartford *Times*, increasingly awkward and uncomfortable. "I am reduced to the alternative of acting with old friends in the support of principles and an Administration that I despise, or to associate with many old opponents on past issues and do what I believe to be right."[91]

Welles chose the latter course, but many other similarly situated Democrats refused to desert old associates. Republicans repeatedly complained of an inability to get Democrats who disagreed with their party's principles and actions to make the final break. A number of such Democrats finally did leave the party: some, like Preston King of New York, rather quickly and without too much hesitation; others, like Hannibal Hamlin of Maine, with greater reluctance and hesitation. But a substantial number, led by Martin Van Buren and his son John,

[90] "Presidential Election and National Parties: Old Issues Dead—Slavery Is the Vital Issue Now," Typescript, Gideon Welles Papers, Library of Congress.

[91] Charles Chapman to John C. Breckinridge, October 1, 1856, Breckinridge Family Papers, Library of Congress; Thurlow Weed to Hamilton Fish, November 11, 13, [1855], Fish Papers; Gideon Welles, Diary, February 9, 1856, Welles Papers, Library of Congress.

simply could not bring themselves to sever old party ties.[92] Nor was such hesitation confined to Democrats. Many old-line Whigs, even after the party had collapsed, still clung to the battered hulk of the once proud Whig party. Luther Bradish, the prominent New York conservative, stubbornly declared in the midst of the 1856 presidential campaign that he had been born a Whig, lived a Whig, and intended to die a Whig. A New York City resident declined to join in launching the Republican party in that state, although he indicated that he sympathized "entirely" with the proposed movement, for it was "impossible for me to leave . . . my old friends."[93]

Even men disgruntled with their party's principles or nominees found it difficult to change their affiliations. A Democrat complained to Franklin Pierce's campaign manager in 1852 that Whigs who did not like Winfield Scott, the Whig nominee, felt uncomfortable voting for Pierce and desired some excuse to avoid doing so. The subsequent course of anti-Nebraska Democrats, who deserted the party in 1854 in anger over repeal of the Missouri Compromise, illustrates the continuing power of old loyalties. For many of these dissidents, their 1854 bolt represented a one-time protest against party policy, and they quickly returned to the party fold. Torn between their party identity and a dislike of the party's national principles, they eliminated the cross pressures they felt, not by abandoning the Democracy, but by gradually adopting new opinions. In a related fashion, throughout the North the Know-Nothing party served as a halfway house for numerous voters who were in the process of changing their party identities but initially could not bring themselves to support an organization they had opposed during most or all of their adult lives.[94]

---

[92] The reluctance of many anti-Nebraska Democrats in Illinois to forsake their party, despite two years of severe conflict with Douglas and his allies, is very apparent in Lyman Trumbull's correspondence. See, for example, letters from John M. Palmer, January 11, February 28, 1856, D. L. Phillips, January 18, 1856, B. B. Wheeler, May 15, 1856, Lyman Trumbull Papers, Library of Congress; Silas Ramsey to Trumbull, December 28, 1855, Lyman Trumbull to Julia Trumbull, April 25, 1856, Trumbull Family Papers, Illinois State Historical Library.

[93] Luther Bradish to Daniel D. Barnard, July 30, 1856, Daniel D. Barnard Papers, New York State Library; Gerardus Boyce to Edwin D. Morgan, March 17, 1856, Edwin D. Morgan Papers. Also see Barnard to Fish, May 23, 1853, Fish Papers; F. Adams to Thomas Ewing, August 21, 1856, Ewing Family Papers.

[94] A. H. Robinson to John H. George, July 26, 1852, George Papers; Welles to My Dear Sir, September, 1855, Copy, Gideon Welles Papers, Connecticut Historical Society; New York *Evening Post*, November 15, 1854.

Future presidential candidate Samuel Tilden cautioned against the belief that the masses were strongly attached to particular leaders rather than to the party generally. "The truth is that four-fifths of the rank & file follow the organization, by whichever leaders it is wielded."[95] There were times, of course, when feelings were so strong that this generalization did not hold. In 1848 Tilden himself had bolted out of personal loyalty to Martin Van Buren. Many other New York Democrats did likewise (though in no other state did Van Buren show such appeal among Democrats, leading one to suspect that the years of bitter factional wrangling in New York were necessary for such a wide-scale, albeit temporary, revolt). Despite such short-term defections, Tilden's analysis normally was valid. In times of political stability, men followed their party. Only in periods of realignment, such as the mid-1850s, did many voters form new identities, and such eras were rare. "Under ordinary circumstances," the Cincinnati *Commercial* noted, "men are holden together in parties by the force of association and organization; and when there is no issue before them that appeals to their moral sense, mere habit is sufficient to control their acts and to supply the place of opinions which they have not the time nor inclination to form."[96] Party identities composed the foundation of the antebellum political system.

Although the large majority of northern voters formed party identities in the antebellum period, they did not maintain these identities with equal fervor. Most were firmly committed to a party, supported it through thick and thin, and were impervious to the opposition's appeals. During the 1856 campaign, a supporter of Millard Fillmore insisted that "it is perfectly useless to attempt to carry a confirmed man when their [*sic*] is great excitement. The labor is wholly lost." Instead, he urged concentrating on doubtful voters. As is true today, the independent, doubtful, and swing voters—those men Hamilton Fish called the "floating mass, which does not properly belong to either party"— often held the balance of power.[97] After the Civil War the *Nation* ob-

[95] "Additional Notes on the Allotment [of Offices under the Pierce Administration]," [March 19, 1853], Tilden Papers.

[96] Cincinnati *Commercial*, September 21, 1852. Also see Washington Hunt to Samuel B. Ruggles, *Private*, October 21, 1852, Washington Hunt Papers, New York State Library.

[97] Harry Bradley to Millard Fillmore, October 2, 1856, Millard Fillmore Papers, State University of New York, Oswego; Fish to Charles G. Dean, May 8, 1852, Copy, Fish Papers; Jamestown *Journal*, November 2, 1860.

served that "the ardent Republicans are never sufficiently numerous to win an election. They have to secure their majority by the help of a few thousand who are only lukewarm Republicans, whose political feelings are not strong, who are affected in voting by diverse collateral considerations, and who, unless they are well looked after, are as likely as not to go over to the enemy on the day of the battle. It is these men who decide political contests in nearly all the closely divided states."[98] As the *Nation* noted, many of these swing voters had only a weak interest in politics and were not well informed, and consequently they were especially susceptible to short-term issues and temporary considerations.

To be sure, some voters who lacked strong attachments to either party displayed a keen interest in politics and kept abreast of the issues. They were the proverbial independents. One such man neatly explained his political motivation: "When I commenced political action, I started with a fixed determination to act according to the dictations of my own conscience, regardless of any party or faction; that I would listen attentively to all apparently fair and candid reasoning, weigh as carefully as I could, whatever might be said upon either side, and be my own umpire as to its correctness; that no man's smiles should charm, nor frowns should drive me from what I believed correct, after careful deliberation."[99] Other examples exist as well. But some historians have written of politics before the Civil War as if such voters constituted the majority. In reality, they were a small minority of the electorate, though in close elections their influence could be decisive.

Modern survey data indicate that, as a rule, voters with the strongest party identities constitute the most informed and aware segment of the electorate. The same situation prevailed in the years before 1861. Of those voters showing an acute understanding of public affairs, the overwhelming majority also displayed an intense commitment to one party. Usually the response of these voters was colored by strong partisan attachment and most, even when temporarily disgruntled, even-

[98] *Nation*, September 19, 1867, quoted in Phyllis F. Field, "Republicans and Black Suffrage in New York State: The Grass Roots Response," *Civil War History*, 21 (June, 1975), 144; Oscar S. Burges to Seward, November 17, 1856, Seward Papers.

[99] Letter from N. A. Alexander, November 18, 1856, Jamestown *Journal*, November 28, 1856.

tually accommodated their views to the party's.[100] It is impossible to determine precisely what proportion of the electorate such men represented. It is likely, however, in view of the great popular interest in politics, the much more important role it occupied in men's lives, and the greater strength of party identities, that the politically aware constituted a larger proportion of the antebellum electorate than is true today. One of the fundamental distinctions between the modern political universe and that of a century ago is that the nineteenth-century electorate was more committed, more informed, more issue conscious.[101]

Philip Converse, as part of his general denial of a fundamentally different electorate in the nineteenth century, challenges the view that voters of the earlier period were more informed or more ideological. He places great emphasis on the impact that increased education has on modern voters' involvement and comprehension, while he observes that educational opportunities were much more limited in the previous century.[102] His argument deserves close scrutiny.

Although advanced education was unusual before the Civil War, literacy was widespread—remarkably so by world standards—in the free states. In addition, sound reasons exist to reject the assumption that education played as important a role in past politics as it does today. Levels of education within the electorate cannot be extracted from prewar data, but it is suggestive that no strong positive relationship exists between participation and various indices of public commitment to education (Table 9). Moreover, it is difficult to reconcile the idea of an ignorant, uninformed electorate with the activities of professional politicians. Parties before the Civil War expended much money and considerable energy in printing and distributing literally thousands

[100] For examples, see Artemas Carter to Charles Sumner, July 17, 1854, John H. Smith to Sumner, March 27, 1855[?], Charles Sumner Papers, Harvard University; Sidney D. Maxwell Diary, 1852–1856, Cincinnati Historical Society; William Corry to William Haines Lytle, February 6, 1856, Lytle Family Papers, Cincinnati Historical Society.

[101] See the discussion in Eric Foner, *Free Soil, Free Labor, Free Men: The Ideology of the Republican Party before the Civil War* (New York: Oxford University Press, 1970), esp. 1–10, 310–17.

[102] Converse, "Change in the American Electorate"; and Philip E. Converse, "Information Flow and the Stability of Partisan Attitudes," *Public Opinion Quarterly*, 26 (Winter, 1962), 578–99.

TABLE 9. Pearson Product Moment Correlations:
Education Indices and Mean Turnout, 1850–1860.

	Illinois	Indiana	Ohio	Pennsylvania
Schools/ Family	.13	.19	−.01	.06
Education Taxes/ Family	−.16	−.04	.14	−.04
Education Taxes/ Schools	−.21	−.07	.02	−.06
School Funds/ Family	.08	.05	.15	−.06
School Funds/ School	−.08	−.07	−.03	−.06
Students/ Children	.01	.37	.20	.13
Illiterates/ Adults	.12	.01	.03	.00
N (counties)	99	91	88	63

SOURCE: Educational data from 1850 United States Census.

and thousands of political documents. Once a campaign was in full swing, national and state party headquarters were besieged with requests for documents. Such efforts dwarf similar activity in recent times. The manager of the 1856 Democratic campaign in Pennsylvania, for example, reported that party workers had distributed at least one document to every household in the county of Philadelphia. Politicians, whose livelihood was at stake, firmly believed that printed partisan material influenced voters.[103]

Everything we know about the antebellum northern electorate indicates that high voter interest, intense mass cognizance, and great emotional commitment prevailed in the absence of extensive educational opportunity. The pervasive attitude that political life was vital spurred mass political involvement much more than did education.

[103] Forney to Buchanan, September 11, October 3, 1856, Buchanan Papers; Roy Franklin Nichols, *The Disruption of American Democracy* (New York: Macmillan Company, 1948), 42–43, 47.

Furthermore, studies of voting in the 1960s and 1970s indicate that ideology is hardly confined to the well educated. In fact, the rise of ideological voting in recent times is directly traceable to the less well educated portion of the electorate.[104] In the face of this evidence, the argument that limited educational opportunity in the pre–Civil War North substantially precluded ideological voting is not persuasive.

Not all voters, of course, were moved by ideological considerations. As with the modern electorate, voter perception in the antebellum period covered a wide spectrum, ranging from a sound grasp of ideology to only the dimmest comprehension of the issues at stake. A wide variety of psychological, social, and intellectual factors influenced northern voting behavior, so that individuals and groups voted for a party for many different reasons. With a larger portion of voters then than now, issue voting and ideology prevailed. But the desire to achieve concrete goals (whether viewed in general, abstract terms or in a more limited context) was not the sole determinant of voting behavior. Also important were party loyalty and tradition, opposition to certain groups in the other party (negative reference groups), and a desire to identify with certain groups (positive reference groups).[105] Moreover, as Richard Trilling's work on modern political behavior suggests, these latter considerations—party loyalty, tradition, and reference group attitudes—have ideological overtones, especially in the creation of a party image as a component of partisan identity, that are not always recognized.[106] For many Americans then as now, party identification was predicated on a party image that reflected a certain degree of issue orientation. Thus men could vote Democratic because they perceived the Whigs as aristocrats and puritans who wished to regulate society. Or, believing that all rum sellers and drunkards were Democrats, a pro-temperance man could vote Whig, even if the party did not specifically endorse prohibition. In such cases, the rational blurred into the irrational. Yet, once a voter embraced an idea it was difficult to dispel.

After the 1856 election, a Connecticut politician outlined the im-

[104] Norman H. Nie with Kristi Anderson, "Mass Belief Systems Revisited: Political Change and Attitude Structure," *Journal of Politics*, 36 (August, 1974), 540–87.

[105] Lee Benson, *The Concept of Jacksonian Democracy: New York as a Test Case* (Princeton: Princeton University Press, 1961), 270–87.

[106] Richard J. Trilling, *Party Image and Electoral Behavior* (New York: John Wiley & Sons, 1976). Also see his article with the same title, *American Politics Quarterly*, 3 (July, 1975), 284–314.

portance of various attitudes in mass voting behavior. The Catholic Irish, he explained, voted solidly Democratic, for they believed that the Republicans would abolish slavery and bring blacks north to take jobs from them; they "love to have *somebody* beneath them and therefore are glad to keep the 'negroes' down." Rum drinkers and sellers along with proslavery men also voted Democratic, for they recognized the Republican party's hostility to their values. But also included among the opposition, he continued, were many of the "better class" of Democrats whose motivation was less apparent. "They are farmers, who think every Republican is an abolitionist; who think the Hartford Times [the Democratic state organ] another Gospel, —mechanics, who think they show their independence by voting the ticket dubbed Democratic; to whom a Republican is an old Whig, and an old Whig an Aristocrat who would be glad to go back to the government of George 3rd." [107]

With some voters, as these remarks imply, one consideration predominated. Undoubtedly with most voters, however, a wide variety of motivations blended into a party identification. A person rarely supports a party for a single reason. Reflected through the prism of party identity, these influences became mutually reinforcing. Much as in our own times, party identity was the means by which nineteenth-century voters sifted information and made sense out of the political universe around them.

That ideology played a greater role in politics before the Civil War does not mean that the rank and file shared the same level of comprehension of public issues or adhered to an equally sophisticated ideology as party leaders. In this period, as more recently, overly abstract appeals were doomed to political failure. Thus a prominent Illinois Republican declared that what the party needed was a practical question, for "it is too difficult to rally the people on a mere abstract principle." Horace Greeley believed that "a large majority of the voters" were not motivated by any grand political principle and that any party which appealed "wholly to [the] mind ignoring material considerations, is doomed to failure." [108] The typical voter's creed embraced a few issues

[107] Orris S. Ferry to Joseph R. Hawley, May 14, 1857, Hawley Papers. I wish to thank Michael F. Holt for a copy of this letter. Also see the New York *Tribune*, September 11, 1852.

[108] Herman Kriesman to Sumner, November 13, 1855, Sumner Papers; Horace

and rudimentary principles, complexly interwoven with rational and irrational beliefs, prejudices, material considerations, and social, cultural, and religious values. The skillful intertwining of these attitudes into a comprehensive and comprehensible world view was largely restricted to articulate party elites.

Nevertheless, voters generally shared the values which underpinned party ideologies in pre–Civil War America, even if they could not elucidate all the ramifications of their beliefs.[109] An appreciation of fundamental values such as the importance of self-government, the dignity of free labor, or the virtue of economic opportunity was not confined to the well educated. These beliefs pervaded northern society, despite significant disagreement on how best to implement, protect, and promote them. Nor is it true that antebellum voters lacked intelligible political beliefs. A high level of abstraction was not necessary to make meaningful political decisions. Men did not need a deep grasp of the constitutional issues involved, for example, to decide whether they disapproved of slavery expanding into Kansas or whether they believed that the liquor traffic, Catholics, southern slave-holders, or some other group threatened what they perceived as their interests, values, and rights.

After the Civil War many northerners, appalled by the shoddy corruption and crassness of the postwar years, wistfully looked back on the two decades before the war as the golden age of American politics. It was, as one commentator recalled many years later, a time when campaigning seemed in flower.[110] To some extent, such comments overlooked the continuities between politics in this period and that which followed. Party identities, to take the most obvious example, would remain the cornerstone of the American political system up to the present day. In other and more important respects, however, the political culture of the antebellum years was fundamentally different from that of today. Mass interest, as recorded by voter turnout, stood at an all-

---

Greeley to Theodore Parker, May 23, 1854, Copy, Theodore Parker Papers, Massachusetts Historical Society.

[109] Works that emphasize ideology during the Civil War era include: Foner, *Free Soil, Free Labor, Free Men*; Silbey, *A Respectable Minority*; Holt, *Political Crisis of the 1850s*; W. R. Brock, *An American Crisis: Congress and Reconstruction, 1865–1867* (New York: Harper & Row, 1963).

[110] Charles B. Johnson, "The Presidential Campaign of 1860," *Transactions of the Illinois State Historical Society* (1927), 117, 119–20.

time high. Ideology lay at the very heart of political conflict, and voters displayed a degree of political commitment and understanding unmatched in our own century. Party loyalty was stronger than at any other time in American history. More than in any subsequent era, political life formed the very essence of the pre–Civil War generation's experience. During this period, as one editor commented at its close, politics formed "the all-absorbing theme of conversation in the barroom, and in the drawing room, on the streets, and in the house, morning, noon and night."[111]

The nature of political culture in the years 1840–1860 had important ramifications for the collapse of the normal political process in 1861. The reasons for this breakdown were many, but one important cause was the interaction between each section's political culture. Party leaders had to seek solutions to the growing sectional crisis within a system that extolled the importance of ideology and stimulated popular fears that political defeat would be fatal to the cause of republican government. Frequent elections kept popular passions overheated and weakened the ability of moderates to check the growing forces of extremism in American society. As events after 1845 increasingly galvanized the emotions of a large and active electorate, politicians had less and less room to seek an acceptable compromise.[112]

Yet, as events after April, 1861, demonstrated, the relationship between the antebellum political universe and the sectional crisis was paradoxical: although the North's political system contributed to the political failure that led to war, once hostilities commenced, it greatly strengthened the Union war effort.[113] The North's political culture, with its emphasis on mass involvement and the widely shared belief in the necessity of safeguarding the experiment of popular government, enabled the Lincoln administration to mobilize northern public opinion behind a successful crusade to preserve the American republic.

[111] Peoria *Transcript*, July 13, 1860, quoted in George H. Mayer, *The Republican Party, 1854–1966* (2nd ed.; New York: Oxford University Press, 1967), 4.

[112] David Donald, "An Excess of Democracy: The American Civil War and the Social Process," *Lincoln Reconsidered* (2nd ed.; New York: Alfred A. Knopf, 1972), 209–35.

[113] Eric L. McKitrick, "Party Politics and the Union and Confederate War Efforts," William Nisbet Chambers and Walter Dean Burnham, eds., *The American Party Systems* (New York: Oxford University Press, 1967), 117–51.

APPENDIX

I used several different methods to estimate the number of eligible voters in the northern states for the period 1840–1860. Although the turnout rates given in Table 1 and elsewhere, like much of the statistical analysis of nineteenth-century American politics, rest on assumptions that cannot be fully verified, I believe that they are more accurate than any previously available estimates for the antebellum period.

I assembled data on the total number of votes cast in the northern states in these elections from a number of sources. The two most important were the archival holdings of the Inter-University Consortium for Political and Social Research and the returns printed in Horace Greeley's *Whig Almanac* (after 1854, the *Tribune Almanac*). Where necessary, I supplemented these sources with the election results given in newspapers, from the official returns contained in state archives, and from Walter Dean Burnham's compilation, *Presidential Ballots, 1836–1892* (Baltimore: Johns Hopkins University Press, 1955).

For all northern states except New York, Ohio, and Rhode Island, I used the number of adult white males as the best estimate of the size of the electorate for the years 1840–1847 (in those few states with black suffrage, I included adult black males as well). I extrapolated linearly for the years between the two end points. The New York state censuses of 1845, 1855, and 1865 indicated the number of voters in the state, so I used these figures to estimate the size of the electorate throughout the entire two decades, again extrapolating between censuses. I followed the same general method for Ohio, using the figures given in the Auditor's Reports for 1855 and 1863. For Rhode Island, I employed the estimates provided by Chilton Williamson in "Rhode Island Suffrage Since the Dorr War," *New England Quarterly*, 18 (March, 1955), 34–50. Wisconsin also represented a special case. Since aliens could vote in Wisconsin, I used the number of adult white males (from the 1850 and 1860 federal censuses) to estimate the state's electorate, beginning with its admission in 1848.

In addition to New York and Ohio, four other states—Connecticut, Indiana, Iowa, and Massachusetts—enumerated voters during the antebellum period. For Iowa, I used the state censuses of 1854, 1856, and 1859, and for Indiana, see the Reports of the State Auditor for 1850, 1854, and 1866. The number of voters in Massachusetts for various years is given in the *Massachusetts Register for the Year 1853*, 322–25; *Manual for the Use of the General Court* (1858), 115–23; and the Commonwealth of Massachusetts, House of Representatives, *House Document No. 65* (1876). The figures for Connecticut are taken from the *Connecticut Register for 1860* (1861). Several earlier editions indicated the number of polls in the state, and I used the 1860 ratio of voters to polls to estimate the number of voters for earlier years. For each state except Indiana, I used these figures to estimate the number of voters between 1848 and 1860.

Indiana's census of voters in this period seriously undercounted the size of its electorate, and thus I disregarded these figures in favor of those given in the federal censuses of 1850 and 1860. Since the 1851 state constitution instituted alien suffrage, I used adult white males as the best estimate of the electorate for the period 1851–1860, extrapolating between the end points. For the years 1848–1850, I corrected for the presence of immigrants by the technique described below. Massachusetts also required a slightly different procedure for part of these two decades. Because the number of adult males in 1840 significantly overestimates the state's electorate (primarily because of the inordinate weight of Suffolk County in the statewide figures), I extrapolated the number of voters from 1840 to 1852, when the state conducted its first census of voters, to reduce the error in my estimates.

For the remaining northern states, it was necessary to make some correction for the number of immigrants who were eligible to vote. Somewhat arbitrarily, I chose 1848 as the base year to begin this adjustment. In making this correction, I utilized the information in the 1856 Iowa and 1855 New York state censuses, which listed not only the native- and foreign-born population, but the number of native-born and naturalized voters as well. Contemporary observers consistently maintained that the ratio of voters to population did not significantly vary, so I employed the New York ratio of naturalized voters to foreign-born population in calculating the number of voters in the eastern states (Maine, Vermont, New Hampshire, Pennsylvania, and New Jersey) and the Iowa ratio for the remaining western states (Michigan, Illinois, and California).

For these eight states, my method was as follows. From the federal censuses I obtained the number of adult white males, foreign-born and native-born inhabitants in a state. Blacks were included in the estimates for those states (Vermont, New Hampshire, and Maine) where they were granted the franchise. I estimated each state's electorate by adding the number of native-born voters (adult males multiplied by the proportion of native-born population) and naturalized voters (the appropriate ratio times the foreign-born population). I ignored the impact of a tax-paying requirement in those few states where one still existed. In his careful study of the suffrage, Chilton Williamson concluded that, except for Rhode Island, these requirements were either innocuous or rarely enforced. Michael Holt reached a similar conclusion concerning the franchise in Pennsylvania, the most important state that still retained a tax requirement.

In calculating the turnout for state elections, I used the vote for the most important office. In a few instances when no state office was contested, I used the vote for congressman. For those states that held state and presidential elections simultaneously, I calculated turnout rates for both the presidential and state contests, but I used only the higher figure in computing a state's mean turnout. Including both percentages would, in effect, weight the election twice and distort the average.

The technique just described, though hardly flawless, yields estimates for the years 1848–1860 that are definitely superior to using simply adult white males. Moreover, the procedure has the advantage that it errs on the side of overestimating the size of the electorate by exaggerating the number of native-born voters (since the foreign-born population contained a proportionately greater number of adult males). As a result, the turnout figures are, if anything, too low for those states for which this method was employed. To a lesser degree, estimates of turnout based on adult males for the pre-1848 period also are conservative. In fact, it is virtually certain that the extent to which my method underestimates the actual rate of voting in the northern states during these decades exceeds any possible electoral fraud.

THOMAS B. ALEXANDER

The Dimensions of Voter Partisan Constancy in Presidential Elections from 1840 to 1860

By 1840 the nation's second two-party system was fully developed in every region.[1] A close, nationwide rivalry between Democrats and Whigs formed the basic configuration of presidential politics, not only in total popular vote but also within most of the states and even within an immense number of counties. Neither party could muster as much as a two-to-one majority in almost three-fourths of the nation's counties in 1840, or even 60 percent in considerably more than one-half.[2] This party system was subjected to such intense strain during the succeed-

[1] A more general research project on the two-party system of the United States between 1836 and 1880, from which this analysis of continuity is drawn, has been facilitated by grants from the Social Science Research Council, the University Research Committee of the University of Alabama, Tuscaloosa, and the University Research Council of the University of Missouri, Columbia. Computing facility staffs at both universities have provided essential services. During the development of the data set, of which the county-aggregate presidential returns are a part, invaluable assistance was furnished by Ross J Cameron, Walter D. Kamphoefner, William W. Beach, Paul E. McAllister, and Harry D. Holmes. Assistance for this specific project was generously furnished by Larry Steven Demaree and Don Wayne O'Hara, as well as by Walter Kamphoefner. No one working with presidential election data for this period of United States history should omit a fervent expression of appreciation to Walter Dean Burnham, whose 1955 *Presidential Ballots, 1836–1892* opened vistas that quickened the pulse of a generation of historians before there was a historical archive of machine-readable data at the Inter-University Consortium for Political and Social Research at Ann Arbor. I am grateful for the generous assistance provided by Richard P. McCormick.

[2] All statements concerning county-level aggregate election data for presidential elections and all analyses of these data are based on the author's set of county-aggregate census and election data. This set incorporates presidential, gubernatorial, and congressional election returns for 1838–1878 and 1850, 1860, and 1870 United States census information. Only the presidential data are used in this essay, except that change in turnout referred to in notes is based, in addition, on population information. The presidential election returns are from Walter Dean Burnham, *Presidential Ballots, 1836–1892* (Baltimore, 1955), adjusted or corrected when internal or other evidence justified changes. The gubernatorial and congressional data were obtained from the Historical Archive of the I.C.P.S.R. at Ann Arbor.

ing two decades, however, that the period is usually portrayed as one of the two or three most revolutionary epochs in the country's party history. Territorial expansion precipitated a storm over the status of slavery in territories, which threatened disaster by 1850, abated after the compromise of that year, and burst forth in 1854 with the Kansas-Nebraska imbroglio. Meanwhile, nativist sentiment flared and intruded sharply into even national politics. When the newly organized Republican party captured the upper North in 1856 with a frankly sectional appeal and then captured the presidency in 1860 in a four-way contest that was virtually a pair of separate elections—one northern, the other southern—it created the impression that sectionalism had destroyed the two-party alignment of the 1840s.[3] Yet, Democrats and their principal opponents actually maintained an almost equal division of the popular vote in presidential elections during the two decades before the Civil War. Each enjoyed the constancy of an impressive bloc of voters who appeared to be almost impervious to the appeals of rival candidates and issues. So close were the contests that usually only trifling aspects dictated which major-party candidate won. Something quite substantial, however, made it possible for electoral outcomes to hinge on trivial considerations. That substantial something was the massive continuity of voter alignment. To estimate the dimensions of that continuity is the objective of this essay.

The theme of continuity has been neglected, when not ignored, in accounts of presidential elections likely to be read by students or laymen. The customary episodic treatments appearing in almost all of the widely used college textbooks of the 1960s and 1970s obscure much of the essential character of the presidential contests of the 1840s and 1850s. To lose sight of continuity, a danger inherent in analyzing each election separately, is to risk a critically distorted view of each individual contest and of the role of presidential electoral politics in the political system. One consequence may be to misunderstand not only the

[3]The voluminous literature on the politics of these decades is synthesized by many scholars, but the most useful for the years of alleged decline and collapse of the party system is the New American Nation series volume by David M. Potter (completed and edited by Don E. Fehrenbacher), *The Impending Crisis, 1848–1861* (New York, 1976). James L. Sundquist, *Dynamics of the Party System: Alignment and Realignment of Political Parties in the United States* (Washington, D.C., 1973), provides a lucid analysis of the 1850s realignment that undeniably occurred but leaves an impression of greater voter shifting than is suggested in this essay.

TABLE 10. Absolute Difference between Percentages of Total Popular Vote Recorded for the Two Major Parties in Presidential Elections, 1840–1860.

State or Region	1840	1844	1848*	1852†	1856†	1860‡
Connecticut	11	5	5	0.4	13	16
Maine	0.5	13§	6§	1§	29	32
Massachusetts	16	11	19	29	53	52
New Hampshire	11§	19§	26§	14§	8	15
Rhode Island	23	20	28	3§	33	23
Vermont	28	18	25	40	59	60
New England	10	2	7	12	35	36
New Jersey	4	1	4	6§	6	4§
New York	3	1§	4§	0.3§	34	7
Pennsylvania	0.1	2§	4	2§	0.2§	18
Middle Atlantic	2	1§	0.3§	2§	18	10
Illinois	2§	12§	3§	4§	12	4
Indiana	12	2§	3§	4§	0.2§	6
Iowa	—	—	4§	1§	19	12
Michigan	4	6§	10§	1§	17	15
Minnesota	—	—	—	—	—	27
Ohio	9	2	5§	4	12	10
Wisconsin	—	—	3§	4§	12	13
North-Central	7	2§	4§	0.1§	10	10
Arkansas	13§	27§	10§	24§	34§	26§
Delaware	10	2	4	0.3	11§	5§
Maryland	8	5	4	7§	10	4§
Kentucky	28	8	15	3	5§	8§
Missouri	13§	14§	10§	12§	9§	9§
North Carolina	15	5	11	1§	13§	7§
Tennessee	11	0.1	5	1	5§	5§
Virginia	2§	6§	2§	12§	20§	8§
Upper South	9	0.5§	4	5§	9§	8§
Alabama	9§	18§	1§	22§	24§	38§
Florida	—	—	17	20§	14§	24§
Georgia	12	2§	3	11§	14§	19§
Louisiana	19	3§	8	4§	3§	20§
Mississippi	7	13§	1§	21§	19§	27§
South Carolina	(presidential electors not popularly elected)					
Texas	—	—	41§	46§	33§	51§
Lower South	5	9§	0.3§	18§	18§	30§

TABLE 10 continued

State or Region	1840	1844	1848*	1852†	1856†	1860‡
California	—	—	—	7§	3	23§
Oregon	—	—	—	—	—	19§
Pacific	—	—	—	7§	3	20§
All Free States	5	1§	0.4§	1	18	14
All Slave States	8	3§	3	8§	12§	15§
United States	6	1§	1	1§	9	5

SOURCES: The basic source for state-level returns and percentages, and by combinations for regional percentages, is Svend Petersen, *A Statistical History of the American Presidential Elections* (New York: Frederick Ungar Publishing Co., 1963). In instances in which these returns differ substantially from the ones found in W. Dean Burnham, *Presidential Ballots, 1836–1892* (Baltimore: Johns Hopkins University Press, 1955), further checking with other sources, including the *Tribune Almanac*, has led to the acceptance of Burnham's for Georgia for 1852, for Pennsylvania for 1856, and for Vermont for 1860.

*Free-Soil vote of New York State added to the Democratic party total for the United States, the Middle Atlantic region, the all-free-state region, and the state of New York.

†Difference between Democratic party percentage and combined opposition parties' percentages of the total vote.

‡Difference between combined Douglas and Breckinridge percentages and combined Lincoln and Bell percentages of the total vote.

§Democratic party majority or plurality.

capstone political institution of the United States but also the essential character of other political systems with which comparisons are made in terms of form rather than substance. On the premise that prevailing treatments of these presidential elections sacrifice perspective to episode, careful attention to the implications of persistence of party alignment appears to be justified.

Table 10 provides a basis for observing the closeness of presidential races between major-party candidates. That 6 percent was the difference between the parties in national popular vote in 1840 is one concise way of describinig a 53 percent Whig versus 47 percent Democratic share of the vote. Only one-half of the percentage difference would be needed to bring about a tie vote, it may be noted, so that

New England's 10 percent difference in 1840 means that a shift of 5 percent of the total vote from the Whig candidate to the Democratic would have made the outcome nearly a standoff. Within regions or individual states, narrow differences were customary in 1840, with the exceptions chiefly of some New England states, Kentucky, and Louisiana. This 1840 election was the first Whig party victory, with William Henry Harrison defeating incumbent Democratic President Martin Van Buren.

In comparing the closeness of contests through the period, it is evident that the 1844 margin of victory by James K. Polk over Whig idol Henry Clay was considerably narrower than Harrison's had been. Continuing close rivalry characterized the 1848 election of General Zachary Taylor over Lewis Cass, long-time Democratic leader from Michigan. Not even the heavy desertions by New York Democrats to the Free-Soil candidate, former President Van Buren, disguises the closeness. These Democrats returned to their party four years later, and adding their number to the Democratic vote in 1848 displays how evenly balanced the major-party contingents remained. The succeeding election, that of 1852, came after the shockingly sectional clash in 1849 and 1850 that culminated in the Compromise of 1850. Nevertheless, this too was a close contest in most of the country. Franklin Pierce carried the Democratic banner to victory with less than 54 percent of the major-party vote cast for himself or for his Whig opponent General Winfield Scott. The Free-Soil party, drawing principally from former Whigs, had fallen back from its 1848 high to only 5.5 percent of the total vote. Less than 1 percent separated Pierce from his combined opposition.

The emergence of the Republican party before the 1856 election helped to create an illusion of revolutionary political realignment. James Buchanan, the Democrat, won with about 45 percent of the popular vote, defeating Republican John C. Frémont and Millard Fillmore, the American party candidate. Fillmore had succeeded to the presidency at the death of Whig President Taylor in 1850 and was supported mostly by southern Whigs in 1856. The party name, American, was a by-product of the nativist surge. Tracing basic party alignments, Democrats against anti-Democrats, reveals only 9 percent separating Buchanan from his opposition. The illusion of revolutionary realignment was enhanced in 1860 by the division of the Democratic party.

TABLE 11. Absolute Change in the Democratic Percentage of the Total
Popular Vote in Presidential Elections, 1836–1860.

Region	1836–1840	1840–1844	1844–1848	1848–1852	1852–1856	1856–1860	1840–1860*
United States	−4	+3	−7 (−3)†	+8 (+4)†	−5	+2	+0.4
New England	−6	+1	−9	+7	−11	−0.5	−13
Middle Atlantic	−4	+1	−14 (−0.1)†	+15 (+1)†	−10	+4	−4
North-Central	−2	+3	−3	+3	−5	+0.3	−1
Upper South	−4	+5	−2	+5	+2	−0.5	+9
Lower South	−4	+7	−4	+9	+0.2	+6	+18
Pacific					−5	+12	
All Free States	−4	+2	−9 (+1)†	+9 (−1)†	−8	+2	−4
All Slave States	−4	+6	−3	+6	+2	+2	+12

*Net changes by state from 1840 to 1860 do not usually vary greatly from regional
changes. Among the states existing in 1840, more than one-half, fifteen, had changes
of less than 10 percent; the only states with more than 15 percent are Louisiana
(+20%), Kentucky (+18%), Massachusetts (−17%), Mississippi (+17%), Vermont
(−16%), and Maine (−16%).

†These are absolute change percentages if the Free-Soil vote of New York State is added
to the Democratic party vote of the United States and of the Middle Atlantic and the
all-free-states regions.

Republican Abraham Lincoln defeated Stephen A. Douglas, the northern Democrat, and won a majority of the electoral vote. In the South,
Democrat John C. Breckinridge ran ahead of Whig John Bell, whose
party used Constitutional Union as its title in this crisis election. Not-
withstanding that two nearly separate elections did occur in 1860,
Democratic vote totals combined against Republicans and Constitutional Unionists show the closeness of continuing party rivalry. For the
entire country and for the regions with most of the voters, the contest
between Democrats and their opponents was closer in 1860 than in the
preceding presidential election.

The continuity of party strength from election to election in aggregate returns is illustrated in Table 11. For the entire United States, for
example, the Democratic percentage of total popular vote in 1836 was
approximately 51 and for 1840 approximately 47, hence an absolute decline of 4 percent. Losses and gains alternated at the aggregate United

States level until 1860. It is notable that over the years from 1840 to 1860, both years of Democratic defeat, the Democrats' percentage of the total national vote changed by less than 1 percent. The change was not the same or in the same direction for each region. The most northeastern part of the country veered more away from the Democrats, while the southwestern part gradually became more Democratic. Nevertheless, in the free-state area as a whole Democrats declined by only 4 percent net from 1840 to 1860, and in the slave-state region Democrats gained by only 12 percent net over the same twenty-year period. Individual state changes in Democratic percentage are not included in Table 11, but the pattern is not significantly different from that offered by the regional analysis.

Admittedly, continuity in proportions of voters aggregated by regions, or even by states, is not convincing evidence that masses of individual voters were constant in their party loyalties. Compensating shifts of voters between parties could account for the same impression of consistency. If party appeals had drawn very different elements of the electorate from contest to contest but had been so nearly equal in impact that the resulting lineup of voters repeatedly almost duplicated aggregates of the foregoing election, both closeness of contest and slightness of change between elections could have prevailed for twenty years. This may tax one's credulity somewhat; but before additional evidence of voter constancy is offered, an examination of the typology of presidential contests pervading textbook accounts can bring into focus the nature and extent of possible distortion.

Candidate personality or reputation, campaign enthusiasm, and the alleged overriding importance of one or another national issue dominate the passages concerned with these elections.[4] When men-

---

[4]The college textbooks used for this analysis of accounts of presidential elections and from which are taken all quotations not otherwise identified are: Thomas A. Bailey, *The American Pageant* (3rd ed.; Boston, 1966); Bernard Bailyn *et al.*, *The Great Republic* (Lexington, Mass., 1977); Leland D. Baldwin and Erling A. Erickson, *The American Quest* (Belmont, Calif., 1969, 1973); John M. Blum *et al.*, *The National Experience* (2nd ed.; New York, 1968); John M. Blum *et al.*, *The National Experience* (4th ed.; New York, 1977); Harry J. Carman, Harold C. Syrett, and Bernard W. Wishy, *A History of the American People* (2nd ed.; New York, 1960); Oliver P. Chitwood, Rembert W. Patrick, and Frank L. Owsley, *The American People* (3rd ed.; Princeton, 1962); James I. Clark and Robert V. Remini, *We the People: A History of the United States* (Beverly Hills, Calif., 1975); Richard N. Current, T. Harry Williams, and Frank Freidel, *American His-*

tion is made of the pivotal impact of one state, usually New York, little attention is paid to other closely contested states in which a total bloc of electoral votes greater than New York's was at stake. It is rare to be able to read as elementary a recognition of the facts as the following: "By 1840 the two parties were almost equally strong not only at the national level but also in every section, in most of the states, and in a majority of the counties." And it is almost unique to find in a textbook, even one appearing as late as 1977, a comment about the 1844 election that "most of the electorate was less swayed by issues than by party loyalty."

The 1840 "log cabin campaign" has been almost universally classified as a campaign ballyhoo classic, in which "claptrap was king" and the Democrats were "hooted out of office by a meaningless hoopla campaign." The panic of 1837 and ensuing depression are usually mentioned as overriding issues, personalized by contrasting the "stern simplicity" of Harrison in his log cabin with Van Buren's "Turkish divan" in the "Royal Splendor of the President's Palace." Apart from panic and depression, personalities get colorful treatment in most accounts: Harrison as a "simple, honest, son of toil" who could turn into a military hero when his people needed him at the battle of Tippecanoe; and "Martin Van Ruin" as "Sweet Sandy Whiskers," "a simpering dandy" and a "slothful and effeminate oriental potentate."

tory: A Survey (New York, 1961) and (4th ed.; New York, 1975); Carl N. Degler et al., The Democratic Experience: A Short History (3rd ed.; Glenview, Ill., 1973); John A. Garraty, The American Nation: A History of the United States (3rd ed.; New York, 1975); Norman A. Graebner, Gilbert C. Fite, and Philip L. White, A History of the American People (New York, 1971); Rebecca Brooks Gruver, An American History (New York, 1972); Oscar Handlin, The History of the United States (New York, 1967); Ralph Volney Harlow, revised by Nelson M. Blake, The United States (4th ed.; New York, 1964); John D. Hicks, George E. Mowry, and Robert E. Burke, A History of American Democracy (3rd ed.; Boston, 1966); Richard Hofstadter, William Miller, and Daniel Aaron, The American Republic (Englewood Cliffs, N.J., 1959); Richard Hofstadter et al., The United States (4th ed.; Englewood Cliffs, N.J., 1976); Dumas Malone and Basil Rauch, Empire for Liberty (New York, 1960); Samuel Eliot Morison and Henry Steele Commager, The Growth of the American Republic (5th ed.; New York, 1962); Richard B. Morris and William Greenleaf, U.S.A.: The History of a Nation (Chicago, 1969); Dexter Perkins and Glyndon G. Van Deusen, The American Democracy (New York, 1964); Dexter Perkins and Glyndon G. Van Deusen, The United States of America: A History (2nd ed.; New York, 1968); Charles Sellers and Henry May, A Synopsis of American History (Chicago, 1963); Charles Sellers, Henry May, and Neil R. McMillen, A Synopsis of American History (4th ed.; Chicago, 1976).

The 1844 campaign is sometimes portrayed in part as a matter of personalities or exciting campaigning, but the omnipresent theme is "manifest destiny" as represented in the Texas and Oregon expansion issue. Although Polk is commonly described as the first "dark horse" candidate and Clay as a popular idol, "easily the most popular man in the country," the decisive influence of the expansion issue stands out. One account even goes so far as to claim that "Texas was the one outstanding issue" and that "the election of Polk indicated that a majority of the voters were in favor of annexation." Unusual, indeed, is one analysis of the outcome as no such mandate, but as decision on vital issues by a minority of voters. Almost as frequent as mention of the expansion issue is reference to the decisive role of New York, where James G. Birney's small Liberty party vote is judged to be from Whig ranks and to account for Clay's loss of that state and with it the election. But no direct reference is to be found to the fact that Clay carried by extremely slender margins such states as New Jersey, Ohio, and Tennessee, aggregating more electoral votes than New York.

The Mexican War and the sectional antagonism aroused by the potential expansion of slavery alarmed the leaders of both major parties. The 1848 election is generally portrayed, therefore, as largely issueless, with both parties eager to avoid real issues because the chief one was slavery expansion. Some emphasis is placed on personalities, General Taylor being offered as a blend of military hero and ordinary American. "Old Rough and Ready" was a "simple, honest soldier, who detested the sophistries of politicians and regarded the slavery question as an artificial abstraction." Lewis Cass was hard to present colorfully, so "colorless old party wheel-horse" was a substitute sobriquet. All accounts bring out the disaffection of antislavery leaders that produced the Free-Soil party, and most accounts emphasize that New York's Free-Soil vote was chiefly from Democratic ranks and cost Cass the state and the election. Rarely is it mentioned that the Free-Soil defections gave Ohio and Indiana to Cass. Some treatments even emphasize an alleged "high degree of political fluidity" in both free-soil territory and the South, where a recovery from the losses of 1844 produced a mild percentage change in favor of the slaveholding Whig general, who claimed Louisiana as his official residence.

The 1852 presidential contest has usually been treated as an example of weariness with strife, which is actually an issue-oriented explanation. Exhausted by the crisis of 1850 and deeply perturbed, leaders of both parties sought to avoid rekindling spent passions. Descriptions of this contest between Pierce and Scott usually emphasize its dullness. The attempts to endow this account with any color usually involve the "Old Fuss and Feathers" label for Scott, or "the hero 'of many a well-fought *bottle*'" for Pierce, who was widely believed to be using alcohol to excess. On the premise that a craving for peace was widespread, the Democrats are usually portrayed as winning because they had supported the Compromise of 1850 more strongly than the Whigs, although both parties endorsed the compromise. Moreover, despite the close contest throughout the nation, nearly every account paints the Whig party as dead or nearly so from the intraparty sectional antagonisms of the crisis period. This latter emphasis is clearly an issue-oriented treatment, engendered, one suspects, more by a look forward to 1854 and 1856 than by anything to be drawn from the election results.

The appearance in presidential politics of the Republican party, with John C. Frémont as its standard-bearer for 1856, is almost uniformly presented as the long-awaited crumbling of party alignments. Few, if any, treatments of this election are concerned with elements of continuity among the anti-Democrats; the Democratic party is left as the sole bearer of partisan continuity. The fact that nativism had surfaced and had been seized upon by many Whigs as a winning issue (hence their party name for the contest, American party) provided another basis for implying that voter alignments were dissolving. The overwhelming emphasis on issues—whether slavery in the territories, nativism, or general sectional rivalry—dominates customary accounts. Some color and personality are introduced. "Free Soil, Free Labor, and Frémont," "Bleeding Kansas," and an emphasis on the dashing reputation of the "Pathfinder" fail, however, to obscure the portrayal of real issues splintering the old parties. Not infrequent mention of a solid South making Buchanan's victory possible, despite his receiving only about 55 percent of the slave-state vote, enhances the impression of deep-rooted sectional conflict and the end of the previous two-party alignment.

Lincoln's election in 1860 is almost universally attributed to issues, although not all go so far as to state: "The one dominating issue was slavery extension. The Republicans managed to convince the plain people of the Northwest that if this were allowed to continue at the Kansas-Nebraska and Dred Scott pace, the Great Plains would be carved into slave plantations instead of free homesteads." Some emphasis, however, is placed on Lincoln's image as a rail-splitter, somehow continuing the log cabin tradition of 1840, and on enthusiastic campaigning with torchlight parades, songs, and banners. Yet the image projected in textbooks consists primarily of response to issues, either by voters or by leaders who presumably were assessing probable voter response.

The Democratic party schism is commonly explained as a clash over the status of slavery in the territories and Douglas' position on that issue. The northern Democrats' pairing of a Deep South Democrat with Douglas (Herschel V. Johnson of Georgia after Benjamin Fitzpatrick of Alabama declined) is presented as a natural effort to mute sectional antagonism. That southern Democrats nominated a border-state leader, John C. Breckinridge of Kentucky, with Joseph Lane of Oregon as running mate, is also attributed to a desire to project sectional moderation.

The choice of Lincoln by the Republicans, in preference to front-runner William H. Seward of New York, is commonly explained as still another decision for moderation in sectional issues. The Republican platform is treated as a shrewd subduing of the party's antislavery image of 1856 and the promotion of economic appeals to the East and West. Lincoln's running mate, Hannibal Hamlin of Maine, is rarely mentioned, probably because his nomination does not fit into a moderate, less sectional mode of interpretation. The Constitutional Union party, composed chiefly of southern Whigs, is portrayed as reacting to the issues by attempting to evade all specific ones as unmanageable and by substituting a generalized faith in the Constitution, the Union, and the enforcement of the laws. Its candidates, John Bell of Tennessee and Edward Everett of Massachusetts, were supposed to reflect the party's national, nonsectional orientation.

Overall, the impression is commonly left that pivotal numbers of voters were uncommitted and that issues, either directly or indirectly through candidate reputation or place of residence, determined voter response. The possibility of continuity of alignment for most voters is not made manifest. Truly exceptional is the one recognition that Republicans paired Hamlin, a Democrat turned Republican, with the former Whig, Lincoln, specifically to weaken the loyalty of the Democratic rank and file. Not even the simple fact that California and Oregon were the only free states to which substantial numbers of southern Democrats had migrated is mentioned as a reason for the selection of an Oregonian as Breckinridge's running mate.

These customary accounts of presidential elections justify concern.[5] Colorful, even trivial characterizations too often result from emphasizing the unique or incidental. Personality, color, issues, and accidents so overwhelm the occasional mention of the continuity of voters' preference for a specific party that certain inferences seem difficult to escape. The casual reader of these accounts might even envision each voter as a free agent ready to weigh his own interests, preferences, and judgments about the general welfare every time he voted in a presidential contest. Only the most inexperienced or naïve would jump to such a simplistic conclusion; but why all the emphasis on candidates, campaigning, and fears and hopes of the electorate unless the reader is meant to conclude that a significant number of voters were, in fact, independent? And if such a conclusion reinforces an exaggerated impression of voter perceptiveness and independence, it may contribute to a chauvinism that is already difficult enough to contain. If the people of the United States are to continue, generation after generation, to compare their political institutions with other peoples', almost always to the disadvantage of the latter, it will be salutary to have an unclouded view of what they are extolling. Although we may agree that the well informed and wary can read the prevalent offerings on presidential elections from 1840 to 1860 without being seriously misled, much remains to be said in the interest of the less wary or less concerned.[6]

---

[5] Perceptive historians, as almost all authors of successful college textbooks may safely be described, have known very well that persisting voter alignment is the basic terrain on which presidential battles are fought. But it is not appealing to comment about one election after another as essentially a repetition of the preceding one except for a few unique aspects of little intrinsic significance. Moreover, a plausible justification for emphasizing the unique is readily at hand: who won is commonly the denouement of the story. If it was a horse race all the way, that is all the more reason to lay great stress on the sometimes almost imperceptible distinctions that, after all, did make the difference between a winner and a loser.

[6] It is instructive to note how deeply ingrained is the habit of episodic treatment of

The habit of continuing to support the party one first chooses to support has been convincingly demonstrated for twentieth-century voters by sophisticated survey research projects beginning with the 1930s.[7] Voters of the 1840s and 1850s cannot be surveyed by interviews, it is true, but much may be inferred about their behavior from surviving information about thousands of individuals. It is suggestive, for example, that only 3 percent of 659 politically active men in Indiana during the 1836–1860 period were identified as having changed party, and that only 7 percent of 1,499 such Tennesseans were so identified (almost all of whom changed during the short period when nativism intruded into national politics).[8] Even more may be inferred from aggregate data such as county-level election returns over as extended a period as twenty years, incorporating six presidential elections. It is through analysis of these data that evidence has been gathered to support the proposition that far fewer voters of the period made lasting party changes than might be supposed and that many of the voters dur-

---

presidential elections. In 1971 there appeared a four-volume treatment of presidential elections, one by one, each by a different author with few exceptions: Arthur M. Schlesinger, Jr., ed., *History of American Presidential Elections, 1789–1968* (New York, 1971). Elections from 1836 through 1860 are by Joel H. Silbey for 1836 (I, 577–640), William Nisbet Chambers for 1840 (I, 643–744), Charles Sellers for 1844 (I, 747–861), Holman Hamilton for 1848 (II, 865–918), Roy and Jeanette Nichols for 1852 (II, 921–1003), Roy F. Nichols and Philip S. Klein for 1856 (II, 1007–94), and Elting Morison for 1860 (II, 1097–1152). Two of these treatments are especially sensitive to voter constancy, and others reveal awareness; but these concerns are injected in spite of the basic organization. Subsequently Schlesinger edited the four-volume *History of U.S. Political Parties* (New York, 1973), in which the essays escape somewhat from the episodic. Aspects of voter constancy are explored by Michael F. Holt in writing about the Democratic party, 1828–1860, and by David Herbert Donald in his treatment of the Republican party, 1864–1876, in which he reflects on the inability of Republicans to attract northern Democrats during the Reconstruction period.

[7] Basic references begin with Angus Campbell *et al.*, *The American Voter* (New York, 1960) and *Elections and the Political Order* (New York, 1966). A convenient listing of other highly relevant references is in Ray M. Shortridge, "The Voter Realignment in the Midwest During the 1850s," *American Politics Quarterly*, 4 (April, 1976), 193–222, and more extensive discussion is in his "Voting Patterns in the American Midwest, 1840–1872" (Ph.D. dissertation, University of Michigan, 1974).

[8] Kit Carson Carter III, "Indiana Voters During the Second American Party System, 1836–1860: A Study in Social, Economic, and Demographic Distinctions and in Voter Constancy" (Ph.D. dissertation, University of Alabama, 1975); Frank Mitchell Lowrey III, "Tennessee Voters During the Second Two-Party System, 1836–1860: A Study in Voter Constancy" (Ph.D. dissertation, University of Alabama, 1973).

Various reasons for voter constancy have been suggested. Most of the hypotheses

ing this period probably saw themselves as maintaining rather than abandoning their prior partisan commitments. Least-squares estimates of voting behavior from county-level aggregate voting returns are the bases for the conclusions presented.[9]

If the reader will bear with me briefly, we can soon return to the electoral history. But first it seems appropriate to make clear the nature, strengths, and weaknesses of the tool that is to be used for making the estimates essential to the argument of this essay. Serious attention to findings is unlikely if the reader has little basis for perceiving how they were obtained. Offering a research design in notes or appendix is probably suitable when readers may be expected to share a clear understanding of the tool used, a comforting situation not to be expected in this instance. With hope that what follows will be of more interest and will be taken more seriously and that the characteristics of the tool will be more apparent when it is observed cutting into familiar

---

reject any notion that the classical model of the informed voter can account for the constancy, although there is some support for a very generalized voter awareness of individual interests being congruent with one major party's dominant thrust. Psychological identification or affective orientation is most commonly stressed, together with a supplementary concept of voter perceptions of political events, issues, or personalities being so thoroughly filtered through party orientation as to deter defection, even when voter interests might clearly be better served by the opposition party. The objective of this essay does not require an explanation of voter constancy, although a more useful assessment of the party system surely will require an explanation. Recent studies of voter constancy are too numerous to be catalogued here but one may begin with *The American Voter, Elections and the Political Order*, and *Dynamics of the Party System*, all mentioned before, and Joel H. Silbey, *A Respectable Minority: The Democratic Party in the Civil War Era, 1860–1868* (New York, 1977), esp. Ch. 1, entitled "A Party of Habits, Prejudices, and Traditions." The provocative character of the present debate may be perceived readily in exchanges among Walter Dean Burnham, Philip E. Converse, Gerald M. Pomper, and Jerold G. Rusk in the *American Political Science Review* in the March, 1965, December, 1970, December, 1971, June, 1972, and September, 1974, issues.

[9] A fascinating comparison of county-level ecological analysis for the 1960 presidential election with comparable conclusions from survey research provides a basis for confidence in the ecological analysis approach: E. Terrence Jones, "Ecological Inference and Electoral Analysis," *Journal of Interdisciplinary History*, 2 (Winter, 1972), 249–62. During 1973 and 1974 three extended research notes that appeared in that journal furnish both an intensive evaluation of ecological regression techniques and an extensive array of relevant references: J. Morgan Kousser, "Ecological Regression and the Analysis of Past Politics," 4 (Autumn, 1973), 237–62; Allan J. Lichtman, "Correlation, Regression, and the Ecological Fallacy: A Critique," 4 (Winter, 1974), 417–33; and E. Terrence Jones, "Using Ecological Regression," 4 (Spring, 1974), 593–96.

historical material, I will discuss the method not as an afterthought but as an integral part of the argument.

A very large number of counties, ranging from small proportions of habitual Democratic party supporters to large proportions of Democrats among the voters, provides substantial stability for least-squares estimates when a high degree of similarity of voting behavior is found to have existed between any pair of presidential elections. Or, if one is permitted to be slightly more technical, very strong associations in a bivariate regression analysis, in which the values of both variables are well distributed over a wide range, make it possible for us to infer with considerable confidence what proportion of those who voted Democratic in 1840, for example, also voted Democratic in 1844.[10]

The assumption underlying the least-squares estimate, as displayed by scattergram presentation in Figure 1, is that a close fit to the least-squares line justifies an inference that the central tendency of Democrats in one election to vote Democratic in a later election has been estimated. Hence, knowing for the first election the Democratic party's percentage of the total vote in a considerable number of counties makes it possible to predict very closely what percentage of each county's vote the Democrats will obtain in the second election. The least-squares line in Figure 1 suggests that for each of the 1,037 counties about 95 percent of those who voted Democratic in 1840 also voted Democratic in 1844. In line with this central tendency, 95 percent is the least-squares estimate of continuity among Democratic voters. Weighting by the number of votes cast in each county is necessary to correct for any substantial difference in voter behavior that is related to the actual size of the electorate in a county, but this type of differential behavior is usually not very great. The weighted regression analysis for this particular pair of elections yields the same estimate of 95 percent, although the weighted regression equation is slightly different (intercept=9 instead of 13; regression coefficient=86 instead of 82).

---

[10]There are disagreements about several aspects of operationalizing and performing ecological regressions on county-level variables. This does not seem an appropriate place to enter the lists in defense of the particular methods used here. The use of party percentages of the total vote actually cast, for example, is rejected by Shortridge, "Voter Realignment in the Midwest During the 1850s," 200, in favor of party percentages of an estimated eligible electorate. I have concluded that this procedure introduces more assumptions about the nature of participation or abstention, not to mention the eligibility

FIGURE 1. Scattergram and Regression Line for Regression Analysis
of Democratic Percentage of County-Level Aggregate Vote
for the Presidential Elections of 1840 and 1844.

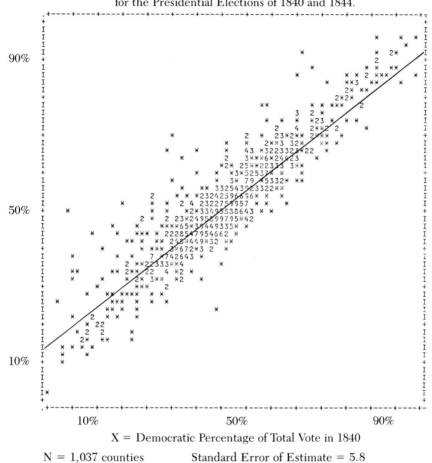

N = 1,037 counties   Standard Error of Estimate = 5.8
r = .91   Least-Squares Estimate
a = 13   of Party Continuity   = 95%
b = .82

As extended over a decade or more in pairwise comparisons of elections, these estimates are not intended to be taken literally as suggesting that a certain proportion of the actual individuals who voted Democratic in one election also voted Democratic in a later one. Deaths, the coming of age of prospective voters, and migrations into or out of a county preclude such literal interpretation. The rising tide of immigration and the speedy addition of immigrants to the voting pool further becloud the meaning of voter constancy estimates by least-squares projection. What a well-founded and very high estimate of continuity of voting alignment over a four-, eight-, or even twelve-year period does literally mean is that the party's proportion of the total vote by county is changed very little from one election to the next. Why this stability existed is not the same question, of course, but it is closely related.

In a single state in which almost every county is closely divided between parties, inference about stability of voter alignment is tenuous. But many counties, whether within one state or from a number of states, that incorporate a wide range of strength for one party (as in Figure 1) provide a far better basis for inference about stability. Compensating shifts of voters between parties can readily be hypothesized where a close division exists. But to assume that compensating shifts just neatly balance regardless of whether the division is 80–20, 75–25, or 20–80 taxes credulity. Surely the most obvious hypothesis in such cases is that men who voted in the two elections rarely switched parties, that deaths and departures were distributed between the parties in proportion to their respective strengths, that voters coming of age commonly accepted their fathers' party preference, and that newcomers to a neighborhood were influenced by the dominant party preference there. It is relevant to this last point that surviving returns from rural voting districts, where the total vote was often less than one hundred, indicate that one of the parties was more likely to be predominant than is the case for entire counties.

On the other hand, counties of the 1840s and 1850s were small enough aggregate voter units to be useful for ecological regression analysis. Nineteenth-century counties had far fewer voters than might be assumed by anyone acquainted with twentieth-century county vote

---

factor, than I am willing to accept. Weighting is debated by some, for another example. All that seems appropriate within this essay is to make explicit the procedures; discussion of alternatives will be happily pursued through appropriate outlets.

totals. In 1840, for example, even in the more densely populated North, 35 percent of the counties recorded fewer than 1,000 votes in the presidential election—and 50 percent fewer than 2,500. Almost two-thirds of the southern counties reported fewer than 1,000 votes. This did not change rapidly between 1840 and 1860 because new counties were created almost in proportion to growing vote totals in many of the states outside the Northeast.

There is no doubt that employing regressions on county-aggregate election data to estimate continuity of voting habit yields imprecise estimates. Moreover, the errors of estimating proportions for each county are substantial, even for a four-year interval, and it could hardly be otherwise for a number of reasons. Rapid increase in total vote in presidential elections together with the substantial death rate for adults assured the presence of many new voters at the second of any pair of presidential elections (Table 12). The voters coming of age within a county might be influenced by family, but the as yet unmeasured heavy internal migration provided many newcomers also. Especially in northern counties, the foreign born became increasingly numerous between 1840 and 1860, and they too moved about considerably within the country. If political party alignment was unrelated to a move to a different county (by no means a certainty, but yet untested), the pool of new voters in the second of a pair of elections would be reflecting division between parties in the areas they had left, which might or might not be similar to that in their new home, as well as responding perhaps to the pressures of new neighbors. Turnout rates varied considerably from election to election, affected by considerations not yet studied systematically but probably including such nonpartisan matters as the weather and the accidents of administering an election.[11] It is not unusual to discover reports that an election box was

[11] The variations from one presidential election to the next in county-level turnout is a serious source of possible random errors of estimate in ecological regression procedure. Little is known about the characteristics of voter participation, and turnout rates varied from the average-per-county turnout change between elections by as much as 10 percent for about one-fourth of the northern counties and more than one-third of the southern counties between any two presidential elections of this period. Change in the turnout rate exceeded 20 percent for more than one-tenth of the counties and between 1848 and 1852 exceeded 20 percent for two-fifths of the southern counties. Since so little is known about the reasons for participation or abstention, what proportion of this variation in turnout may have been randomly distributed between parties is also unknown.

TABLE 12. Rate of Increase in the Total Popular Vote in Presidential
Elections, 1840–1860.

Date Interval	Rate (percent)
Four-Year:	
1840–1844	12
1844–1848	7
1848–1852	10
1852–1856	28
1856–1860	16
Eight-Year:	
1840–1848	19
1844–1852	17
1848–1856	40
1852–1860	48
Twelve-Year:	
1840–1852	31
1844–1856	49
1848–1860	63
Twenty-Year:	
1840–1860	95

NOTE: The proportion of voters in the second of each pair of elections who could not
have voted in the first is much greater than suggested directly by rate of increase, for
an unknown proportion of new voters was required to replace those who died or
moved away during the date interval simply to maintain a zero rate of increase. Moreover, at the level of county aggregate vote, further increases in the proportion of
voters who had not voted there in the preceding election are attributable to unknown
but substantial internal migration rates.

not opened because of such an unpredictable circumstance as the absence of any firewood to use in the stove. Even the accidental or deliberate falsification of the election returns probably had the effect of in-
troducing greater apparent variation in voting proportions than in fact
existed. Poll officials were known to send in election returns in some
instances showing the margin of victory rather than the totals for each
candidate. And many an instance is documented of whole boxes not
getting counted in time to be included in the official totals. In the face
of these beclouding circumstances, the closeness of fit to a regression
(or least-squares) line displayed in Figure 1 is impressive evidence that

some forces were at work holding party division of the actual vote close to a stable ratio. The hypothesis supported in this essay is that the preponderant force was the near rigidity of individual partisanship.

In addition to the fact that considerably less than a perfect fit to a regression line is not unusual, the regression equations in almost all of the comparisons used here are similar in having an intercept above zero and a regression coefficient lower than 1.0, yielding a least-squares estimate below 100 percent. It has been suggested that the addition of new voters for the second of a pair of elections being compared biases the estimate toward the mean because the new voters are likely to be more closely divided than the repeating voters in a county that is disproportionately controlled by one party.[12] The effect to be expected from this plausible proposition is, of course, to raise the Y values in the low range of X values, to lower the Y values in the high range of X values, and therefore to tilt the regression line away from zero intercept and 100 percent least-squares estimate to something like an intercept of 10 and an estimate of perhaps 90. Preliminary effort to test this hypothesis by excluding the rapidly growing counties has been fruitless, and more investigation is needed here. There is also the possibility, yet untested, that a higher turnout of the voters is more likely to incorporate the less committed and to suffer disproportionate losses in the succeeding election attributable to nonvoting or defection. This possibility should be testable, but such testing will require extremely careful controls and perception of the many possible mutually canceling considerations. Whatever may be concluded about this characteristic of the regression equations, it is a fact that the least-squares estimates offered here are almost always biased downward slightly for both parties, even in a straightforward two-party contest. Some of this difference between the estimates and 100 percent is probably a valid reflection of voter switching, but a substantial portion appears to be artifactual consequences of applying a linear assumption to a slightly curvilinear relationship and of elements not yet identified.

The dimensions of voter constancy in party alignment in presidential elections from 1840 to 1860 are estimated from computations displayed in tables for pairwise comparison of elections at four-year, eight-year, and twelve-year intervals. The tables are largely self-explanatory,

---

[12] Shortridge, "Voter Realignment in the Midwest During the 1850s," 203.

but some preliminary comment is needed. The counties employed in regressions are necessarily limited to those unaffected by major boundary changes resulting from creation of new counties between the dates of the two elections. For some parts of the country this necessitates eliminating a large number of counties for even a four-year interval. Consequently, some areas of rapidly growing population, together with other areas of unmeasured demographic and economic attributes, are underrepresented. The only practical alternative to such exclusion is the recombining of geographic areas so as to retain identical aggregate-data units for the two elections. But this procedure introduces extraneous considerations, especially the extensiveness of area and oversized population when one employs large areas comprising as many as a dozen counties, a situation not uncommon in states in which county creations were frequent in the years involved. Although the recombination approach serves useful purposes under certain conditions, it has not been selected for this overview essay. A few counties in remote frontier stretches have been excluded by requiring that at least one square mile of improved land be reported in farms within the county.

The number of counties with usable returns for the two elections is shown for each analysis. Every usable county has been incorporated from all of the states admitted before 1860 except for California and Oregon. The regional grouping of states is as normally expected, but to avoid uncertainty it is noted that Delaware is included in the Middle Atlantic, Missouri in the South, and Arkansas in the Upper South. The values offered arise from weighting each county percentage by the total vote cast in that county in the first of the two elections. Unweighted regressions in almost every instance reported here yield closely comparable values and serve as bases for scattergram inspection, but overall estimates of individual voter constancy rest on weighted regressions.

The standard error of estimate is provided as a summary measure of closeness of fit in addition to the commonly used product-moment correlation coefficient r. The reason for this additional statistic is that r, being the square root of the computed value R^2 (sometimes designated the coefficient of determination), is a measure of proportional reduction of error. Error is defined as the total variance in a frequency distribution, and proportional reduction is the percentage of that variance that can be eliminated by employing the regression equation for estimating the value of the dependent variable for each case. In terms of the picture presented by a scatterplot such as that in Figure 1, variance (total error) is the sum of the squared distances of every point from a horizontal line representing the mean of all Y values (vertical axis, 1844 Democratic percentages in this instance). The sum of the squared vertical distance of every point from the regression line is designated residual error. Proportional reduction of error (R^2) is total error minus residual error divided by total error. The magnitude of R^2, and hence of r, is therefore dependent not only on the closeness of fit of the points about the regression line but also on the initial closeness of fit of the points about the mean line for Y values.

Given a specified closeness of fit about the regression line, the value of r depends upon the amount of variance for Y. If, therefore, the counties of a state are all closely divided between parties, variance about the mean for, say, Democratic percentages for 1844 will be small and reasonable closeness of fit to a regression line will not yield much proportional reduction of error. If, however, the counties of a state are widely dispersed over a broad range of Democratic percentages in 1844, a comparably close fit to the regression line will yield a much higher value for R^2 and r. The points on Figure 1 representing the usable 29 counties of Michigan are all close to the regression line, but the 1844 Democratic percentages are concentrated between 40 percent and 60 percent and provide a very small variance. The points on Figure 1 representing the 93 usable counties of Georgia, on the contrary, do not fit the line as well but are widely dispersed in Democratic percentage value for 1844 from below 10 percent to above 90 percent. The value of r for a regression on the Georgia counties separately is .92 but for the Michigan counties separately is only .73. This is an accurate reflection of difference in proportional reduction of error, and it carries implications of greater confidence in the predictive power of the regression equation. Yet, the Michigan configuration is compatible with a hypothesis of greater consistency than is the Georgia one. The standard error of estimate, being the square root of the average-per-case variance about the regression line, is approximately a measure of average distance of point from line and serves as an additional clue to closeness of fit. For Michigan in this instance it is 4.0, while for Georgia it is 6.7.

The tables that follow display for the United States and for various regions not only the values of r and the standard error of estimate but also the values of the regression coefficients, the intercept a and the slope b (multiplied by 100), and the least-squares estimate (a plus 100 times b). The intercept is the value of Y where $X=0$ and the least-squares estimate is the value of Y where $X=100$. Very informally stated, the intercept for a pairwise regression analysis of county-aggregate data for two consecutive elections estimates what percentage of the total vote the party would receive in the second election in a theoretical county in which that party had received no votes in the earlier election. Consequently, the value of the intercept in such instances as that portrayed in Figure 1 may be taken as an estimate of the percentage of the opposition party vote of 1840 transferred to the Democratic party in 1844. The least-squares estimate may be treated as the percentage of the total vote expected to be Democratic in 1844 in a theoretical county in which the Democratic vote in 1840 had been 100 percent, hence the percentage of the Democratic supporters of 1840 continuing to vote Democratic in 1844. With one more reminder of the pitfalls and unavoidable weaknesses inherent in this type of estimating from regressions on county-level aggregate election data, we may turn to the tables.

The estimates of continuity of voter alignment for the four-year interval from 1840 to 1844 are 95 percent for Democrats and 87 percent for Whigs, with the regional estimates falling close to the national ones (Table 13, Part A). Correlation coefficients are uniformly very high, and standard errors of estimate generally are between 3 and 5 percent. Figure 1 displays the scattergram for the unweighted Democratic percentages for these two elections and provides an opportunity to observe some of the characteristics of the regression attributable to reasonably well-known circumstances. Democratic percentages are about 2.5 percent higher for 1844 than for 1840, and Whig percentages about 4.5 percent lower. The Liberty party received only about .25 percent of the total vote in 1840 but more than 2.25 percent in 1844. Only 35 northern counties reported even 1 percent Liberty vote in 1840, 28 had only 1 percent, 6 had 2 percent, and 1 had 3 percent. In 1844, however, 113 northern counties, more than one-fifth the total, reported 5 or higher percent Liberty, and 30 counties reported 10 percent or more. The injection of even this limited a third-party vote in 1844 weakens the correlation, introduces unpredictable effects on the regression coefficient, and probably lowers excessively the least-squares estimate for Whig continuity because the Liberty vote came principally from Whig ranks.

The artifactual effect of linear assumption in the regression analysis is well illustrated on Figure 1 by the scattering of counties, most in the Lower South, in which the Democrats made spectacular gains in percentage of total vote, from the 5-to-20-percent range to the 30-to-50-percent range. The effect of this configuration on the regression line, which is in a sense anchored in the center of the scattergram by the great number of counties near the 50-50 point, is to draw the line upward at the left and (given the straight-line assumption) to depress the line at the right. The least-squares estimate for Democratic continuity is thereby reduced simply because the Democrats made such unusual gains in some areas of their greatest weakness four years earlier. Also, the intercept is higher in value than it would otherwise be, exaggerating the proportion of Whigs switching to the Democrats between 1840 and 1844. Conversely, estimates of Whig continuity, apart from the effect of losses to the Liberty party, are artifactually depressed by these same losses to Democrats in the high range of Whig percentages of 1840. There is no generally employed procedure for making adjustments for such a configuration, apart from removing the offending cases from the regression and encountering indignant charges of "cooking" the data. Until some general agreement has been reached about employing a least-squares linear regression model when the model's assumptions are not met by the data, perhaps it is safe merely to note that the intercept ought to be lower and the estimate higher for both Democrats and Whigs.

The succeeding four-year interval, 1844–1848, cannot profitably be analyzed without controlling for the effect of the large Free-Soil party vote. With former Democratic president Martin Van Buren as the candidate, the Free-Soil party split the Democratic voters of Van Buren's home state, New York, and cut deeply into the two-party vote in many counties elsewhere. Approximately one-half the northern counties reported at least 5 percent Free-Soil vote, one-third at least 15 percent, one-sixth at least 25 percent, and almost one-tenth at least 33 percent. Voters returned to their former two-party alignment substantially by 1852, so that the 1848 election may be classified as a deviating one. It is also a harbinger of realignments to come in 1856 with the Republican

TABLE 13. Party Continuity, 1840–1848 (Regression Values for County-Level Party Percentage of Total Vote Weighted by Total Vote in the First Election).

Elections Compared	Geographic Area	Number of Counties	Democratic with Democratic					Whig with Whig				
			r	Std. Err. Est.	a	100 × b	Least Sq. Est. (percent)	r	Std. Err. Est.	a	100 × b	Least Sq. Est. (percent)
Part A	United States	1,037	.92	4.2	9	86	95	.91	4.3	4	81	87
	North	436	.92	3.3	7	89	96	.88	3.9	5	82	87
1840	Northeast	183	.94	2.7	4	94	98	.88	3.9	3	86	89
with	North-Central	253	.91	3.7	11	83	94	.90	3.8	6	77	84
1844	South	601	.94	5.3	12	84	96	.94	5.3	3	84	88
	Upper South	379	.94	5.2	12	83	95	.94	5.2	5	83	88
	Lower South	222	.94	5.0	14	85	98	.94	5.0	2	85	86
Part B	United States	1,130	.72	10.1	-6	95	89	.84	6.0	5	88	93
	U.S. (counties less than 5% Free-Soil, 1848)	942	.95	3.8	3	89	92	.95	4.0	8	89	97
1844	North	472	.61	11.1	-9	98	89	.77	5.9	5	85	90
with	North-Central	276	.86	4.8	3	88	91	.62	7.0	13	63	76
1848	South	658	.95	4.3	3	88	91	.95	4.3	9	88	97
	Upper South	422	.96	3.9	2	91	93	.96	3.9	7	91	96
	Lower South	222	.94	4.7	2	85	87	.94	4.7	12	85	97

Part C		994	.60	11.6	5	76	81	.75	7.3	10	71	81
1840 with 1848	United States	994	.60	11.6	5	76	81	.75	7.3	10	71	81
	U.S. (counties less than 5% Free-Soil, 1848)	756	.92	4.8	11	78	89	.91	4.9	10	78	88
	U.S. (excl. N.Y.)	938	.83	7.1	6	84	90	.77	7.6	9	73	82
	North (excl. N.Y.)	362	.78	7.4	−1	95	94	.61	7.8	13	62	75
	New England	61	.85	7.0	−18	123	105	.71	7.3	−2	82	81
	Mid.-Atlantic (excl. N.Y.)	63	.83	5.2	7	80	87	.84	5.0	10	80	90
	North-Central	238	.82	5.3	12	75	88	.61	6.7	17	51	78
	South	576	.93	5.0	12	78	90	.93	5.0	10	78	88
	Upper South	354	.94	4.7	11	79	91	.94	4.7	9	79	89
	Lower South	222	.92	5.5	12	75	88	.89	5.5	12	75	87

party's first presidential campaign. The large majority of the defectors in the Northeast were undoubtedly Democrats, with the probable illusion that they were remaining loyal to their party and state faction leaders as long as their votes went to a former Democratic president. Some northeastern defectors and many North-Central region defectors were Whigs, who were more decisively rejecting their party, at least for this one election. The estimate of continuity for Democrats at the national level is lower than for Whigs, whether the counties reporting 5 percent or more Free-Soil vote are excluded or not (Table 13, Part B). But with the exclusion of these northern counties the regression equation is more nearly comparable with that for the Democratic 1840–1844 comparison. Compatible with the general Whig gain over the Democrats, estimates of Whig continuity are higher than for the preceding four-year interval.

For the eight-year interval from 1840 to 1848, both years of Whig presidential success, party continuity estimates are close to the 90 percent level if the counties with as much as 5 percent Free-Soil vote in 1848 are excluded (Table 13, Part C). The regional estimates from all usable counties (excluding all New York counties from the North and from the Middle Atlantic region) are usually close to 90 percent except for the lower estimate for north-central Whigs, who furnished the bulk of defectors to the Free-Soil party in that region. The regression equation for New England illustrates the distortion that can result from widespread defection to the third party when the number of cases is as small as 61.

Comparison of 1848 with 1852 patterns requires the same kind of adjustment for the 1848 Free-Soil vote because the Free-Soil party in 1852 fell back from its 1848 high to about 5.5 percent of the total vote. Exclusion of counties with not less than 5 percent Free-Soil vote in 1848 almost certainly accomplishes the desired exclusion of counties with an appreciable Free-Soil vote in 1852. The Democrats, winning in 1852, are estimated at high levels of continuity in the northern counties with less than 5 percent Free-Soil vote, and the Whigs at close to 85 percent continuity (Table 14, Part A). Northern regional estimates excluding only the state of New York are still very high for Democrats and slightly lower for Whigs except for New England, with only 79 percent estimate for Whig continuity.

The crisis of 1850 damaged party loyalties somewhat in all parts of

the country. It is Georgia, however, that provides the most serious interference with continuity estimates. The 1850 crisis produced such
turmoil there that an Independent Whig and an Independent Democrat presidential ticket together garnered almost 17 percent of the total
vote in 1852, making shambles of continuity estimates for the state.
With Georgia counties removed, the estimates of southern Democratic continuity are close to 100 percent and for the Whigs close to 90
percent. The Upper South counties yield a higher estimate for Whigs,
and the Lower South a 76 percent estimate, arising from a less predictable pattern than for any other region ($r=.78$ and the standard error of
estimate$=8.1$). Many Whigs, especially in Alabama and Mississippi,
appear to have abstained.

Estimates from the eight-year span from 1844 to 1852 encounter
the handicaps of changes during the longer time interval but are free
from the effects of the 1848 Free-Soil surge and, additionally, compare
two elections in which Democrats were victorious. Estimates for Democratic continuity are about 97 percent if Georgia counties are excluded—98 percent for the North and 95 percent for the South (Table
14, Part B). Estimates of Whig continuity are close to those obtained
from 1848 to 1852 comparisons, especially when counties reporting as
much as 10 percent Free-Soil vote in 1852 are excluded. This exclusion
increases the estimate of Whig continuity in the North-Central region
from 76 to 85 percent and from 82 to 86 percent for the North.

Estimates from the twelve-year interval, 1840 to 1852, predictably
encounter a somewhat weaker correlation, yet the decline in strength
of correlation is remarkably slight (Table 14, Part C). For the entire
country excluding Georgia counties, the value of r for Democratic percentages is .84 compared with .89 for the 1844 to 1852 regression, and
.81 compared with .87 for the Whig percentages. For Democratic continuity the estimates are well above 90 percent except for the North-
Central at 91 percent. This 1840 to 1852 comparison is between a
Democratic losing year and a Democratic winning year, which helps to
account for the generally high estimates for Democratic continuity.
Whigs, encountering the reverse, are found to have consistently lower
estimates of continuity than from 1844, lower by 8 or 9 percent, falling
near 75 percent and ranging from 82 percent for the Upper South to 68
percent for the North-Central. The counties with at least 10 percent
Free-Soil vote in 1852 are not excluded from these analyses; were they

TABLE 14. Party Continuity, 1840–1852 (Regression Values for County-Level Party Percentage of Total Vote Weighted by Total Vote in the First Election).

Elections Compared	Geographic Area	Number of Counties	Democratic with Democratic					Whig with Whig				
			r	Std. Err. Est.	a	100 × b	Least Sq. Est. (percent)	r	Std. Err. Est.	a	100 × b	Least Sq. Est. (percent)
Part A	United States	1,301	.72	7.8	26	57	83	.76	6.7	11	69	80
1848 with 1852	U.S. (counties less than 5% Free-Soil, 1848)	1,009	.87	6.0	11	86	98	.79	7.8	4	81	85
	U.S. (excl. N.Y., Ga.)	1,163	.90	5.1	12	84	96	.87	5.2	9	75	85
	North (excl. N.Y.)	470	.88	4.8	15	77	92	.86	4.2	12	69	86
	New England	64	.91	4.9	14	79	93	.81	5.0	13	67	79
	Mid.-Atlantic (excl. N.Y.)	76	.88	4.2	15	78	93	.91	3.4	6	79	85
	North-Central	330	.83	5.1	13	78	91	.87	3.8	13	71	84
	South (excl. Ga.)	693	.93	5.3	9	92	101	.90	6.1	0	89	89
	Upper South	464	.98	3.7	8	91	100	.96	3.7	1	91	91
	Lower South (excl. Ga.)	229	.85	7.3	16	87	102	.78	8.1	1	75	76
Part B	United States	1,070	.86	5.7	6	90	95	.78	6.4	7	76	83
1844 with 1852	U.S. (excl. Ga.)	990	.89	4.9	5	92	97	.87	4.8	6	80	86
	North	460	.88	4.6	2	97	98	.81	4.4	9	74	82
	North (counties less than 10% Free-Soil, 1852)	361	.89	3.4	10	84	93	.88	3.4	8	78	86
	Northeast	192	.86	4.9	1	98	99	.84	4.1	6	79	85

	n										
Northeast (counties less than 10% Free-Soil, 1852)	141	.88	3.5	10	84	94	.86	3.4	8	78	86
New England	64	.83	6.4	−1	98	97	.81	5.0	7	72	79
Middle Atlantic	128	.88	3.6	6	91	97	.90	3.0	5	83	88
North-Central	268	.91	3.8	3	94	97	.74	5.0	14	63	76
N. Central (counties less than 10% Free-Soil, 1852)	220	.91	3.3	9	84	93	.90	3.3	8	78	85
South	610	.85	7.6	11	82	93	.77	10.1	5	79	84
South (excl. Ga.)	530	.93	5.3	9	86	95	.92	5.7	5	85	89
Upper South	389	.94	4.7	9	85	94	.94	4.7	6	84	90
Lower South	221	.69	11.6	17	74	90	.49	13.2	11	50	61
Lower South (excl. Ga.)	141	.87	7.1	10	86	96	.82	7.5	6	76	82
Part C United States	943	.80	6.8	13	79	92	.73	7.1	9	66	75
U.S. (excl. Ga.)	863	.84	6.0	11	81	93	.81	5.6	8	70	77
1840 North	407	.83	5.3	6	90	96	.73	5.2	11	62	74
with Northeast	177	.85	5.1	1	98	100	.74	5.1	9	68	77
1852 North-Central	230	.85	4.8	15	76	91	.72	5.0	16	52	68
South	536	.83	8.3	20	73	93	.74	10.7	6	69	75
South (excl. Ga.)	456	.90	6.2	18	77	94	.89	6.7	5	75	81
Upper South	330	.92	5.4	17	75	93	.92	5.4	7	75	82
Lower South	206	.69	11.8	25	66	91	.52	13.0	9	47	52
Lower South (excl. Ga.)	126	.86	7.5	21	75	96	.83	7.7	5	67	72

TABLE 15. Absolute Change in the Democratic Percentage of the Total Popular Vote in Presidential Elections between 1836 and 1852.

Region	Net Change
United States	down 0.3% from 50.94% to 50.65%
New England	down 7.7% from 51.65% to 44.01%
Middle Atlantic	down 2.1% from 52.97% to 50.86%
North-Central	up 2.0% from 47.96% to 50.00%
Upper South	up 2.8% from 49.56% to 52.40%
Lower South	up 7.6% from 51.34% to 58.90%
All Free States	down 1.8% from 51.20% to 49.39%
All Slave States	up 4.1% from 49.97% to 54.04%

excluded the estimates for Whig continuity would be higher by a few percentage points.

Voters, riding out the stormy national controversies from 1848 through the Compromise of 1850, were able to regroup for the 1852 presidential election nearly in the party pattern of the elections of 1840 and 1844. This is striking evidence of the power of party labels to direct the response of all but a small proportion of voters. The deviations of 1848 were substantial principally because of Van Buren's name and the comfort it gave to Democratically aligned voters aroused to cast a protest vote on either ideological or party factional grounds. The restored pattern in 1852 belies an interpretation that a fundamental realignment occurred in 1848. Between 1840 or 1844 and 1852 a modest amount of shifting away from the Democratic party in New England and the northern counties of the North-Central region balanced a modest pro-Democratic drift in the South, especially in the Lower South. These shiftings may have been a harbinger of an irresistible sectional current which would tug at party attachment, but even so it was by 1852 certainly no tidal wave and hardly a perceptible swell. To illustrate this point, regional stability in Democratic percentage of total vote over sixteen years between the Democratic victories of 1836 and 1852 is summarized in Table 15.

Between 1852 and 1856, striking political developments presented the voters with an apparently new and different set of alternatives. Yet, northern and southern Democrats stood opposed to largely the same segments of the electorate that they had opposed for a decade or more.

It is true that the newly organized Republican party of the North was by no means the continuation of Whiggery and that the American party of 1856, seeking to capitalize on nativism to rejuvenate and extend Whig appeal in the South and border North, attracted a few Democrats and repelled some Whigs. Nevertheless, the number of voters shifting either into or out of the Democratic ranks may easily be exaggerated.

The divided opposition to the Democrats in 1856 makes it difficult to trace continuity among the anti-Democrats of the North, and the above-mentioned splintering of the presidential vote in Georgia in 1852 again points to the advisability of examining continuity with the Georgia counties excluded. Moreover, the voters of New York State revealed in 1856 how much their party ties had been weakened by the 1848 Free-Soil defection. Probably those who had voted Free-Soil consciously and preponderantly out of ideological enthusiasm were likely candidates for defection to the Free-Soil party again in 1852 and to the Republican party in 1856. But a great many of the defecting Democrats of 1848 had only been following their state Democratic chieftain, Martin Van Buren, in opposing his bitter intraparty rival Lewis Cass of Michigan, the Democratic nominee of 1848. These Democratic voters may have been less susceptible to Free-Soil appeals in 1852 but were probably more likely than the consistent Democrats to vote Republican in 1856. The New York counties for an 1852 to 1856 regression yield an r value of only .68, but more important even than this modest strength of association is the fact that almost every New York county falls far lower in Democratic percentage in 1856 than in 1852, from an average of about 50 percent to an average of about 33 percent. On a scattergram for all usable counties in the country, comparable with Figure 1, the points for New York counties lie generally across the center but well below the regression line. They do not greatly affect the regression equation, but they do weaken the association and produce lower values for r and higher standard errors of estimate. New York as well as Georgia is therefore excluded from appropriate regressions (Table 16, Part A).

Texas was growing so rapidly between 1852 and 1856 that comparing counties across even four years is not helpful. The Texas counties alone show weak association for the 1852 to 1856 regression ($r=.48$). The exclusion of Texas makes little difference, however, for the poor fit

TABLE 16. Party Continuity, 1844–1856 (Regression Values for County-Level Party Percentage of Total Vote Weighted by Total Vote in the First Election).

Elections Compared	Geographic Area	Number of Counties	Democratic with Democratic					Whig with American				
			r	Std. Err. Est.	a	100 × b	Least Sq. Est. (percent)	r	Std. Err. Est.	a	100 × b	Least Sq. Est. (percent)
Part A	United States	1,356	.72	10.2	−4	96	92					
1852 with 1856	U.S. (excl. N.Y., Ga., Tex.)	1,171	.79	8.5	−2	96	94					
	North	578	.71	9.2	−7	98	91					
	North (excl. N.Y.)	522	.80	7.5	−4	98	94					
	Northeast	201	.69	9.8	−10	100	90					
	Northeast (excl. N.Y.)	145	.81	7.9	−7	103	96					
	New England	60	.91	4.6	−6	89	82					
	North-Central	377	.77	7.0	0	90	90					
	South	778	.74	9.9	13	77	90	.73	10.0	13	74	86
	South (excl. Ga., Tex.)	649	.76	9.5	9	84	92	.77	9.4	7	85	91
	Upper South	482	.80	8.7	7	88	95	.81	8.6	4	89	93
	Lower South	296	.56	11.9	24	55	79	.59	11.6	22	59	81
	Lower South (excl. Ga., Tex.)	167	.61	11.9	16	70	85	.65	11.4	12	78	90

Part B

	N										
United States	1,213	.81	8.6	9	84	93					
U.S. (excl. Ga., Tex.)	1,097	.82	8.5	9	85	93					
1848 with 1856											
North	517	.82	7.5	9	79	89					
Northeast	190	.89	7.9	10	80	89					
New England	60	.86	5.1	5	73	79					
Middle Atlantic	130	.79	7.1	12	82	94					
North-Central	327	.75	6.7	5	88	92					
South	696	.81	9.6	16	78	94	.75	9.6	5	78	84
Upper South	419	.61	8.6	12	84	96	.81	8.5	3	85	88
Lower South	277	.60	11.1	26	62	88	.61	11.1	12	62	74
Lower South (excl. Ga., Tex.)	161	.60	11.7	23	69	92	.60	11.7	8	69	77

Part C

	N										
North	440	.59	10.9	−5	93	88					
North (excl. N.Y.)	385	.70	9.3	−3	95	93					
1844 with 1856											
Northeast (excl. N.Y.)	123	.69	10.2	−6	100	94					
New England	59	.75	7.4	−9	93	83					
Mid-Atlantic (excl. N.Y.)	64	.60	7.9	19	62	81					
North-Central	262	.72	7.5	4	85	89					
South	498	.80	8.8	14	78	92	.80	8.7	7	79	86
Upper South	313	.83	8.1	11	83	95	.84	8.0	5	84	89
Lower South	185	.71	9.9	20	67	87	.71	9.9	12	67	79

to a regression line of these Texas counties is largely offset for a national or Southwide regression because almost all of the counties reported greater than 60 percent Democratic proportion for both elections. These 64 cases fall well into the upper-right quadrant of a scattergram and enhance the positive association strength of a larger set with well-distributed values for the Democratic percentage.

The estimates of Democratic continuity are usually above 90 percent for this 1852 to 1856 comparison, highest at 95 percent for the Upper South. The 85 percent estimate for the Lower South is probably that low because of the Whig resurgence under the label American from the poor showing of 1852 in those states. The estimate of 82 percent for New England reflects a real erosion of Democratic strength all across that region. The r value is .91, the standard error of estimate is only 4.6, and the indication of almost uniform decline in Democratic percentages across the region is compatible with the aggregate vote changes in New England. For the South, the Whig to American party continuity is estimated at about 91 percent with Georgia and Texas excluded. That the values of r are lower than those noted for regressions previously discussed warns of less uniform voter behavior across the counties of the South. Although the estimates may be close for all southern voters taken together, the level of consistency in party alignment appears to have been declining, as somewhat less predictable divisions of the electorate occurred in an increasing number of counties.

Comparing the elections of 1848 and 1856 reveals as much voter constancy as does the 1852–1856 interval and even greater continuity in some regions even though this eight-year period was one of rapid growth in the total vote cast. The tendency of the Free-Soil voters of 1848 to become Republicans in 1856 contributes to the strong association between these two election patterns, and New York counties need not be excluded from this comparison. Georgia's major deviation from continuity was in 1852, so that slight change in either r or the regression equation is accomplished by the exclusion of Georgia counties (Table 16, Part B). Estimates of Democratic continuity are above or near 90 percent for the country and for each region apart from New England, for which the 79 percent estimate has already been recognized as reflecting a real erosion of Democratic strength. Estimates of Whig continuity from the 1848 to 1856 comparison are lower than from the 1852 to 1856 comparison probably because of the recovery from the poor showing of 1852 in the Lower South. The 1848 to 1856 estimates form a better indicator of the trend of Whig losses in the Lower South.

The twelve-year span from the 1844 Democratic victory to the 1856 Democratic victory under very different circumstances cannot be expected to provide a trustworthy basis for estimating continuity. Nevertheless, accepting somewhat lower values of r and standard errors of estimate of 7 to 10, an impressive level of continuity is suggested by these estimates (Table 16, Part C). New York counties are again a source of interference because the changing alignments there did not begin until 1848. Even with New York counties excluded, the 94 percent estimate for the rest of the Northeast is disturbingly inconsistent with more credible estimates of 83 and 81 percent for each of the component parts, New England and Middle Atlantic. Otherwise, the entire set of estimates comports well with those made from the 1848 to 1856 comparison, when it is recognized that 1844 was a winning year for Democrats and that larger defections should be more likely than from the losing year 1848.[13]

The presence of four parties in the presidential contest of 1860 gives the appearance of an uprooting of the two-party system; yet, as in 1856, the lineup of Democrats against their opponents provides evidence of substantial party continuity (Table 17, Parts A and B). Comparing any earlier election with that of 1860 introduces some thorny problems. There were very nearly two separate elections, with Republicans against Douglas Democrats in the North and Constitutional Union supporters of John Bell (former Whigs and then American party adherents generally) against Breckinridge Democrats in the South. But support for Breckinridge and Bell in the North and for Douglas in

[13]The inconsistency in estimates for the Northeast and its subregions results from the New England counties' being considerably lower in Democratic percentage than Middle Atlantic counties. Inspection of scattergrams for unweighted regressions readily reveals the source of the inconsistent estimates. New England counties lie lower and more to the left, with a slope of .93 from a very low intercept of -9, while Middle Atlantic counties lie higher and more in the center of the plot, with a slope of .62 from a high intercept of 19 (regression values from weighted analyses). As combined, the two subregions provide the configuration of lower-left concentration (New England) and higher center-range concentration (Middle Atlantic) that yield the much steeper slope (1.00) from the low intercept (-6) that together produce the least-squares estimate of 94 percent. This is an example of the difficulties of estimating when r is as low as .69 with a standard error of estimate above 10.

TABLE 17. Party Continuity, 1856–1860 (Regression Values for County-Level Party Percentage of Total Vote Weighted by Total Vote in the First Election).

| | | | Democratic with Douglas and Breckinridge | | | | | Republican with Republican Southern American with Bell | | | | |
Elections Compared	Geographic Area	Number of Counties	r	Std. Err. Est.	a	100 × b	Least Sq. Est. (percent)	r	Std. Err. Est.	a	100 × b	Least Sq. Est. (percent)
Part A												
	North	628	.79	7.1	15	68	83	.80	6.7	33	47	80
	North (excl. Pa.)*	568	.84	6.4	13	77	90	.90	5.0	27	57	84
1856	New England	64	.95	2.9	4	87	91	.94	2.9	13	79	92
with	Mid-Atlantic (excl. Pa.)*	82	.88	4.8	21	75	96	.89	4.7	29	55	84
1860	North-Central	422	.92	4.1	9	83	91	.88	5.4	27	56	82
	South	829	.84	7.6	12	81	93	.80	8.6	7	78	85
	South (excl. Mo., Ga., Tex.)	591	.86	7.1	12	81	93	.85	7.4	7	80	87
	Upper South	507	.88	6.3	11	79	90	.80	8.4	10	76	85
	Upper South (excl. Mo.)	415	.89	6.2	10	81	91	.87	6.9	9	80	89
	Lower South	322	.80	7.6	20	77	97	.80	7.6	3	77	80
	L. South (excl. Ga., Tex.)	176	.84	6.3	25	70	94	.84	6.3	6	70	76

		Democratic with Republican or Bell					American with Breckinridge				
Part B											
1856 with 1860											
North	628	−0.79	6.9	82	−67	14					
North (excl. Pa., Del.)	565	−0.83	6.2	82	−72	10					
New England	64	−0.74	5.8	80	−58	22					
Mid-Atlantic (excl. Pa., Del.)	79	−0.89	4.7	79	−78	1					
North-Central	422	−0.90	4.9	91	−87	4					
South	829	−0.80	8.6	84	−78	6	−0.60	16.1	80	−83	−3
South (excl. Mo., Ga., Tex.)	591	−0.85	7.5	86	−79	7	−0.67	13.3	81	−79	1
Upper South	507	−0.80	8.5	84	−76	9	−0.59	15.6	74	−77	−3
Upper South (excl. Mo.)	415	−0.87	6.8	87	−78	9	−0.69	13.0	80	−80	1
Lower South	322	−0.80	7.6	80	−77	2	−0.61	14.2	88	−82	6
L. South (excl. Ga., Tex.)	176	−0.84	6.3	75	−70	5	−0.58	12.8	80	−66	15

*Pa. and Del. excluded from Republican analysis.

the South disturbs continuity estimates unless combinations are used. The combined Douglas and Breckinridge percentages are used for estimating 1856 to 1860 Democratic continuity in both North and South. Estimating anti-Democratic continuity is not so simple, for in the North the Republicans in 1860 acquired much but not all of the American party vote of 1856. Moreover, the northerners who voted for John Bell, though traditionally anti-Democratic, were passionately anti-Republican in 1860, had almost surely been as anti-Republican in 1856, and hence are better left out of the 1856 to 1860 estimates of Republican continuity. The one state for which no really acceptable continuity study is feasible is Pennsylvania, where a desperate fusion effort on Breckinridge rather than Douglas electors dismayed Democratic voters and led to a sharp decline in turnout clearly attributable to Democratic abstention. Excluding Pennsylvania from the regression is one of the ways used to evade this difficulty. Delaware, a slave state included in the Middle Atlantic region, is also excluded from estimates of Republican continuity.

Missouri was the only southern state to divide its vote substantially among all four candidates; Lincoln received more than 10 percent, Breckinridge almost 20 percent, and Douglas and Bell nearly tied at more than 35 percent each. For some analyses, therefore, Missouri is excluded. The extreme frontier conditions in much of Texas and the continuing distractions in Georgia justify an examination of continuity estimates with these two states excluded as well. Georgia in 1860 gave Douglas 10 percent of its vote, and a considerable amount of this support must have come from former Whigs following the leadership of Alexander H. Stephens, who had deserted to the Democrats earlier and supported the northern candidate Douglas in 1860.

Democratic continuity from 1856 to 1860 (Table 17, Part A) is estimated at 90 percent or higher for all parts of the country apart from Pennsylvania. Excluding Missouri, Georgia, and Texas makes very little difference in the South. Republican continuity is estimated at 84 percent apart from Pennsylvania and above 90 percent in New England. These estimates are almost certainly skewed downward by the large gains Republicans made between 1856 and 1860 in counties in which their percentage had been low in 1856, when so many former Whigs held out for the last time against the Republican surge by supporting the American party. These counties appear on each scattergram as a cluster of points far above the 0-to-100 diagonal line toward the left side of the plot, producing a high intercept. With great numbers of counties clustered near the 50-50 intersection, each regression line is tilted substantially away from a slope near 1.0 and provides a least-squares estimate near 85. Inspection of the unweighted scattergrams makes it clear that these estimates for Republican continuity would be close to 100 percent without the impact of the approximately one hundred counties where Republicans in 1856 received less than 30 percent of the vote but in 1860 received from 30 to 70 percent. Anti-Democratic continuity in the South, estimated on the basis of comparing the American party vote in 1856 with the Constitutional Union party vote in 1860, is about 85 percent, higher in the Upper South outside Missouri.

A different approach to estimating continuity is to estimate directly the proportion of defections by comparing one party's percentages in an election with the opposition percentages in the subsequent one (Table 17, Part B). Comparing Democratic 1856 percentages with 1860 Republican or southern Constitutional Union percentages provides estimates of defection of 10 percent in the North (excluding Pennsylvania and Delaware) and 6 percent in the South. Estimates are highest for New England and lowest for New York and New Jersey. Southern Democratic defections to Bell are estimated as greater in the Upper South—9 percent—than in the Lower South. Comparison of 1856 American party percentages with 1860 Breckinridge percentages produces r values uncomfortably low and provides estimates that few if any American party adherents of 1856 were supporting the southern Democrat Breckinridge in 1860.

The eight-year interval from 1852 to 1860 provides a comparison with the most recent two-party presidential contest (Table 18). For this comparison not only can Democratic percentages be compared with combined Douglas and Breckinridge percentages but also Whig percentages can be compared usefully with combined Lincoln and Bell percentages in the North. With Pennsylvania, Missouri, Georgia, and Texas excluded, estimates for Democrats are about 95 percent for both North and South. The New England estimate is lowest at 78 percent, and the North-Central is 88 percent. The Upper South estimate is slightly higher than that for the Lower South. Estimates of Whig continuity in the North are critically flawed by exceedingly low r values.

TABLE 18. Party Continuity, 1852–1860 (Regression Values for County-Level Party Percentage of Total Vote Weighted by Total Vote in the First Election).

Elections Compared	Geographic Area	Number of Counties	Democratic with Douglas and Breckinridge					Whig with Lincoln and Bell Southern Whig with Bell				
			r	Std. Err. Est.	a	100 × b	Least Sq. Est. (percent)	r	Std. Err. Est.	a	100 × b	Least Sq. Est. (percent)
Part A	North	570	.78	7.0	−3	93	91	.27	10.9	40	41	80
	North (excl. Pa.)	512	.80	7.0	−4	98	94	.19	11.4	43	31	75
1852	New England	59	.90	4.5	−3	81	78	.37	9.4	49	47	96
with	Mid-Atlantic (excl. Pa.)	78	.75	6.8	−9	110	101	.36	9.5	23	69	92
1860	North-Central	375	.78	6.4	4	84	88	.21	10.0	43	27	70
	South	733	.79	8.3	13	79	92	.79	8.6	8	77	85
	South (excl. Mo., Ga., Tex.)	537	.83	7.6	11	83	95	.85	7.2	4	86	90
	Upper South	461	.83	7.2	11	82	92	.84	7.5	3	87	91
	Upper South (excl. Mo.)	373	.87	6.6	9	86	95	.86	6.8	4	87	91
	Lower South	272	.67	9.5	29	59	88	.58	10.4	17	52	69
	L. South (excl. Ga., Tex.)	164	.67	8.5	30	59	89	.76	7.5	8	69	78

		Northern counties less than 5% Free-Soil, 1852; southern counties less than 10% Douglas, 1860.									
Part B											
1852	North	342	.64	7.2	7	79	85	.59	7.5	18	76	94
with	North (excl. Pa.)	294	.65	6.7	9	79	87	.57	7.2	17	74	91
1860	Mid-Atlantic (excl. Pa.)	52	.64	6.0	2	95	96	.63	6.3	6	94	100
	North-Central	229	.66	6.8	13	70	83	.61	7.2	20	69	88
	South	470	.85	7.7	10	85	95	.86	7.4	6	84	90
	South (excl. Mo., Ga., Tex.)	381	.87	7.0	9	87	96	.90	6.2	3	89	93
	Upper South	268	.90	6.1	7	90	96	.91	6.0	3	91	94
	Upper South (excl. Mo.)	266	.91	6.0	6	90	97	.91	5.9	3	91	94
	Lower South	202	.65	9.6	30	57	87	.63	9.9	14	59	73
	L. South (excl. Ga., Tex.)	115	.65	7.9	34	52	86	.77	6.6	10	67	77

Although the resulting least-squares estimates are high and within a credible range, there is no assurance that major compensating shifts are not incorporated. An estimated 90 percent of southern anti-Democrats in 1852 continued to vote anti-Democratic in 1860. However in the Lower South, even excluding Georgia and Texas, the estimate is only 78 percent, an estimate that is compatible with other kinds of evidence.

An additional basis for estimating continuity from 1852 to 1860 is to use only counties not seriously affected by the northern Free-Soil vote of 1852 or the southern Douglas vote of 1860. Approximately two-fifths of the northern counties reported 5 percent or more Free-Soil vote in 1852, and this includes all but 13 of the New England counties. More than one-third of the southern counties, including almost all of Missouri, reported at least 10 percent Douglas vote. One should not attempt to disguise the simple fact that these counties are the ones where voters were less rigidly aligned; it may be useful, however, to examine continuity estimates for the substantial majority of the country's counties in which third-party appeals were not effectively made. In this way the direct interchange between major parties may better be estimated (Table 18, Part B). Analyses of northern Democratic continuity produce lower r values than for all usable counties, but the fact that standard errors of estimate are no larger reflects merely a reduction in variance of Democratic percentages, principally because many counties very low in Democratic percentage are excluded. The estimates are somewhat lower but closely parallel to those derived from all usable counties. It is the northern Whig comparison with combined Lincoln and Bell percentages that is sharpened by the exclusions, not surprising considering that the 1852 Free-Soil vote came substantially from Whig ranks. Very high estimates of Whig continuity from 1852 to 1860 now appear for these counties not seriously affected by third-party defections, and the r values are better than for all usable counties, even though too low to justify confident estimates of individual behavior. The regressions for the South and for the border or Upper South yield higher r values and higher estimates of continuity for both Democrats and Whigs.

The twelve years from 1848 to 1860 involved too much growth and change in the North to provide a usable basis for continuity analysis (Table 19, Part A). Only the estimate for the North-Central region for the percentage of Democrats of 1848 voting Republican in 1860 is based on even a barely usable r value, and the estimate of 6 percent is reasonable in light of other kinds of evidence. In the South, on the other hand, continuity can be estimated with reasonable confidence over this twelve-year interval, although with greater difficulty for the Lower South (Table 19, Parts B and C). A 98 percent continuity is estimated for southern Democrats, and the estimate is even higher for those counties with less than 10 percent Douglas vote in 1860. Southern Whig continuity of about 80 percent is higher in the Upper South and much lower in the Lower South. For Whigs the estimates change little with the exclusion of the 10-percent-or-more Douglas counties.

In general, then, for the voters of the nation in 1860, standing with the Democratic organization or against it was far more habitual than crossing this line. Of those who voted in 1860 and who had been able to vote in 1856 or earlier, probably 90 percent of the former Democrats voted for Douglas or Breckinridge. The proportion was larger in the South and smaller in the Northeast. Among the anti-Democrats of the 1848 or 1852 elections, probably 90 percent voted for Lincoln or Bell in 1860. This proportion was probably larger in the North and in the Upper South and smaller in the Lower South. Without seeking to belittle a shift in proportions of voters that dominates the outcome of an election, and surely without underestimating the gravity of having almost separate northern and southern presidential elections in 1860, one should still be able to get some perspective on the relative importance of change and stability in voter alignments. Political leaders were dealing with largely intractable masses of voters, who were not likely to accept a conscious change of party. Whatever labels were used, at least the perception of the negative reference group remained substantially intact. And it was within the limits of latitude permitted by the preponderant partisan inertia of voter response that leaders had to maneuver for victory in presidential contests. In almost every respect this was quite different from some theoretical situation in which the more attractive candidate, issue position, or popular appeal should have won a majority of an open-minded electorate.

Descriptions of the presidential elections from 1840 to 1860 would differ markedly from customary accounts if historians properly incorporated the persistence of voting behavior into their narratives. They would then focus attention on those groups in the electorate whose

TABLE 19. Party Continuity, 1848–1860 (Regression Values for County-Level Party Percentage of Total Vote Weighted by Total Vote in the First Election).

Elections Compared	Geographic Area	Number of Counties	Democratic with Republican									
			r	Std. Err. Est.	a	100 × b	Least Sq. Est. (percent)					
Part A	North	508	−0.55	9.3	72	−45	27					
	Northeast	129	−0.45	9.7	68	−35	34					
1848	New England	59	−0.57	7.5	76	−38	37					
with	Middle Atlantic	125	−0.46	9.4	65	−33	32					
1860	North-Central	324	−0.75	7.2	90	−85	6					

Elections Compared	Geographic Area	Number of Counties	Democratic with Douglas and Breckinridge					Whig with Bell				
			r	Std. Err. Est.	a	100 × b	Least Sq. Est. (percent)	r	Std. Err. Est.	a	100 × b	Least Sq. Est. (percent)
Part B	South	656	.75	9.1	21	73	94	.76	9.0	3	76	79
	South (excl. Mo., Ga., Tex.)	484	.79	8.4	19	79	98	.80	8.3	2	79	81
1848	Upper South	398	.83	7.1	17	77	93	.83	7.6	3	81	84
with	Upper South (excl. Mo.)	325	.87	6.5	15	82	97	.87	6.7	3	82	85
1860	Lower South	258	.66	9.5	33	61	94	.66	9.5	6	61	67
	L. South (excl. Ga., Tex.)	159	.68	8.4	34	62	96	.68	8.4	4	61	66
	Southern counties less than 10% Douglas, 1860											
Part C	South	423	.82	8.4	18	81	98	.82	8.2	1	81	82
	South (excl. Mo., Ga., Tex.)	344	.83	8.0	17	82	99	.83	7.8	0	83	83
1848	Upper South	233	.90	6.1	13	86	99	.91	6.0	1	86	87
with	Lower South	190	.68	9.1	33	61	95	.68	9.1	6	61	67
1860	L. South (excl. Ga., Tex.)	112	.69	7.5	36	60	95	.69	7.5	5	60	65

shifting allegiance, indifference, or unusual turnout could actually determine the outcome of the political contests of this era. The scope of this essay prohibits any attempt to rewrite the history of these contests. What follows, therefore, is merely a plea for such a rewriting and, meanwhile, for cautious handling of prevailing accounts. The remaining discussion suggests the types of revision that might be helpful and speculates about the possible consequences of such revisions for our understanding of the significance of presidential politics.

One suggestion is that the outcome of presidential elections from 1840 through 1852 depended upon a host of episodes (most of which were probably trivial) and consequently should not be presented as the result of decisive voter response to candidates, specific issues, or the "packaging" of party wares. The Whig victory in 1840—a landslide in the electoral count, 234 to 60—nonetheless might have been reversed by a few minor mishaps. Despite all the log cabins, hard cider, and frontier imagery, the Whigs gained only half the needed votes from western states. It was in the Atlantic seaboard states that the Whigs achieved their victory, for six of these states switched from the Democratic column in 1836 to the Whig in 1840. An examination of the closeness and fortuitous nature of these outcomes is revealing.[14]

The Whigs carried Pennsylvania by only 239 votes out of a total of almost 300,000—that is, by approximately one-tenth of 1 percent. Important to this Whig victory was the final stage of fusion of Anti-Masons and Whigs, and any wavering or reluctance among Anti-Masons would surely have given the state to Van Buren. In New York, Harrison's margin over Van Buren was 3 percent of the total popular vote. The Whig organization there was, in some senses, also a final fusion of elements under cooperating leadership of such accomplished political managers as Thurlow Weed, William H. Seward, Francis Granger, Millard Fillmore, and Horace Greeley. The Whigs could have spared very little of their good fortune and still retained a margin of victory in New York.

Without either New York or Pennsylvania in his column, Harrison could have won by some combination of several of the other states he gained, but not one of these combinations was assured against small

[14]Richard P. McCormick, *The Second American Party System: Party Formation in the Jacksonian Era* (Chapel Hill, 1966), provides a lucid account of the circumstances within each state that had a direct bearing on the outcome of the presidential election of 1840.

exigencies. Even the comfortable Whig margin in North Carolina was the result of fortunate timing. North Carolina Whigs were in 1840 in the final stages of emerging as the majority party in the state through a combination of exceptionally able leaders, who took credit for a popular new state constitution in 1835. That Harrison profited from this timing is neither entirely accidental nor altogether causally related; a substantial element of good fortune was involved.

The outcome of the 1840 election is difficult to see as related significantly to anything other than a backlash from panic and depression, which probably gave Harrison the needed advantage in eastern states. Without New York and Pennsylvania, any other losses totaling 16 electoral votes would have wiped out his landslide victory.

Polk's victory over Clay in 1844 is not so easily attributed to expansion fever as might be thought at first glance. The depression following the panic of 1837 was fading, and voting patterns returned closely to the 1836 alignment. Polk would have lost had only 33 electoral votes been switched to Clay. With almost half the total electoral vote from states balanced so closely that any minor misadventure might have reversed the outcome, the election of Polk must be attributed to numerous unknown and possibly irrelevant circumstances. As it turned out, not all his gains in the West, where enthusiasm for territorial expansion was keenest, could have elected him without New York or Pennsylvania.

The allegation that the Liberty party cost Clay the electoral votes of New York and hence the election requires examination. Almost certainly the 3 percent of the popular vote that went to Birney came principally from the Whig ranks and did cost Clay whatever chance he had in New York. The Liberty party vote probably cost him Indiana and Michigan as well. Yet, with so many states closely contested, a reversal of Polk's narrow losses in, say, Tennessee, New Jersey, and Delaware would have preserved his victory without New York, Indiana, and Michigan. To whatever extent the Texas and general expansion issues tipped the balance in 1844 through interposition of the Liberty party, that party's effect was the reverse, at least in the short run, of its public policy position. There is, all things considered, little justification for viewing this remarkable exhibition of voter loyalty to party as a mandate for or against any national policy.

Taylor's victory over Cass in 1848 was close enough in the electoral count that a change of 19 votes would have reversed the result. New York, Pennsylvania, and Ohio each had more than 19 votes. The almost universally assigned role of the Free-Soil party as decisive in Cass's defeat cannot bear close scrutiny. Van Buren's winning of 26 percent of New York's popular vote destroyed whatever chance Cass might have had in that state. It is not at all certain, however, that Cass would have carried New York in a two-party contest. It is far more likely that in Ohio the Free-Soil vote came preponderantly from Whig ranks and gave Cass that state. But had Cass won New York and lost Ohio, he would still have fallen 6 votes short of victory. Moreover, it is possible that a Democratic victory in Michigan and Wisconsin would not have occurred if Free-Soil appeals had not drawn off some Whig votes. Pennsylvania, the other pivotal state, would have been closely divided without a Free-Soil vote, but the addition of the Free-Soil vote to the Democratic total there was still not enough to carry the state for Cass. Perhaps the only way to lay Cass's defeat to Free-Soil voters is to argue that a Liberty party candidate such as Birney would have drawn more Pennsylvania voters from Whig ranks than from Democratic ranks and delivered the state to Cass. This is a possibility, but to make such close reckoning about a state that remained on the razor's edge until after the 1856 election is hazardous at best.

In the 1852 victory the Democrats blanketed the nation with electoral votes. Pierce received 86 percent of these. Scott won only Vermont and Massachusetts in the East and Kentucky and Tennessee in the West. Yet the Democrats garnered less than 51 percent of the national popular vote and fared no better in the Middle Atlantic and Old Northwest sections. The Democratic percentage was less than 53 in the Upper South. Only in New England, where the Democratic vote was 44 percent, and in the Lower South, where the Democrats received almost 60 percent, was an uncommonly wide margin found. Apparent abstentions among southern Whigs were alarmingly large and suggestive of possible disaster ahead for that party, but certainly not proof that resurgence was impossible. Descriptions of the terminal illness of the Whig party cannot safely be based upon an analysis of these election returns but must rest upon other evidence of collapse in party structure. As mentioned before, one cannot avoid a suspicion that the "mortal sickness" interpretation grew out of a glance ahead to events after 1852. A different interpretation can be wrung from the actual

votes. A summary comparison of 1852 with the first Democratic victory under a fully developed two-party system, that of 1836, illustrates
this possibility. The Democratic percentage of the total popular vote of
the nation and its principal regions had changed between 1836 and
1852 (despite a doubling of the number of voters and sweeping internal
migration as well as immigration) by the small percentage alterations
shown in Table 15.

The election of 1856 cannot profitably be analyzed in terms of close
state contests that might have ended differently. The critical consideration in 1856 was that widespread antislavery sentiment encouraged
many prominent former Whigs in the North to believe that they could
draw into a common anti-Democrat party almost all Free-Soilers if
southern Whigs were jettisoned. This is what the Republican party accomplished in the Upper North. The three-way contest in the border
North, however, kept too many traditional anti-Democrats away from
the Republican fold in support of Fillmore. The Republicans were
counting on continuity of anti-Democratic alignment to give them the
bulk of former Whigs, even those not greatly agitated about slavery expansion, and in addition on Republican appeal to those former Democrats who had already shaken loose from habitual voting in support of
the Free-Soil principle. The perfectly obvious strategy of Republican
party managers was to try to take advantage of the fact that, in a two-
party contest throughout the North, the Democrats were likely to slip
behind their combined opponents in almost every state. As long as
southern anti-Democrats had to be appeased, it had become apparent,
no fusion of all anti-Democrats of the North could be effected. A manifestly sectional party was clearly dangerous, and truly independent
voters might have recoiled in great numbers. The long-standing habit
of voting against the Democratic party was probably an essential component of Republican hopes for eventual victory.

By 1860 the Republicans were ready to cash in on their strategy.
Lincoln's reputation and place of residence, together with a more mod-
erate platform than in 1856, were obvious appeals to the border North.
The likelihood that the election would eventually be settled in the
House of Representatives is integral to understanding party strat-
egy among the opponents of Lincoln. The Democratic convention in
Charleston split in early May, bringing into the open the probability
that no candidate would win in the electoral college. A few days later

the Constitutional Union party placed its candidates in the field, further guaranteeing a division of electoral votes. And in mid-May the Republican and the two Democratic slates were nominated. The lame-duck session of the House that might have had to decide among the leading three candidates had delegations from 33 states, so that 17 would be required for a majority. Republicans controlled 15 state delegations; northern Democrats controlled 3; southern Democrats controlled 11, if Missouri's is included; and southern Whigs controlled only Tennessee's delegation. Kentucky, Maryland, and North Carolina delegations were apparently tied between Bell and a Democrat, presumably Breckinridge. If Lincoln could have been denied a majority in the electoral college, the selection of one of his opponents would have been almost a certainty.

Voters generally performed as might have been expected from their former party alignments, except for those in Pennsylvania. In a frantic final effort to stave off almost certain defeat, Douglas men attempted to support Breckinridge electors. It meant little besides the major objective of getting the election into the House, but it evidently baffled or angered many Democrats and caused them to abstain. The dominating element in the election had proved to be the eminently successful strategy of the anti-Democratic politicians of the North. Counting on a massive continuity of voting habit to keep out of Democratic reach those who had long opposed that party, Republicans had achieved a rare success in realigning permanently a limited but decisive segment of former Democrats of the North.[15]

An appreciation of the importance of voter attachment to party, the theme of this essay, ought to lead to more satisfactory accounts of presidential elections between 1840 and 1860. Surely the significance of the

---

[15]There is no doubt that very high proportions of voters changed party affiliation in some places at several times during the two decades from 1840 to 1860. Findings to this effect are numerous in special and local studies and are entirely compatible with the more general estimates of voter constancy drawn from least-squares procedures. A strong association does not rule out the possibility of large deviations for some of the cases, and several counties do fall far from the regression pattern in many of the comparisons used in this essay. Particularly pertinent is the fact that counties with relatively small population may well have altered political alignment dramatically without seriously affecting the strength of association in a weighted regression for many counties. The issue is not whether a realignment occurred during the 1850s, for it surely did; the issue lies more in the question of relative importance of constancy and change and of the perceptions of contemporary political leaders at the time of critical strategy decisions.

presidential electoral process during the larger part of this twenty-year period, 1840 through 1852, must be sought in a context different from voter response to men or measures. Leaders of each party were free in most respects to pursue objectives along a poorly defined but real corridor of mass acceptance. Which side won was probably more a consequence of chance than of anything else. To the extent that this electoral process helped prohibit extreme departures, it did serve a definite purpose. Whether that purpose was appropriate and desirable is a subject of study altogether apart from the teapot tempests of the campaigns.

The last two elections of the period, those of 1856 and 1860, witnessed presidential politics notably different from the preceding elections. But even then, open voter choice among clearly perceived alternatives was not the primary characteristic of the contests. The great majority of voters had little sensible choice to make other than to follow visible and familiar political figures from either the Democratic or the anti-Democratic half of the political firmament. The responsibility for clarifying the alternatives offered and the consequences of such delimiting of options lay with a small coterie of political managers on each side. These men could plot courses with considerable assurance of the response they would get from party-oriented electorates, even though they could have little assurance that their leadership would command the slenderest margin of victory at the polls. The presidential electoral arrangements operating in 1856 and 1860 were without doubt significant, but not as arrangements for a popular mandate. One key question, applicable to the process before 1856 as well, is whether the latitude permitted the actual option makers was more or less desirable than that which might have been provided by other ways of selecting chief executives.

Electing presidents with firm rival alignments of voters in a two-party system is after all a means, not an end. Such an electoral arrangement should be judged by its contribution to outcomes deemed desirable by those advancing the judgments.[16] Painting these elections as

[16]There is certainly an extensive literature on this subject, but rarely incorporating the historical dimension reaching back into the nineteenth century until very recently. Sundquist's *Dynamics of the Party System* and Silbey's *A Respectable Minority* are examples of the welcome attention to history. And Richard P. McCormick's *The Presidential Game: The Origins of American Presidential Politics* (New York, 1982), appearing while this essay was in press, is singularly relevant. The notes for this essay began with

New England town meetings on a canvas of continental proportions, or as quadrennial circus parades, can only obscure the role they have played in the nation's history.

---

acknowledgment of a great debt to Walter Dean Burnham for his 1955 *Presidential Ballots, 1836–1892.* It seems fitting to end them with reference to his early contributions to the historical dimension: Burnham, *Critical Elections and the Mainsprings of American Politics* (New York, 1970), and William Nisbet Chambers and Burnham, eds., *The American Party Systems: Stages of Political Development* (New York, 1967).

MICHAEL F. HOLT

Winding Roads to Recovery: The Whig Party from 1844 to 1848

THE Whig party won the presidency for the second and last time in November, 1848, when General Zachary Taylor, a Mexican War hero and Louisiana slaveholder, was elected to the White House. Four years earlier many Whigs would have found this triumph inconceivable. In 1844 they had run Henry Clay, "the embodyment and polar star of Whig *principles*," as one had called him, against the Democrat James K. Polk, and the Whigs had been convinced that they had both the superior candidate and the superior position on the issues of the day. They would win in 1844, or else, many thought, they could never win. Thus one Whig paper had proclaimed on the eve of the election, "If J. K. Polk prevails over Henry Clay, the WHIG PARTY IS NO MORE." Clay's narrow loss to Polk, therefore, filled Whigs with "gloom and consternation" and shattered their faith in popular government. "The people have been appealed to and have elected a mere *Tom Tit* over the old Eagle," protested one Kentuckian. "Our strongest man has been beaten by a mere John Doe." Or, as Millard Fillmore, who himself lost the 1844 gubernatorial election in New York, wrote in despondency, "If with such *issues* and such *candidates* as the national contest presented we can be beaten, what may we not expect. A cloud of gloom hangs over the future. May God save the country, for it is evident the people will not." An equally dismayed Virginian evinced more anger: "With a most emphatic by God, I do say it is a disgrace, a lasting disgrace to our God Almighty – God damn – raggedy arse – hyena-made Republic to have elected over H. Clay that infernal poke of all pokes James K. Polk of Tenn." Gauged against this background of defeat and demoralization, the election of Taylor in 1848 marked a dramatic recovery for the Whig party.[1]

[1] J. W. Mighels to Henry Clay, November 11, 1844, Henry Clay MSS, Library of Congress, microfilm ed.; Richmond *Whig*, November 1, 1844, quoted in William J.

Rather than stressing the Whigs' resiliency, however, many historians portray the very nomination of Taylor as a sign of the party's bankruptcy and a portent of its impending demise. By this interpretation, Taylor's victory in a campaign in which the Whigs refused to adopt a national platform, like that of William Henry Harrison in 1840, demonstrated that the Whigs could prevail only when they ran a military hero and fudged the issues. They could not win on their policies and principles. Actually Taylor was even more apolitical than Harrison. He had never voted before 1848, and, as in the case of Dwight D. Eisenhower a century later, he was initially considered by both major parties as a potential presidential candidate. Since 1847 Taylor had been presented as a "no party" or "people's" candidate for president and had frequently vowed that he would never accept a regular party nomination from a convention or run a party administration. In the spring of 1848 he had threatened to remain in the race even if the Whigs nominated someone else, and only shortly before the Whig convention had he publicly admitted that he was a Whig though not, he emphasized, an "ultra Whig." Patently, as both Whig and Democratic contemporaries were quick to point out, Taylor was not a devoted champion of traditional Whig programs.[2]

Because of Taylor's fame and popularity, he also appealed to many outside the ranks of normal Whig voters. The Whigs needed precisely such a candidate in 1848, many historians argue, because their policies were sterile and obsolete. A campaign on those issues would have been hopeless. By 1848, according to Allan Nevins, the Whigs had lost their ideas and integrity. "They lacked any vital doctrine to give them real cohesion. They had been beaten on the tariff, on the United States

---

Cooper, Jr., *The South and the Politics of Slavery* (Baton Rouge: Louisiana State University Press, 1978), 225; Richard W. Thompson to Millard Fillmore, January 8, 1845, Millard Fillmore MSS, State University of New York, Oswego, microfilm ed.; Leslie Combs to John M. Clayton, November 20, 1844, John M. Clayton MSS, Library of Congress; Fillmore to Clay, November 11, 1844, Clay MSS; William M. Cooke to William C. Rives, December 14, 1844, William C. Rives MSS, Library of Congress.

[2]The "no party" campaign for Taylor is described in Holman Hamilton, *Zachary Taylor: Soldier in the White House* (Hamden: Archon Books, 1966), 38–81; George R. Poage, *Henry Clay and the Whig Party* (Gloucester, Mass.: Peter Smith, 1966), 154–58; and Michael F. Holt, *The Political Crisis of the 1850s* (New York: John Wiley & Sons, 1978), 62, 72–73. The public avowal of being a Whig but not an ultra Whig came in the first Allison letter, April 22, 1848.

Bank, and on generous national appropriations for internal improvements; it was plain that national sentiment was against their main ideas." In his splendid study of Abraham Lincoln's economic thought, Gabor S. Boritt also contends that the Whig strategy in 1848 "sadly implied that the Whigs had failed to get their message across, that their policies were not viable enough to be carried to victory by party regulars, at least in 1848." By backing Taylor, Lincoln joined other Whigs in "attempting to bring their principles to triumph through the back door." Similarly, William R. Brock has written recently that by August, 1846, the Whig program was "dead beyond the hope of recovery" and that the Whigs were "intellectually barren." Whig economic policies "were an inevitable casualty when the economy flourished without their adoption and prophecies of doom went unfulfilled." Taylor had been adopted in desperation. When he reached the White House "the Whigs became a party without a head . . . [and] the heady stimulant of Taylor's popularity would leave the party too weak for survival."[3]

There is considerable evidence, however, that the Whig party was more robust and that its issues were more vital than this interpretation indicates. The superb quantitative studies of roll-call voting in Congress by Thomas B. Alexander and Joel H. Silbey, for example, demonstrate that Whigs did remain internally cohesive and sharply divided from Democrats on most issues through the summer of 1848, despite sectional rifts over the Wilmot Proviso. Elsewhere, I have argued that the economic and expansionistic policies of the Polk administration and Democratic Congress, including the Mexican War, sharpened party lines in the states in 1846 and 1847 and enabled the Whigs to conduct successful campaigns in the off-year state and congressional elections as well as in the presidential election of 1848.[4] Certainly the results of

---

[3] Allan Nevins, *Ordeal of the Union: Fruits of Manifest Destiny, 1847–1852* (New York: Charles Scribner's Sons, 1947), 194; G. S. Boritt, *Lincoln and the Economics of the American Dream* (Memphis: Memphis State University Press, 1978), 145; William R. Brock, *Parties and Political Conscience: American Dilemmas, 1840–1850* (Millwood, N.Y.: KTO Press, 1979), 151–52, 188. See also David M. Potter, *The Impending Crisis, 1848–1861*, edited and completed by Don E. Fehrenbacher (New York: Harper & Row, 1976), 181.

[4] Thomas Alexander, *Sectional Stress and Party Strength: A Computer Analysis of Roll-Call Voting in the House of Representatives, 1836–1860* (Nashville: Vanderbilt University Press, 1967); Joel H. Silbey, *The Shrine of Party: Congressional Voting Behavior,*

those crucial elections between 1844 and 1848 belie the notion of a bankrupt party. If Whig issues were so defunct that the party needed a military hero to win in 1848, one would expect the party to have sustained drubbings in those off-year elections when it lacked the coattails of such a leader. Yet in the congressional elections of 1846–1847 the Whigs picked up 38 new seats in the House while the Democrats lost 35 seats. Put another way, in the Twenty-ninth Congress which enacted Polk's policies in 1846, the Democrats had a majority over the Whigs of 143 to 77. In the next Congress the Whigs would have a majority of 115 to 108 and control of the House for the first time since 1841. More important, 30 of those new seats came from states Clay had lost in 1844. The Whig gains in New York, Pennsylvania, Virginia, and Indiana were especially significant. Nor was that all. Between 1844 and 1848 Whigs won the governorship in Georgia, New York, and New Hampshire and control of the legislatures in New York, Georgia, Louisiana, and Indiana—all states that Clay had lost. Over the same period they maintained control of the state governments of such Whig strongholds as Massachusetts, Vermont, Connecticut, Kentucky, Tennessee, North Carolina, and Ohio.[5]

By these measures, surely, the Whig party was hardly an invalid as the election of 1848 approached. Since 1844 it had bounced back strongly at virtually all levels of the federal system and seemed to be flourishing. Why, then, did the Whig party find it necessary to select a candidate in 1848 whose very nomination signaled to Whigs and Democrats alike an abdication of Whig principles?

One answer has been offered by those historians who stress the centrality of the slavery issue in 1848 and the sectional nature of Taylor's support. Whatever the reasons for Whig gains after 1844, they argue, by 1847 and 1848 slavery expansion, crystallized by sectional divisions in both parties over the Wilmot Proviso, had become the major political issue of the day. The Polk administration may have revived economic issues in northern states. But in the South, where slavery monopolized political attention and where each party jockeyed to

---

1841–1852 (Pittsburgh: University of Pittsburgh Press, 1967); Holt, *Political Crisis*, 39–66.

[5] Figures on party strength are in U.S. Bureau of the Census, *Historical Statistics of the United States: Colonial Times to 1970* (2 vols.; Washington, D.C.: Government Printing Office, 1975), II, 1083.

prove itself a better proslavery party than its opponent, economic issues were dead by 1846. In this view, southern Whigs were in an especially desperate position. Democratic state parties vowed to reject any Democratic presidential candidate who was not pledged against the proviso, and John C. Calhoun was calling on all southerners to abandon the major parties and form a new Southern Rights party to resist northern agressions. Pressed by the need to prove that the Whig party was safe on the proviso issue, southern Whigs seized on the candidacy of Taylor not only because he was a military hero but also because they could argue that his status as a large slaveholder guaranteed that southern rights would be protected in the controversy over slavery extension. Thus, according to this interpretation, southern Whigs were the driving force behind the Taylor candidacy. Southern Whig congressmen formed the core of his initial support and orchestrated the Taylor boom. Southern Whigs provided the votes for Taylor at the Whig National Convention, and Taylor's nomination should be regarded as a victory of the southern wing of the party over its northern leaders, virtually all of whom opposed slavery extension and many of whom publicly advocated passage of the Wilmot Proviso.[6]

There is much to be said for this interpretation. Southerners were integral to the initial Taylor movement, and southerners did back him solidly at the Whig convention. Three-fourths of the slave-state delegates cast votes for Taylor on the first ballot, and they constituted over three-fourths of his total. On the fourth and final ballot, 106 of 110 southerners supported Taylor. Moreover, the Whig party *was* divided over the slavery issue, and many northern Whigs, especially in Massachusetts and Ohio, did perceive Taylor's nomination as a triumph of the South and an insult to the North. In 1847 a Massachusetts Whig had warned, "The southern Whigs want to go for Taylor on the ground of slavery, even if they knew it would break up the Whig party." After the convention another angrily fulminated that the southern Whigs "have trampled on the rights and just claims of the North sufficiently long, and have fairly shit upon all our Northern statesmen and are now trying to rub it in and I think now is the time and just the time for the

---

[6] For a forceful restatement of this argument, see Cooper, *The Politics of Slavery*, 225–68. See esp. 228–31 for the disappearance of economic issues in southern states.

North to take a stand and maintain it till they have brought the South to their proper level."[7]

Yet there is much that this thesis fails to explain. For one thing, the implication that all southern Whigs wanted Taylor only to neutralize or capitalize on the slavery issue oversimplifies their motivation; a variety of circumstances pointed southerners in that direction. For another, Taylor had northern support for the nomination from the time his name was first mentioned in 1846, and that support was clearly not based on his being a safe proslavery candidate. For example, New York's Whig boss Thurlow Weed was attracted to Taylor in 1846, a year in which he had tried to court antislavery voters in New York by pushing for black suffrage in the new state constitution. Two of the so-called Young Indians, the initial congressional supporters of Taylor, were northerners, and one of these was the influential Truman Smith of Connecticut, who came closer to being the equivalent of a modern national party chairman than any other Whig of the day. By March, 1848, Abraham Lincoln, then a Whig congressman from Illinois, wrote that not only he and Smith but also two Whig representatives from Indiana, three from Ohio, five from Pennsylvania, and four from New Jersey supported Taylor. Like Lincoln, all of these men had been elected in the Whig sweep of 1846–1847. Most important, of course, solid southern support alone did not secure Taylor's nomination at the Whig National Convention in June, 1848. One-fourth of Taylor's votes on the first ballot and almost two-fifths of his support on the final ballot came from free-state delegates.[8]

Taylor's northern supporters on that final ballot constituted 38 percent of the free-state delegates. By the final ballot another 37 percent of the northern delegates voted for General Winfield Scott, the other

[7] Charles Hudson to William Schouler, June 28, 1847, William Schouler MSS, Massachusetts Historical Society; William H. Howe to Roger Sherman Baldwin, Jr., July 25, 1848, Baldwin Family Papers, Sterling Library, Yale University.

[8] On Weed, see Robert F. Dalzell, Jr., *Daniel Webster and the Trial of American Nationalism* (Boston: Houghton-Mifflin Company, 1973), 125–26; Abraham Lincoln to Usher F. Linder, March 22, 1848, in Roy F. Basler, ed., *The Collected Works of Abraham Lincoln* (9 vols.; New Brunswick: Rutgers University Press, 1953), I, 45. For voting on the different ballots I have used the report of the Whig convention printed in the appendix of Glyndon G. Van Deusen, "The Whig Party," in Arthur M. Schlesinger, Jr., ed., *History of U.S. Political Parties* (4 vols.; New York: Chelsea House and R. W. Bowker, 1973) I, 433–44.

hero of the Mexican War and a man whose credentials as a champion of Whig policies were almost as negligible as those of Taylor. In sum, not only did virtually all southern Whigs support a military hero rather than a known advocate of Whig programs but so too did fully three-fourths of the northern Whigs. On the final ballot Henry Clay and Daniel Webster, the two contenders for the nomination who were prominent proponents of Whig measures, together garnered a meager 25 percent of the northern delegates and 16 percent of the total vote.[9]

One of the reasons some northern Whigs supported Scott and Taylor was indeed the divisiveness of the Wilmot Proviso. Early in the spring of 1848 several shrewd Whigs like Thurlow Weed recognized that the party would need a malleable candidate who had taken no public position on the proviso so that the party could conduct a two-faced campaign in 1848, running as a free-soil, pro-proviso party in the North and as an anti-proviso, pro–southern rights party in the South.[10] But there were orthodox civilian Whig politicians who met that need and still had a record on Whig policies. Moreover, it is difficult to believe that most northern delegates who backed Taylor or Scott did so because they calculated on this two-faced strategy to salvage the election. It is much more likely that those delegates were primarily attracted to the generals' appeal as military heroes and by the promise, especially in Taylor's case, that they could lure thousands who had never voted Whig.

Thus the questions arise again. If the Whigs had done so well in the off-year elections between 1844 and 1848, if they had already made a dramatic recovery from the narrow yet psychologically crushing defeat of 1844, why did so many apparently believe in 1848 that they couldn't win on traditional issues with an orthodox Whig politician? Why did so many think, as the evidence makes abundantly clear they did think, that they required a military hero not only to capture the White House but also to help the Whigs win the congressional and state elections that were simultaneously being conducted that year?

Why the Whigs thought they needed a military candidate in 1848 and why Taylor won the Whig nomination are related but separate

---

[9]On the first ballot, Clay and Webster together won 42.6 percent of the total vote and 58 percent of the northern vote. Even then, military heroes attracted the support of the majority of the convention and of a large minority of northern delegates.

[10]Holt, *Political Crisis*, 61–62.

questions. The latter involves delineation of complex considerations, such as intraparty factional maneuvering for advantage in virtually every state, that are beyond the scope of this essay. My concern here is with the first question, and the best way to answer it is to take a closer look at the nature of, and the reasons for, the apparent Whig recovery in the off-year elections between 1844 and 1848. Such an examination reveals that there was no single road to Whig recovery after 1844. Rather the fortunes of the party and the strategies it pursued varied both geographically and chronologically, from state to state and from year to year. The winding paths Whigs followed after 1844 and the changing fortunes that befell them along those roads greatly help to explain why many Whigs believed that yet another route was necessary to achieve victory in 1848.

Theoretically the Whigs could have traveled several different roads as they sought recovery after 1844, but in essence these narrowed to three alternatives, which they could pursue singly or in some combination. The choice depended upon their answer to the following question: could they win by emphasizing and clarifying traditional differences with the Democrats or would they have to change the party's image and broaden its appeal? In other words, should they work to retain majorities where they already had them or attempt to build new ones where they did not? The first possible course was to abandon national issues in favor of state and local concerns in the hope of forging statewide majorities in off-year elections that could be retained on the basis of party loyalty in the next presidential election. Most Whigs and Democrats in this period considered control of state governments to be as important as control of the national government anyway, and a resort to state issues often seemed an efficient way to capture statehouses. A second possibility was to attack the Democrats on national issues in off-year elections. These issues could be old ones like the tariff and territorial expansion that had dominated the 1844 campaign or new ones generated by the Polk administration and the Democratically controlled Congress that would meet in December, 1845. Finally, they could resort to nominating a presidential candidate in 1848 who had broader appeal than Clay had had in 1844.

The attractiveness of these alternatives or the necessity of employing them depended upon a number of factors. These included varying Whig perceptions of why they had lost in 1844, the availability of viable state issues that could be separated from national issues, and the presence or absence of minor parties that threatened to siphon off crucial Whig votes. But the most important variable by far was the competitiveness of a state's Whig party with the Democratic opposition. It is fruitful, accordingly, to divide the states into three groups: (I) states Whigs carried for Clay in 1844, however closely; (II) states they lost narrowly in 1844; and (III) states they lost decisively, that is, where the margin between the Democrats and Whigs exceeded ten percentage points (Table 20).

The behavior of Whigs in the states composing Group III is easiest to understand. For all practical purposes Whig prospects in these states, Illinois, Mississippi, Maine, Missouri, Alabama, New Hampshire, and Arkansas, were hopeless. To this group should be added Texas, which entered the Union in 1845, a state where the Whig party bore the crippling stigma of having opposed Texas' admission in the first place. True, the Whigs picked up three extra congressional seats from Mississippi, Alabama, and New Hampshire in 1847, and they won the New Hampshire gubernatorial election in 1846. But those gains were ephemeral and exceptional. In New Hampshire, for example, the Whigs won only because of a coalition with the Liberty party and dissident antislavery Democrats led by John P. Hale. In 1846, when no candidate received a popular majority in a three-way gubernatorial race, this coalition in the legislature elected a Whig governor. Yet his own share of the popular vote was less than 32 percent, and in 1847, when turnout was higher than in 1844 and the Whigs picked up a congressional seat, they received only 35 percent of the statewide vote. Similarly, the telling fact in Alabama, Mississippi, and Arkansas was the Whigs' decision not even to contest gubernatorial elections during most of these years and to write off a number of congressional seats as well. The Whigs were so weak in Missouri, finally, that their historian argues that they constituted more of a pressure group than a viable political party.[11]

Whigs and Democrats alike commented on the bleak Whig position in these states. In 1845, for example, Mississippi's Whigs moaned in

[11] John Vollmer Mering, *The Whig Party in Missouri* (Columbia: University of Missouri Press, 1967). Data from uncontested elections, as well as the data on most off-year elections in this essay, come from the voting returns listed annually in the *Whig Tribune Almanac*.

TABLE 20. The Strength of Whig State Parties
Ranked by the Percentage of the 1844 Vote.

	Whig	Democratic	Liberty	Major Party Margin*
Group I				
Rhode Island	60.0	39.9	0.0	+20.1
Vermont	55.0	37.0	8.0	+18.0
Kentucky	53.9	46.1	0.0	+ 7.8
North Carolina	52.7	47.3	0.0	+ 5.3
Maryland	52.4	47.6	0.0	+ 4.8
Massachusetts	51.7	40.0	8.3	+11.7
Delaware	51.2	48.7	0.0	+ 2.5
Connecticut	50.8	46.2	3.0	+ 4.6
New Jersey	50.4	49.3	0.2	+ 1.1
Tennessee	50.1	49.9	0.0	+ 0.2
Ohio	49.6	47.7	2.6	+ 1.9
Group II				
Georgia	48.8	51.2	0.0	− 2.4
Louisiana	48.7	51.3	0.0	− 2.6
Pennsylvania	48.5	50.6	0.9	− 2.1
Indiana	48.4	50.1	1.5	− 1.7
New York	47.8	48.9	3.3	− 1.1
Virginia	47.0	53.0	0.0	− 6.0
Michigan	43.5	49.9	6.5	− 6.4
Group III				
Mississippi	43.4	56.6	0.0	−13.2
Missouri	43.0	57.0	0.0	−14.0
Illinois	42.4	54.4	3.2	−12.0
Alabama	41.0	59.0	0.0	−18.0
Maine	40.4	53.8	5.7	−13.4
Arkansas	37.0	63.0	0.0	−26.0
New Hampshire	36.3	55.2	8.5	−18.9

*A plus sign indicates the Whigs carried the state; a minus sign indicates that the Democrats carried the state.

despair, "We have no hope as a party in this state—you know we are in the egyptian darkness of Locofocism." Similarly, a Mississippi Democrat confidently predicted victory in the 1847 gubernatorial election because "the Whigs offer no organized opposition to our state candidates," and he ridiculed as well the refusal of Whigs to accept congressional nominations because their cause was futile.[12] In Illinois a prominent Whig legislator lamented in early 1845, "I have hardly the faintest hope of this State ever being Whig." By the end of that year he had determined to leave politics for private business because "there is precious little use for any Whig in Illinois to be wasting his time and efforts. This state cannot be redeemed. I should as leave think of seeing one rise from the dead." He was right. The Whigs, who had won a pathetic 42 percent of the popular vote in 1844, did even worse in the congressional and gubernatorial elections of 1846, elections in which Whigs elsewhere were making a comeback (Table 21).[13]

In short, however much new state and national issues might help Whigs elsewhere, they were simply not enough to generate Whig recovery in these states. Here Whigs could not win on their program; here they needed a presidential candidate who could cut into the Democratic vote. It is no wonder, then, that Whigs from these states favored Taylor's candidacy overwhelmingly. Historians have long pointed out the delicious irony that Lincoln, the future Republican president, was an original member of the "Young Indians," the small group of congressmen who began the boom for the slaveholder Taylor. Lincoln, in fact, was not a Young Indian, for he did not arrive in Congress until December, 1847, long after the Taylor bandwagon was rolling.[14] Still he was an ardent Taylor booster, as were other Illinois Whigs who publicly endorsed Rough and Ready in the summer of 1847. He was well aware that he was the lone Whig congressman from Illinois and that the Whigs had to reach far beyond their own ranks to carry the state. Only Taylor could win the presidency for the Whigs, Lincoln insisted over and over, and only Taylor could help the Whigs in Illinois:

[12] Duncan McKenzie to Duncan McLaurin, November 2, 1845, Duncan McLaurin MSS, Perkins Library, Duke University; B. F. Dill to John A. Quitman, September 7, 1847, John F. H. Claiborne MSS, Mississippi Department of Archives and History. See also P. B. Barringer to Daniel M. Barringer, June 26, 1845, Daniel M. Barringer MSS, Southern Historical Collection, University of North Carolina, and John P. Stewart to Duncan McLaurin, July 11, 1845, McLaurin MSS.

[13] David Davis to John Henry, February 11, 1845, Davis to John Rockwell, December 17, 1845, and Davis to William P. Walker, December 6, 1846, David Davis MSS, Chicago Historical Society.

[14] Among the historians who repeat this error are Hamilton, *Zachary Taylor*, 63; Poage, *Clay and the Whig Party*, 157–58; Cooper, *The Politics of Slavery*, 245; and Joseph G. Rayback, *Free Soil: The Election of 1848* (Lexington: University Press of Kentucky, 1970), 38.

TABLE 21. Fluctuations in the Major Party Proportions of the Vote.

	1844		1845		1846		1847	
	Whig	Democrat	Whig	Democrat	Whig	Democrat	Whig	Democrat
Group I								
Rhode Island	60	39.9	49.1	50.4*	49.8	49.2*	57.4	36.3
Vermont	55	37	47.9	39.1	49.1	36.5	48.7	36.7
					47	32.4†		
Massachusetts	51.7	40	48.8	35.3	53.9	32.7	50.8	37.5
					55.4	32.9†		
Kentucky	53.9	46.1	51.6	48.4†	—	—	53.1	44.3†
North Carolina	52.7	47.3	42.9	57.1†	54	46	52.4	47.6†
Maryland	52.4	47.6	43.3	54.6†	—	—	49.5	50.5
							50	50†
Connecticut	50.8	46.2	51	45.3	48.6	47.5	50.5	45.9
			51	44.8†			50.8	46.1†
Delaware	51.2	48.7	—	—	49.4	50.6	—	—
					50.6	49.4†		
Ohio	49.6	47.7	—	—	48.3	47.3	—	—
New Jersey	50.4	49.3	—	—	51.4	46†	48.1	51.9
Tennessee	50.1	49.9	49.4	50.6	—	—	50.4	49.6
Group II								
New York	47.8	48.9	—	—	51.5	48.5	53.6	41.7‡
Indiana	48.4	50.1	46.8	51.8†	48.3	51.7	50.1	49.9†
Pennsylvania	48.5	50.6	38.1	51.1§	51.3	48.7†	44.6	50.8
					47.9	43.5§		
Georgia	48.8	51.2	51.1	48.9	46.9	53.1†	49.1	50.9
Louisiana	48.7	51.3	N.A.		44.1	53.2	47.2	52.8†
Virginia	47	53	N.A.		—	—	48.8	51.2†
Michigan	43.5	49.9	—	—	43.8	50.1	—	—
Iowa	—	—	—	—	48.9	51.1	48	52†
Florida	—	—	49.6	51.1†	50.8	49.2†	—	—
Group III								
Illinois	42.4	54.4	—	—	36.7	58.2	—	—
					40.3	54.4†		
Mississippi	43.4	56.6	35.2	64.8	—	—	33.6	64.7″
Maine	40.4	53.8	40.2	50.7	40.1	46.9	37.2	51.3
Missouri	43	57	N.A.		N.A.		N.A.	
Alabama	41	59	Two Dems.		—	—	44.7	55.3
New Hampshire	36.3	55.2	34	51.2	31.8	48.7	34.9	51
Arkansas	37	63	—	—	No Contest		—	—

*I have listed the Law and Order percentage under the Whigs and the Liberation party under the Democrats.

†These are returns from congressional races. All other returns after 1844 are for gubernatorial races except where otherwise indicated.

‡The returns in New York in 1847 are for comptroller.

§These returns in Pennsylvania are for canal commissioner.

″In this Mississippi election the Whig candidate was a volunteer. The party made no official nomination.

"In Illinois, his being our candidate, would *certainly* give us an additional member of Congress, if not more, and *probably* would give us the electoral vote of the state. That with him, we can, in that state, make great inroads among the rank and file of the democrats, to my mind is certain; but the majority against us there, is so great, that I can no more than express my *belief* that we can carry the state."[15] To Lincoln, the slavery issue was irrelevant in 1848. He backed Taylor because Taylor was a winner, because Taylor was the only hope Whigs in states like Illinois had.

This same consideration motivated Whigs from other states where the party had been badly defeated in 1844, most of which were slave states. It is true that by 1848 southern Whigs needed a candidate to neutralize Democratic and Calhounite positions on the proviso issue. But Whigs from Texas, Arkansas, Missouri, Mississippi, and Alabama would have needed an ostensibly nonpartisan and enormously popular candidate like Taylor even without the slavery issue. Only with such a presidential candidate could they hope to broaden their voting base sufficiently to triumph. Thus delegates from these states to the Whig National Convention in 1848 provided Taylor with his most solid support. Fully 71 percent of those delegates backed Taylor on the first ballot and 85 percent on the final ballot. The totals for Scott and Taylor together were even higher. Indeed, there was an almost perfect correlation between the competitiveness of Whig parties in different states and the level of support those states gave Taylor at the convention (Table 22).[16] Where the Whig party was weakest, it needed a military hero to have a fighting chance.

However logical and important was the Whig support for Taylor from these normally Democratic states, it provides only a partial answer to the puzzle raised at the beginning of this essay. The Whigs' comeback in off-year elections did not center on those states; rather it occurred in the states the Whigs had carried in 1844 and especially in

[15] Lincoln to T. S. Flournoy, February 17, 1848, Basler, ed., *Collected Works*, I, 452; see also Lincoln to Taylor Committee, February 9, 1848, Lincoln to Usher F. Linden, February 20, March 22, 1848, and Lincoln to Jesse Lynch, April 10, 1848, *ibid.*, 449, 453, 457–58, 463–64.

[16] Without New Hampshire the total for Taylor on the first ballot would have been 81 percent. New Hampshire was unusual in that Whigs there depended on coalitions with antislavery Democrats and the Liberty party for the meager success they enjoyed; hence New Hampshire delegates were especially unlikely to back a slaveholding candidate.

TABLE 22. Proportions of Votes Cast for Military Candidates
by Group at the Whig Convention.

Percentage for Taylor		
	First Ballot	Final Ballot
Group I	29.5	56
Group II	37	56
Group III	70.8	85

Percentage for Taylor and Scott Combined		
	First Ballot	Final Ballot
Group I	48.5	80
Group II	55.5	86
Group III	73	92

NOTES: Groups are those defined by Table 20. Group II includes Iowa and Florida as based on margins in 1846. Group III includes Texas.

the states they had lost narrowly like New York, Pennsylvania, Indiana, and Georgia. To solve the riddle of why an apparently robust party needed a military candidate who was not associated with its principles, one must examine the performance of the Whigs in those states after 1844. Such an examination reveals a predictable variety in the strategies and fortunes of Whig parties in different states. More important, it also shows that the Whig comeback in off-year elections was not as substantial as a mere count of congressional seats and statehouses won seems to indicate. Rather, those victories were based on razor-thin margins, idiosyncratic conditions that could not be re-created, or issues whose salience and appeal proved ephemeral. The result was that even where the Whig party had flourished in 1845, 1846, or 1847, many Whigs believed by the spring of 1848 that nominating a Mexican War hero was necessary to win in the state, congressional, and presidential elections of that year.

For a year or so after Clay's defeat, stunned Whigs experimented with several different routes toward recovery, but most of these proved to be dead ends. By the spring of 1846 the party was generally in worse shape than it had been in November, 1844—listless, worried, and internally divided. In the South the major Whig priority in 1845, a year of important congressional and gubernatorial elections, was to bury the national issues which Whigs thought had hurt them in 1844—the tariff and especially Texas annexation. As one Georgia Whig wrote of the Texas issue, "This question was in our way last year, it is in our way now, and will be a thorn in our side until it is . . . put to rest in some way." Thus Whigs in Virginia, Tennessee, and Georgia urged their congressmen and senators to support annexation by joint resolution in February, 1845, to prevent Democrats from "making party capital" of the Texas issue in gubernatorial elections. And even though a number of Whig senators from the South opposed annexation by that measure, its passage did resolve the issue. At the same time, the lack of concrete tariff proposals in 1845 allowed the Whigs to dodge the tariff issue where they wanted to.[17]

Problems remained for southern Whigs, however. When they did manage to bury the supposedly deleterious national issues of 1844, they usually found that they then had nothing else to run on. In Georgia they clung to the coattails of the popular incumbent Governor George W. Crawford, whose management of state finances was universally praised. They also went out of their way to prevent the Democrats from focusing the campaign on the record of Whig Senator John M. Berrien, who had resolutely defended the Whig tariff of 1842 and opposed Texas annexation and who was up for reelection in 1845.[18] In this way Georgia's Whigs captured the governorship and one house of the legislature in a key southern state that Clay had lost. But this strat-

---

[17] For the quotations, see N. C. Barnett to John M. Berrien, February 18, 1845, John M. Berrien MSS, Southern Historical Collection, University of North Carolina, microfilm ed., and Joseph H. Peyton to William B. Campbell, February 16, 1845, Campbell Family Papers, Perkins Library, Duke University. On the general desire to bury the Texas and tariff issues, see, on Virginia, W. E. Sutton to William C. Rives, January 31, 1845, J. J. Fry to Rives, January 23, 1845, James F. Strother to Rives, November 17, 1844, February 2, 1845, Rives MSS; on Tennessee, Arthur Campbell to David Campbell, November 17, 1844, Campbell Family Papers; on Alabama, H. M. Cunningham to Alexander H. Stephens, December 21, 1844, Alexander H. Stephens MSS, Library of Congress, microfilm ed.; and on Georgia, David S. Anderson to Alexander H. Stephens, February 16, 1845, in U. B. Phillips, ed., "The Correspondence of Robert Toombs, Alexander H. Stephens, and Howell Cobb" in *The Annual Report of the American Historical Association for the Year 1911* (Washington, D.C., 1913), II, 60–64, and Charles J. Jenkins to John M. Berrien, February 3, 15, 1845, Toombs to Berrien, February 13, 1845, Berrien MSS.

[18] See the sources on Georgia in the previous note and Charles J. Jenkins to John M. Berrien, April 22, 1845, C. B. Strong to Berrien, May 9, 1845, J. R. A. Merriwether to Berrien, May 10, 1845, and Francis S. Bartow to Berrien, July 30, August 3, 1845, Berrien MSS.

agem clearly could not be repeated in future Georgia elections; Crawford, indeed, had been very reluctant even to run for reelection.

Elsewhere in the South the Whigs apparently had no viable state issues, and as a result their performance was dismal. They lost the governorship in Tennessee, a state Clay had carried, even though their candidate, Ephraim Foster, had supported Texas annexation in the United States Senate. In Virginia, where internal regional rivalries prevented a coherent stand on any state issues, they unexpectedly lost the legislative elections of 1845 and one U.S. Senate seat and elected just one of fifteen congressmen.[19] North Carolina's Whigs captured only three of nine House seats, and two of those were not contested by the Democrats. Moreover, in the districts the Democrats did contest, the Whig share of the vote dropped from 46.3 percent in 1844 to 42.9 percent in 1845. In Kentucky the Whigs gained an additional congressional seat but suffered a drop in their proportion of the vote. They also lost a special gubernatorial election in Louisiana in January, 1846, with a smaller share of the vote than Clay had attracted in 1844. Worst of all was the Whig experience in Maryland, a state Clay had carried handily. Controlling all six of the state's congressional seats going into the 1845 election, the Whigs lost four of those seats and saw their share of the vote plummet from 52.4 to 43.3 percent. Despair, apathy, and a lack of viable issues obviously contributed to these reverses, for in every southern state except Georgia the Whig drop-off in voter turnout since 1844 was significantly higher than Democratic drop-off (Table 23). By early 1846 the Whig party in the South was clearly in trouble.

In sharp contrast to their southern brethren, northern Whigs initially tried to keep the issues growing out of the 1844 campaign alive as long as possible. They thought they could profit from them, even in the northern states they had lost. Thus the influential New York *Tribune* argued shortly after Clay's defeat that Whig principles were "approved by a large majority of the American people. . . . We are beaten not because we were in favor of Protection and opposed to Annexation, but because our opponents concealed or mystified these vital issues throughout two-thirds of the Union." The road to Whig victory, editor Horace Greeley concluded, lay in clarifying the real differences be-

---

[19] For the Whig expectations and disappointment in Virginia, see J. J. Fry to William C. Rives, January 23, 1845, and Jno. Pendleton to Rives, May 1, 1845, Rives MSS.

TABLE 23. Drop-off Rates of Major Parties in Selected States after 1844.

	1845		1846		1847	
	Whig	Democrat	Whig	Democrat	Whig	Democrat
Vermont	22.6	5.8	14.5	5.4	10.6	−0.4
Massachusetts	23.5	28.2	18.8	36.3	20.4	23.9
Rhode Island	−5.1	−62.3	−2.1	−51.8	6.3	10.7
Connecticut	10.1	12	15.2	8.8	8.2	8.2
New York	—	—	14.4	21.1	24.8	42.7
Pennsylvania	44.4	28.6	39	46.8	20.1	12.7
Ohio	—	—	24.6	23.2	—	—
Indiana	13.3	7.1	15.2	12.4	0.5	4.2
Maryland	33.8	8.3	—	—	6.4	−5
Virginia	N.A.		—	—	17.1	24.4
North Carolina	17	4.7	7.2	12.1	22.6	21.9
Georgia	13.7	21.4	34.5	29.4	0.4	1.8
Kentucky	7.7	−14.3	—	—	−6.2	−3.8
Tennessee	5.6	2.7	—	—	−2.1	−0.9
Louisiana	—	—	15.1	2.9	0.4	1.8

NOTE: This table is based on the same returns as Table 21. When congressional and statewide elections were held in the same year, I used the statewide return to calculate drop-off. On Rhode Island, I again put the Law and Order party in the Whig column and the Liberation party in the Democratic column. A negative drop-off indicates that a party drew more votes in that election than it had in the presidential election of 1844.

tween the two parties on those issues as sharply as possible.[20] Such a tack might galvanize the loyalty of Whig voters and convert people who had supported Polk because they had been hoodwinked by the Democratic campaign. It also might win back the crucial Liberty party vote in closely divided states like Connecticut, New York, Pennsylvania, Ohio, Indiana, and Michigan. Holding this belief, Whigs kept up a steady drumfire against Texas annexation in editorials, party platforms, and legislative resolutions, even after Congress offered and Texas accepted annexation in 1845.[21] While the issue remained salient, it

[20] New York *Tribune*, November 16, 1844.

[21] See, for example, Daniel Webster to Robert C. Winthrop, January 10, 1845, Robert C. Winthrop MSS, Massachusetts Historical Society, microfilm ed.; Webster to Samuel Hurd, March 8, 1845, Daniel Webster MSS, Dartmouth College, microfilm ed.; copy of anti-Texas resolution passed by the Massachusetts legislature, March 31, 1845, in

clearly helped the Whigs. In April, 1845, the Whigs swept to victory in Connecticut, winning the governorship and replacing the entire congressional delegation of Democrats with Whigs. The Democrats' support of annexation by joint resolution, the triumphant Whigs explained, accounted for this rout.[22]

Yet the Texas issue was severely limited so far as northern Whigs were concerned. It was finite. Once Texas accepted annexation to the Union in July, 1845, and its admission by the impending session of Congress seemed assured, the issue lost impact. Indeed, further agitation of it only divided Whigs in states like Massachusetts. Nor could they find different strategies for wooing Liberty party voters that did not also fragment the party. In New York, for example, the Weed-Seward-Greeley wing of the party bid for antislavery voters by pushing for revision of the state constitution to broaden black suffrage. Conservative New York Whigs, however, vehemently opposed such a change, and their hostility neutralized any lure the Whig party as such had for political abolitionists in the state legislative elections of 1845.[23]

Without a powerful unifying national issue like Texas, in fact, the Whig party fragmented almost everywhere in the North in 1845 and early 1846. Ohio was an exception. There the party was in sharp conflict with the Democrats over state banking policy, and it scored impressive gains in the October legislative elections. Pennsylvania was more typical. Whigs from the eastern and western ends of the state, like Democrats, were dividing over the rival claims of the Baltimore & Ohio and Pennsylvania railroads for chartered routes to Pittsburgh. This battle would completely disrupt Whig cohesion in the legislative session that began in January, 1846. Similarly, Indiana's Whigs split

---

Adams Family Papers, Massachusetts Historical Society, microfilm ed.; New York *Tribune*, February 6, September 27, 1845; D. T. Disney to William Allen, December 3, 1844, and C. B. Flood to Allen, December 3, 1844, January 16, 1845, William Allen MSS, Library of Congress; Samuel Sample to Schuyler Colfax, June 8, 1845, Schuyler Colfax MSS, Northern Indiana Historical Society; and Holt, *Political Crisis*, 44–45.

[22] William Ellsworth to Roger Sherman Baldwin, April 9, 1845, and Baldwin to S. C. Phillips *et al.*, July 3, 1845, Baldwin Family Papers.

[23] On Massachusetts, see Kinley J. Brauer, *Cotton versus Conscience: Massachusetts Whig Politics and Southwestern Expansion, 1843–1848* (Lexington: University of Kentucky Press, 1967). On New York, see New York *Tribune*, January 13, April 26, May 17, July 2, 1845; Horace Greeley to Schuyler Colfax, January 26, 1846, Greeley-Colfax MSS, New York Public Library.

over issues like slavery, state internal improvements, and the repudiation of state bonds issued for construction of the Wabash & Erie Canal, and those divisions apparently contributed to the party's defeat in the congressional and legislative elections of August, 1845.[24]

Rhode Island provides yet another example of Whig vulnerability to divisive state issues following the settlement of unifying national questions. In 1844 the Whigs had rolled up a higher percentage of the vote in Rhode Island than in any other state, but in the April gubernatorial elections of 1845 and 1846 the Whig coalition virtually disintegrated. Legacies of the Dorr Rebellion, those campaigns were conducted by state-oriented parties called the Law and Order and the Liberation parties, each of which ran a Whig as its candidate. The party fractured so badly that in March, 1846, a furious Whig berated the folly of his party's newspapers for making so much of the law and order issue. They should make clear, he advised, that the tariff was at stake in the 1846 legislative elections. Whig Senator James F. Simmons, a stalwart on that matter, was up for reelection, and intraparty squabbles over state issues endangered his seat. Only by focusing attention on national issues, in short, could the Whig party be saved from its suicidal internal bloodletting.[25]

Perhaps the most dramatic evidence of how a lack of salient national issues damaged the Whigs came in Connecticut, the state the Whigs had swept so impressively in April, 1845, on the tariff and Texas issues. In the absence of concrete action from the new Congress, Democrats managed to focus the state election of April, 1846, on a state issue, temperance, which divided the Whigs internally and cost them votes among the foes of liquor laws. As a result the Whigs lost their statewide majority, and the Democrats captured the legislature,

[24] On Ohio, see Stephen Maizlish, "The Triumph of Sectionalism: The Transformation of Politics in the Antebellum North, Ohio, 1844–1860" (Ph.D. dissertation, University of California at Berkeley, 1978), 74–95; on Pennsylvania, see Holt, *Political Crisis,* 112, and Henry R. Mueller, *The Whig Party in Pennsylvania,* Columbia University Studies in History, Economics, and Public Law, Vol. 101 (New York, 1922), 131–32; on Indiana, see Godlove Orth to Schuyler Colfax, August 16, 1845, Godlove Orth MSS, Indiana State Library.

[25] Thomas J. Stead to Samuel F. Man, March 18, 1846, Thomas Jenckes MSS, Library of Congress. Without statistical analysis, it is impossible to say precisely how the Whig vote divided, but see Table 21 for the apparent division of the Whigs' 1844 vote between the two parties.

which then elected a Democratic governor. Almost concurrently both the Whig and Democratic parties were splitting internally over the question of bridging the Connecticut River at Middletown to build a railroad from New Haven to Boston. New Haven and Hartford Whigs, along with their respective regional allies, would war with each other over this disruptive issue for two years.[26]

Adding to the disarray caused by intrastate regional divisions and damaging issues in specific states was a more general legacy of the 1844 campaign—the existence of independent nativist or antiimmigrant parties. To the Whigs, such parties posed both a problem and an opportunity. They might drain off Whig voters, and yet they might help to broaden the party's base. Many angry Whigs blamed Clay's defeat on a large and illegal immigrant vote for Polk, and some even wanted to merge with the Native American or American Republican party, as it was called in different places. The threat such a development posed for Whig fortunes became clear soon after the presidential election. In December, 1844, an independent nativist party defeated both Democrats and Whigs in the Boston mayoral election. A few months later in the spring of 1845, there were other disturbing signs—many Whigs continued to back the American Republican party in New York City's municipal election, and nativist parties made overtures to Whig voters in other cities such as Philadelphia, Baltimore, and Richmond. The threat to Whiggery intensified when nativists nominated their own state tickets in Massachusetts, Louisiana, and Pennsylvania.[27]

In the face of this growing challenge, Whig politicians opposed formal mergers that entailed abandoning the Whig name and did what they could to offset the minor parties' appeal to their voters. For example, in order to establish their own nativist credentials, Whigs made

[26] Roger Sherman Baldwin to S. D. Hubbard, March 28, 1846, Emily Baldwin to Edward Baldwin, April 12, 1846, Baldwin Family Papers; A. E. Burr to Gideon Welles, June 17, 1846, Gideon Welles MSS, New York Public Library; Welles to Isaac Toucey, June 23, 1846, Gideon Welles MSS, Library of Congress. Emily Baldwin wrote to Edward Baldwin on May 12, 1847, that there were so many divisions in the state over the question of bridging rivers that "sectional feelings overcome party lines." Baldwin Family Papers.

[27] L. Saltonstall to Henry Clay, December 10, 1844, Clay MSS; Geo Wm. Boyd to John Quincy Adams, April 7, 1845, Adams Family Papers; New York *Tribune*, November 28, 1844, April 10, 1845; S. M. Troutman to James M. Bell, November 13, 1844, James M. Bell MSS, Perkins Library, Duke University; J. J. Fry to William C. Rives, November 13, 1844, Rives MSS.

a concerted attack on illegal immigrant voting. In November, 1844, Webster made a strong speech in Boston calling for reform of the naturalization laws, and Whigs in the Massachusetts legislature passed a resolution to the same effect the following March. Whig governors in Kentucky and Maryland demanded new registration laws to stop illegal immigrant voting in January, 1845, and Whig newspapers and meetings in Virginia and Connecticut called on Congress for action. One result of this pressure was that the Whig-controlled Senate Judiciary Committee undertook a well-publicized, if futile, investigation of illegal naturalization and reported a bill to remedy it during the second session of the Twenty-eighth Congress (December, 1844–March, 1845).[28]

None of these measures stopped the hemorrhaging of Whig voters toward nativist ranks. Separate nativist and temperance tickets cost the Whigs a congressional seat in Baltimore in October, 1845, even though their own candidate had called for reform of the naturalization laws. As the Massachusetts gubernatorial election approached, Whigs there despaired of holding their support. Frantically they tried to portray their familiar candidate, George N. Briggs, as a foe of immigrants, but to no avail.[29] In November a Native American candidate drew 8 percent of the vote, as large a share as the Liberty candidate, and the Whigs lost their absolute statewide majority. A month earlier, the Whigs had been smashed in the race for canal commissioner in Pennsylvania. Their vote plummeted from 48.5 percent to 38.1 percent while the Native American candidate attracted 9.6 percent of the vote. Worse still from the Whig point of view, overt attempts to woo nativists were counterproductive in two regards. They bitterly divided the

[28] New York *Tribune*, November 11, 26, 1844, January 7, 9, 1845; Daniel Webster to David P. Hall, November 16, 1844, and Webster to Robert C. Winthrop, December 13, 29, 1844, Webster MSS; copy of the Massachusetts legislative resolution, March 31, 1845, in Adams Family Papers; John H. Pleasants to William C. Rives, December 23, 1844, Rives MSS; the pressures on the Senate Judiciary Committee can be followed in the papers of its chairman John M. Berrien.

[29] On Maryland, see New York *Tribune*, September 26, 1845; John P. Kennedy to Philip C. Pendleton, October 9, 1845, John P. Kennedy MSS, George Peabody Division of the Enoch Pratt Free Library of Baltimore, microfilm ed. On Massachusetts, see Abbott Lawrence to William C. Rives, January 17, 1845, Rives MSS; Robert C. Winthrop to John P. Kennedy, September 30, October 9, 1845, Kennedy MSS; and Boston *Courier*, quoted in *Pennsylvania Telegraph* (Harrisburg), October 29, 1845.

party, especially in New York where the Seward-Weed-Greeley wing vehemently opposed that strategy, and they probably drove immigrants toward the Democratic party in large numbers. Certainly this tactic did not prevent Democratic victories in New York and Pennsylvania in 1845, any more than in Maryland or Virginia. Recognizing the futility of this path, Whigs abandoned it in 1846. In Congress and in the states, Whig spokesmen renounced any plans to merge with nativists or change naturalization laws.[30] Broadening the party's base by a direct appeal to nativists had proved another dead end. The Whigs would have to find a different road to recovery.

By the spring of 1846, in sum, northern Whigs, like their southern colleagues, had made a series of false starts. Routes that had seemed like shortcuts to power turned out to be blind alleys. In the few states they carried they had either exploited ephemeral issues or suffered serious erosion of their voting support. They had failed to come back in the key states of New York, Pennsylvania, and Indiana and seemed in danger in former strongholds like Rhode Island, Connecticut, and Maryland. To pull back apathetic and defecting voters, the Whigs clearly had to look elsewhere for winning issues. An indication of where most would look came from a discouraged Indiana Whig in January, 1846. Pessimistic about capturing the state's impending gubernatorial election on state issues that divided the party internally, he wistfully yet accurately predicted, "Congress may kick up some deviltry out of which we can make something to put in our pipes."[31]

The actions of the Polk administration and of the Democratic Congress in 1846 and 1847 indeed provided the basis for the Whig party's dramatic comeback in the congressional and state elections of those years. Polk negotiated and the Senate ratified a treaty establishing the northern boundary of Oregon at the forty-ninth parallel, a treaty viewed as a betrayal by both Whigs and Democrats in the Midwest.

---

[30] On the splits in New York, see New York *Tribune, passim* for 1845; for the changes in 1846, see William Henry Seward to Thurlow Weed, January 1, 1846, and John Tayler Hall to Weed, February 17, 1846, Thurlow Weed MSS, Rush Rhees Library, Rochester University.

[31] Godlove Orth to Schuyler Colfax, January 27, 1846, in J. Herman Schauinger, ed., "The Letters of Godlove S. Orth: Hoosier Whig," *Indiana Magazine of History*, 39 (1943), 378–80.

Polk initiated and Congress declared war against Mexico, a war that dragged on until the spring of 1848 and became increasingly unpopular. Whigs throughout the nation denounced the war itself as an immoral aggression, Polk's management of it as partisan and inept, and the prospect of territorial annexation from it as dangerous to North and South alike. At Polk's urging as well, Congress enacted three important economic measures in the summer of 1846 that together marked a frontal assault on the Whig economic program: the Independent Treasury Act, which removed government revenues from private banks and required the government to deal exclusively in specie; the Walker tariff, which lowered most rates on manufactured goods, raised rates on a number of raw materials imported by American manufacturers, and substituted *ad valorem* for specific duties; and the Public Warehouse Act, which in effect gave government credit to importers and foreign manufacturers by allowing them to deposit imports in government warehouses for up to a year before paying customs duties rather than paying the tariff immediately upon the arrival of the goods. To compound matters, Congress defied Polk's wishes and passed a massive rivers and harbors improvement bill, which Polk vetoed. Polk's veto, of course, offended all the intended recipients of government aid.

All of these actions provided the Whigs with something they could put in their pipes, but initially the Democratic economic program formed the chief target. Almost as soon as the election of 1844 was over, Whigs had predicted that Democratic ascendancy meant economic disaster for the country. Yet some Whigs were prepared to let the Democrats have their way on the tariff and subtreasury because the inevitable depression would spark a Whig comeback. Clay himself confidently forecast that "errors" by the Polk administration would offer "abundant cause of public dissatisfaction." So hopeful were the Whigs of the tariff issue that as early as April, 1846, Truman Smith, who was trying to organize a central Whig congressional committee to coordinate state and congressional campaigns in 1846, planned to send Whig tariff speeches to every congressional district in the country. By June, as the Walker bill progressed through the House, Georgia's Whigs were said to anticipate the final law "with the eagerness of hyenas and jackals waiting only for the final onslaught to be over to rush on to the work of mutilation" because the bill included new duties on coffee and tea, while Whigs in Pennsylvania and New York declared that passage of the tariff would doom the Democrats in the ensuing elections.[32]

Lest they lose such a potent issue at the last moment, congressional Whigs put the construction of a winning platform ahead of the economic interests of their constituents. They had no hope of stopping the Democratic steamroller in the House, but the Senate was closely divided and contained a number of protariff Democrats. Businessmen therefore beseeched Whigs to modify the Walker bill in the Senate to offer them more protection and to save specific duties at all costs. Daniel Webster, after extensive consultation with businessmen in the Northeast, prepared a compromise tariff as an amendment to Walker's bill, one that would lower rates more gradually and preserve specific duties. Webster was confident he had the votes to adopt the substitute in the Senate and kill the whole bill when it returned to the House. But he never even offered the amendment because other Whigs would not support him. They wanted the Walker tariff passed, regardless of businessmen's pleas. The worst tariff possible would make the best platform possible. As Webster himself put it, Whigs opposed his amendment because they preferred "the continuance of the controversy to a reasonable and safe settlement of it." Similarly, a bitter manufacturer concluded with perfect accuracy that Whig politicians were "striving to make political capital to overthrow the present administration at whatever cost to the country."[33]

Once the Democratic program passed Congress, Whigs gleefully seized it as an invincible combination of issues. A Massachusetts Whig attempted to console Webster by suggesting that the party could sweep northern congressional elections and secure the next president

[32] New York *Tribune*, December 20, 1844, January 7, 17, 18, August 14, 1845; Thurlow Weed to Francis Granger, February 12, 1845, Francis Granger MSS, Library of Congress; Henry Clay to John J. Crittenden, November 28, 1844, Clay MSS; Clay to John M. Clayton, December 2, 1844, Clayton MSS; Truman Smith to Nathan Appleton, April 9, 1846, Nathan Appleton MSS, Massachusetts Historical Society; John B. Lamar to Howell Cobb, June 24, 1846, in Phillips, ed., *Correspondence*, 82–84; H. King to Thomas Butler King, June 22, 1846, Thomas Butler King MSS, Southern Historical Collection, University of North Carolina; James Bowen to Thurlow Weed, July 21, 1846, Weed MSS.

[33] The negotiations over an abortive attempt at amending the Walker bill can be followed in great detail in the Daniel Webster MSS for July, 1846. For the quotations, see Daniel Webster to Fletcher Webster, July 27, 29, 1846, and Joseph Balch to Webster, July 25, 1846, *ibid*.

on the tariff issue. "It is an ill wind that blows no one any good," he wrote. Agreeing, Thomas Corwin of Ohio predicted that Whigs could carry the entire Midwest by attacking the tariff, the subtreasury, and Polk's veto of the rivers and harbors bill. William Bebb, Ohio's Whig gubernatorial candidate, was exultant: "If the repeal of the Tariff, the passage of the Sub Treasury, the veto of the river and harbor bill and other measures of this administration added to our *state issues* fail to 'stir up the very stones to meeting' we may as well hereafter hang our harps on the willows." At last, Whigs everywhere believed, they had discovered the long-sought road to recovery.[34]

The Whigs, in fact, made extraordinary progress in the 1846 elections. They picked up fourteen additional congressional seats in New York, one in New Jersey, five in Pennsylvania, three in Ohio, and one in Georgia. They held all their seats in other northern states, including the entire Massachusetts delegation, and they won governorships in New York, Ohio, North Carolina, and Massachusetts, where they did much better than in 1845. Although they narrowly lost the gubernatorial election in Indiana in August, they won control of the legislature. More important for the future, the Whigs won a larger proportion of the vote in the fall elections of 1846 than they had in 1844 in every state except Delaware, Georgia, and Ohio and Vermont, two states where the Liberty party cut into their ranks.

Nevertheless, perceptive Whigs might have found cause for concern even in the midst of this truly impressive performance. Attacks on the Polk record by themselves did not give the Whigs control of the crucial states they would need to carry the presidency in 1848. In Georgia, for example, reapportionment of the congressional districts by the Whig legislature was probably more responsible for the Whigs' success in carrying four of eight seats than the Walker tariff, which in its final form did not contain the tea and coffee duties Georgia's Whigs had anticipated so eagerly.[35] Even so, Whigs won only 47 percent of the popular vote, evidence of both the effectiveness of their gerrymander and how hazardous their position in a statewide race re-

[34] Moses Stuart to Daniel Webster, August 3, 1846, Webster MSS; Thomas Corwin to Thomas Ewing, August 1, 1846, and William Bebb to Ewing, August 10, 1846, Ewing Family Papers, Library of Congress. See also R. Fisher to Thomas Butler King, August 3, 1846, and S. Jardin to King, August 6, 1846, King MSS.

[35] On the Whigs' delight with the reapportionment, see Robert Toombs to Alexander H. Stephens, January 1, 1844, in Phillips, ed., *Correspondence*, 52–53.

mained. Pennsylvania's Whigs won the statewide election for canal commissioner in 1846, but with less than a majority of the vote. The Native American candidate still drew 7.5 percent, and Democrats suffered a significantly larger drop-off than the Whigs. Manifestly, Pennsylvania's Whigs were still vulnerable to a full Democratic turnout. Even in New York, where Whigs scored their biggest gains, they depended in 1846 on conditions that went beyond their platform. According to editor Horace Greeley, they had elected the governor and as many as five congressmen only by capturing the Anti-Rent vote and exploiting the growing division between Hunker and Barnburner Democrats.[36]

New York provides a marvelous microcosm of the trial and error method by which Whigs tried to find a winning strategy between 1844 and 1848. Until late in the spring of 1846, the dominant wing of the party, led by Greeley, Weed, and William Henry Seward, had attempted to broaden the Whig coalition by adding antislavery, black, and even immigrant voters to it. To accomplish that goal, they had focused on the state constitutional convention that was to meet in the summer of 1846 and had pushed for the adoption of alien suffrage and broader black suffrage in the new constitution. When it became apparent by late spring that both measures would fail and that both seriously divided the party and might alienate more old Whig voters than attract new ones, the Whig leadership jettisoned that strategy for a different one. They recognized that Hunkers and Barnburners were deeply split over provisions of the new constitution and over control of the state Democratic machine. The Seward Whigs had previously cooperated informally with the Barnburners to call the convention, but now they turned to the Hunkers. Hunker Democrats privately assured them that, if the Whigs chose an acceptable gubernatorial candidate, the Hunkers would sit the election out and allow the Whigs to win. Their main goal was to strip Barnburners of the state patronage controlled by incumbent governor and Democratic candidate Silas Wright. With Democrats and hence Barnburners out of power, the Hunkers believed their chances of winning control of Democratic party machinery would be enhanced. At the same time, the Whigs perceived a bloc of voters other than immigrants and the Liberty party that might be up

---

[36] Horace Greeley to Henry Clay, November 15, 1846, Clay MSS.

for grabs—the Anti-Renters, who despised Democratic candidate Wright. To appease the Hunkers and lure the Anti-Renters, the Whigs nominated John Young for governor in 1846. Democratic abstentions and additional Anti-Rent voters provided him with a narrow margin over Wright and made him the only Whig to win on the statewide ticket. Significantly, it was precisely the summer of 1846 when the cagey Thurlow Weed, who had been forced to abandon his blatant bid for antislavery votes, embraced Taylor as the Whig nominee in 1848. He may have realized even then that exploiting Young's popularity among Anti-Renters was a temporary expedient at best, a tactic that could not be repeated in the future. In any event, because Young alienated virtually every important faction of the Whig party once he took office, it was soon clear that the Whigs would not renominate him for governor in 1848. They would then have to pursue some other course to win the state, congressional, and presidential elections in New York.[37]

Despite these indications that their comeback in 1846 was less solid and more evanescent than it first appeared, most Whigs believed that they had won by attacking the Polk administration's record and that they could continue to ride those issues into the White House in 1848. As one Whig proclaimed of the results in New York, "Whiggism ascends. The present administration are your best recruiting officers, tho' rather expensive." Marveling at the Whig capture of Congress, a Georgian gushed to his congressman, "Did you ever see such a rapid and tremendous revolution. . . . I congratulate you on the signs of the times, for I cannot now have a doubt of your receiving in 1849 [from a new Whig president] some distinguished post." Ohio's Whigs explicitly interpreted their victory as a repudiation of Polk's policies and pre-

---

[37]The complex machinations in New York can be followed in Horace Greeley to Schuyler Colfax, January 22, April 22, 1846, Greeley-Colfax MSS; John Bush to Millard Fillmore, March 11, 1846, Fillmore MSS, State University of New York, Oswego; William Henry Seward to John McLean, March 20, 1846, William Henry Seward MSS, Library of Congress; and Benson Rose to Thurlow Weed, February 6, 1846, Greeley to Weed, March 13, 1846, Charles Boynton to Weed, March 17, 1846, Seward to Alvah Worden, March 22, 1846, Washington Hunt to Weed, April 4, 1846, Seward to Weed, April 5, August 10, 1846, Greeley to Weed, May 14, 1846, and Seth Hawley to Weed, August 24, 1846, Weed MSS. On divisions over the black suffrage issue and the eventual Whig abandonment of it, see also John L. Stanley, "Majority Tyranny in Tocqueville's America: The Failure of Negro Suffrage in 1846," *Political Science Quarterly*, 84 (September, 1969), 412–35.

dicted triumph in 1848 on those issues. No better statement of Whig faith that they could disdain evasive tactics and win on substantive issues can be found than that of Massachusetts Senator John Davis to Henry Clay. The tariff, he asserted, explained the Whig sweep: "We have at length reached an open palpable issue which all can understand, and the policy of the administration is enough to excite alarm without coonskins, hard cider, or even a song or a hurrah. As far as my observation has extended the revolution has been accomplished without any argument or effort. The sense of the public is manifestly opposed to the doings of Congress. The war is daily becoming unpopular and the revenue act meets with condemnation everywhere."[38]

Utterly convinced that they could win the next presidential election on economic issues, Whigs worried only that Webster might derail their express by reintroducing his compromise tariff proposal when Congress met in December, 1846. Across the North nervous Whigs wrote that Webster must be stopped in order to retain their trump card. His plan "is regarded by the most eminent statesmen in the Whig ranks as calculated to produce the overthrow of that ascendancy which we are now gaining with the country and ought to preserve in 1848," wrote a Whig newspaper correspondent. Pennsylvania's Whigs would oppose Webster because they had "secured positive superiority in Pennsylvania through the influence of the Tariff issue, as contrasted with the present impotent scheme & to maintain it we cannot afford to surrender any of the ground." Senator Davis assured Clay that he and other Massachusetts Whigs would not support Webster if he reintroduced the bill. Even Massachusetts manufacturers, who liked Webster's plan, would back a Whig platform demanding a complete return to the tariff of 1842. "If this is the best issue to keep before the public and the great end which we have in view can be obtained by it then it is our best policy to adhere to it and I have no doubt Mass. will acquiesce in that policy." By the end of November, Whigs rejoiced that Webster had abandoned his scheme; their winning issue had been kept intact.[39]

[38] John Couper to Thomas Butler King, November 17, 1846, R. R. Cuyler to King, November 12, 1846, circular of the Whig State Central Committee of Ohio, October 17, 1846, and Robert C. Shenck to King, October 25, 1846, King MSS; Davis to Clay, November 13, 1846, Clay MSS.
[39] James E. Harvey to William Hayden, November 6, 29, 1846, William Schouler

Buoyed by the results of the 1846 elections and the apparent power of their new issues, Whigs who faced congressional and gubernatorial campaigns in 1847 were convinced at the end of 1846 that they could maintain the party's momentum. Virginia Congressman John Pendleton exulted, "For my part, I have never doubted since the new Tariff and the war, that the Whigs must carry the election the next time." Whoever the presidential candidate might be in 1848, moreover, "we shall beat them and beat them badly." Even long-time Virginia Democratic boss Thomas Ritchie agreed, at least, that the tariff would be the dominant issue through 1848. As early as August, 1846, a jubilant Tennessee Whig had predicted that "from the signs of the times . . . the canvass next year will be the easiest one for the Whigs since 1840. We have them on the defensive now." By the end of the year other Tennessee Whigs confidently anticipated victory in 1847 and 1848 because of disgust with Polk. A North Carolina congressman argued as well that anger at the war, hostility to territorial acquisition from Mexico, and the virtual certainty that the tariff and subtreasury measures would bankrupt the government ensured Whig victories in that state's impending congressional elections. Finally, Indiana's long-suffering Whigs, who had searched in vain for popular issues they could use against the Democrats since 1844, believed that they had at last found them. As late as July, 1847, for example, Whig congressional candidate Richard W. Thompson was urged to "attack the Administration at every vulnerable point—upon the Oregon question—the veto of the River and Harbor bill—the subtreasury with a raking fire at the Mexican War, and the attempts of the Administration to prostrate Gen. Taylor." Thompson, who directed his campaign primarily against the war and territorial acquisition, himself declared, "If we can't sustain the issues on which we now stand—we are gone."[40]

MSS, Massachusetts Historical Society; Davis to Clay, November 13, 1846, with Abbott Lawrence to John Davis, November 12, 1846, enclosed, Clay MSS; see also Walter Forward to Millard Fillmore, October 26, 1846, Fillmore MSS.

[40] Jno. C. Pendleton to William C. Rives, November 3, 1846, January 31, 1847, Rives MSS; Thomas Ritchie to Edmund Burke, October 21, 1846, Edmund Burke MSS, Library of Congress; Sam W. Fite to William B. Campbell, August 13, November 24, 1846, John Bell to William B. Campbell, November 22, 1846, Campbell Family Papers; Alfred Dockery to Duncan McLaurin, January 9, 1847, McLaurin MSS; T. H. Nelson to R. W. Thompson, July 5, 1847, Richard W. Thompson MSS, Indiana State Library; Thompson to H. J. Hilton, July 16, 1847, Richard W. Thompson MSS, Lilly Library, Indiana University.

Despite the volume and sincerity of the Whigs' bravado, their optimistic belief that they could recapture the presidency on the basis of economic issues and antiwar sentiment soon proved unfounded. Once again they had chosen a pathway to power that would lead them away from their goal. Whig momentum did continue into the spring and summer of 1847. In April they rebounded strongly in Connecticut, where once again they swept the state and congressional elections on the tariff and antiwar issues, and in Rhode Island, where the new national issues allowed them to campaign for governor as Whigs for the first time in three years and to amass 57 percent of the vote.[41] That month, as well, they picked up five additional congressional seats in Virginia and made gains in the state legislature for their strongest showing in the Old Dominion in years. In August they captured two new congressional seats in Indiana, winning a statewide majority of the vote, added three new seats in North Carolina, and recaptured the governorship of Tennessee.

The Whig tide crested in August, however, and it ebbed markedly by the fall of 1847. Although Whigs were victorious, their vote was down in Massachusetts and Ohio, where their margin in the legislature was narrower than in either 1845 or 1846. They carried the state officers in New York, but only because of massive Democratic abstentions stemming from the Hunker-Barnburner feud. As the Whigs in New York well knew, their future there depended upon preventing the Democrats from reuniting.[42] On the other hand, Georgia's Whigs continued to stumble in 1847. They lost the governorship because they could not match the growing Democratic vote among nonslaveholders in north Georgia. Worst of all were the results from the Middle Atlantic states, where the Whigs continued to campaign hard on the tariff. They lost governorships in Maryland, New Jersey, and Pennsylvania, where the Native American party still siphoned off vital voters from them. Thus, in the fall of 1847, Whig prospects sagged most dramat-

[41] On the impact of the war and tariff issues in Connecticut, see John M. Niles to Gideon Welles, April 11, 1847, and William G. Pomeroy to Welles, May 11, 1847, Welles MSS, New York Public Library; A. E. Burr to Welles, April 13, 1847, Gideon Welles MSS, Connecticut Historical Society.

[42] For example, the Whig margin in the Ohio state assembly fell from 26 seats in 1845 to 6 seats in 1847; in the state senate the margin dropped from 6 seats in 1845 to 2 seats in 1847. On the New York Whigs' recognition of their dependence on Democratic factionalism, see Horace Greeley to Schuyler Colfax, September 18, 1847, Greeley-Colfax MSS.

ically in precisely those states where one year earlier they had boasted that economic issues could carry them to the White House.

Economic issues in fact probably did not contribute much to earlier Whig triumphs in the spring and summer, except in New England. In other states Whigs campaigned primarily against the war, against any absorption of Mexican territory, and against Polk's partisan mistreatment of Generals Taylor and Scott. Even so, they probably gained congressional seats in North Carolina in 1847, as they had in Georgia in 1846, more because of a Whig-engineered reapportionment of districts than because of the issues they raised.[43] In four of the six districts they carried, their share of the vote was lower than it had been in 1844. However impressive their performance in Virginia, moreover, it still left them with only six of fifteen congressional seats and less than a statewide majority in an election where the Democrats suffered a much heavier drop-off than the Whigs. Even in victory, Virginia Whigs had to doubt their ability to carry the state in 1848. The fact that Whig candidates tried to ride on the coattails of Taylor's popularity by endorsing him for president in Virginia, Maryland, Tennessee, and Georgia indicated that those southern Whigs believed that they could not win in 1847, let alone 1848, on the basis of issues alone.[44] To be sure, one motive for this action was the southern Whigs' fear of the slavery issue and their perceived need to offset it. But the tactic demonstrated as well, just as did election results in the North, that campaigning against the Democratic economic record had lost its punch. Back in November, 1846, even as he exuberantly cheered the "tremendous revolution" in Whig fortunes, a Georgia Whig had worried, "The only fear is that the revolution has come too early, and that its effects

[43] On North Carolina's reapportionment, see Alfred Dockery to Duncan McLaurin, January 9, 1847, McLaurin MSS; David Outlaw to Emily Outlaw, February 24, 1848, David Outlaw MSS, Southern Historical Collection, University of North Carolina; and Marc Wayne Kruman, "Parties and Politics in North Carolina, 1846–1865" (Ph.D. dissertation, Yale University, 1978), 6–7.

[44] On Virginia, see Jno. C. Pendleton to William C. Rives, November 3, 1846, William Ballard Preston to Rives, February 28, 1847, Rives MSS; on Tennessee, Meredith P. Gentry to William B. Campbell, February 20, 1847, William B. Campbell to David Campbell, January 23, 1848, Campbell Family Papers; on Georgia, Iverson S. Harris to John M. Berrien, May 9, 1847, Berrien MSS, and Berrien to Daniel Webster, June 21, 1847, Webster MSS. See also Cooper, *Politics of Slavery*, 246–47; and Rayback, *Free Soil*, 41–44.

may wear out before the next Presidential election." Unfortunately for the Whigs, he was right.[45]

What, we must ask, had happened? Whig campaigns in 1846 and early 1847 in fact had been based on predictions of what would happen to the economy under the Democratic program, not on the actual impact of that program. Most of their triumphs and most of their boasting occurred before that economic legislation even went into effect. The Walker tariff did not begin operation until December 1, 1846, and the Independent Treasury Act until January 1, 1847. Indeed, the requirement of the latter law that the government pay out only specie or treasury notes didn't take effect until April 1, 1847. What happened, simply, was that most Whig predictions turned out to be wrong. Despite the authentic conviction of Whig politicians and businessmen alike that the economy would be plunged into disaster, the nation instead prospered in 1847 and the Democrats reaped the benefits. They could and did say, in effect, "I told you so."

In the Whig scenario, the tariff and subtreasury would drain the country of specie and hence dry up credit for commercial transactions. Lowering the tariff would increase imports and cause specie to flow to Europe to pay for them. Democrats argued that the concurrent reduction of Britain's Corn Laws in 1846 would allow increased grain sales to England and therefore America would enjoy a favorable balance of

[45] R. R. Cuyler to Thomas Butler King, November 12, 1846, King MSS. Another index of the disappearance of the Whigs' advantage on economic issues by the fall of 1847 is the way the two parties handled the issues in party platforms and newspaper appeals. In Pennsylvania, for example, though the Whigs continued to attack the Walker tariff in 1847, the Democrats were defending it in 1847 and 1848 as "the most judicious and equitable that has ever been established." Democratic state platforms can be found in the Philadelphia *Pennsylvanian*, March 8, 1847, September 8, 1848. The quotation is from the resolutions of the Allegheny County Democratic Convention, Pittsburgh *Morning Post*, January 13, 1848. In New York, Whigs abandoned economic issues entirely in their official address to voters in 1847 while Democrats continued to boast of the tariff and subtreasury. In 1846, 42 percent of the Whig Address had been devoted to economic issues, whereas in 1847 it focused entirely on the war and slavery extension issues. The Democrats, in contrast, devoted 26 percent of their 1846 address to a defense of the Polk economic measures but 35 percent of their 1847 address to that defense. These figures are based on a content analysis in Gillis Harp, "The Character of Party Dialogue: Democrats and Whigs in New York State, 1844–1852" (seminar paper, University of Virginia, 1980), 30–32. North Carolina's Whig state platform of February, 1848, similarly tried to shift attention explicitly from economic issues to the Mexican War. It can be found in the *National Intelligencer*, March 2, 1848.

trade. The Whigs responded that under the Corn Laws American farmers already enjoyed favored-nation status in British grain markets vis-à-vis Russian and other European competitors and still didn't sell enough grain to balance payments. Hence the repeal of the Corn Laws would only increase European grain sales to England, not American profits. Farmers would suffer from the new tariff, indeed, because the purchasing power of American workers would drop, thereby forcing farm prices down. While the lower tariff would propel specie out of the country, according to Whigs, the subtreasury would suck what was left from the private economy. Under that bill the government would require all payments for tariff duties, land sales, and excise taxes in gold, and then, rather than recirculating that gold through the economy by depositing it in private banks which could issue bank notes based on it, the government would simply hoard its gold in public vaults. Given the low levels of federal expenditure in the nineteenth century, such a critique was plausible, especially since it had been standard Whig fare since Martin Van Buren first introduced the subtreasury idea in 1837. Even Democratic businessmen had constantly denounced the scheme's deflationary implications. The end result would be disaster. Depleted of gold by unfavorable foreign trade balances and governmental accumulation, the economy would see its bank note circulation and commercial credit shrink, and eventually it would grind to a complete halt.[46]

If the economy in general would suffer from Democratic programs, argued the Whigs, the lower tariff and warehousing act would inflict a one-two punch on manufacturers in particular. Three aspects of the Walker tariff were especially pernicious. First, those manufacturers who used imported raw materials complained that, because of higher rates on raw materials and reduced differentials between duties on raw materials and those on finished goods, their production costs would increase to the point where they could not compete with foreign manufacturers. Second, the general reduction of rates would expose all manufacturers to cheap foreign competition, drive them out of busi-

---

[46] The summary of the Whig case against the Democratic economic program is based on a reading of speeches in the *Congressional Globe*, 29th Cong., 1st Sess., the extensive correspondence of businessmen to Daniel Webster in the summer of 1846, and other correspondence such as Abbott Lawrence to William C. Rives, January 17, 26, 1846, Rives MSS.

ness, and throw hundreds of thousands of workers out of their jobs. It was a calamity, Whigs iterated and reiterated, to expose American labor to the competition of European pauper labor. Finally, the *ad valorem* rates would encourage fraud that would reduce the protective barrier of the tariff still further. Importers and foreign manufacturers would undervalue imports since the tariff duty was a fixed percentage of the invoice price. Even if they didn't cheat, *ad valorem* duties would drop as the price of foreign imports dropped, thus providing less protection than specific duties on precisely the goods that were most dangerous to American manufacturers.

As if this weren't bad enough, Whigs complained, the warehousing act in effect subsidized foreign competitors by allowing them to accumulate large inventories in government warehouses before paying any duty and then to sell only when prices were high enough that even with the cost of tariff duties added to their goods they could undersell American manufacturers. Put another way, Whigs charged that the warehousing act would allow foreigners to sell only when profitable rather than run the risk of paying duties immediately and carrying an inventory they could not sell at a profit. The law, that is, permitted foreigners to build up inventories in anticipation of sales, ample enough to meet all demand. Thus it negated the advantages American manufacturers gained by their proximity to customers and by their ability to fill orders before foreign goods could be ordered and shipped from abroad. Under the Public Warehouse Act, according to the Whigs, cheap foreign goods would always be readily at hand in government warehouses.

While American businessmen, workers, and farmers would be ruined, so would the government, Whigs predicted. It was suicidal to lower the tariff after declaring war on Mexico, they argued, because lower tariff rates, even with increased imports, would mean lower government revenue just when the government needed more money to pay for the war. Nor would the government be able to sell bonds, for banks would have no gold with which to buy them. The Independent Treasury Act would require the government to accept only gold for bonds, and what little gold banks had left after the removal of government deposits and shipments of specie abroad would quickly be used up as they physically transferred their gold to government vaults to pay for early bond issues. Lest this augury seem too farfetched, Bray Hammond has pointed out that precisely such a dilemma paralyzed bond sales during the first year of the Civil War.[47]

In 1847, however, almost every one of these predictions proved fallacious. Because of the Irish potato famine and crop failures in Europe, foreign demand for American grain soared. Secretary of the Treasury Walker's rosy analysis of the impact of the reduction of the Corn Laws on American farmers misidentified the source, but grain exports did increase enormously in 1847. As a result the nation enjoyed its most favorable balance of trade in years. Gold and silver flowed into the economy from abroad in record amounts, eastern cities were awash in specie, and farmers enjoyed unprecedented profits. Nor in a time of war could the government sit on its revenues. It had to spend its money on war contracts, thus providing a stimulus to war-related industries. Further to help manufacturers and give a more protective edge to his own tariff, Walker ordered customs collectors to add the cost of shipping, insurance, and exchange to the invoice price of goods when they calculated the *ad valorem* duties. Commerce, agriculture, and industry all flourished.

The forecast of government bankruptcy also went awry. Government revenues did decline just as Whigs said they would, and so did the circulation of state bank notes. But Walker ingeniously financed the war in a way that replaced bank note circulation and increased the general prosperity. He had to borrow money to pay for the war, but instead of issuing long-term bonds in large denominations, which would suck money from the private sector, he relied primarily on short-term treasury notes in small denominations, which could be used as currency. Moreover, to facilitate funding of this debt by bankers, he waived provisions of the Independent Treasury Act and accepted installment payments in certified checks rather than in gold. Because treasury notes earned interest and could be used to pay tariff duties, there was a huge demand for them by businessmen. Bankers, sensing the large profits to be made from the sale of treasury notes, scrambled to handle the loans. The government, in short, pumped much more money into the economy than it took out of it. Instead of the shrunken money supply and deflation Whigs had dreaded, the amount of cir-

---

[47] Bray Hammond, *Sovereignty and an Empty Purse: Banks and Politics in the Civil War* (Princeton: Princeton University Press, 1970), 37–163.

culating currency jumped sharply in 1847 even though the number of bank notes declined, wholesale prices rose, and prosperity prevailed.[48]

Both Whigs and Democrats were well aware of these developments. As early as November, 1846, a Boston Democrat had argued that the Polk economic program was eminently defensible, even in Whiggish Massachusetts. The Warehouse Act was a boon to importing merchants, he said, and any deflationary impact of the subtreasury system would be offset by the flow of English and French gold and by treasury notes, which would be in large demand because they could be used to pay tariff duties. In December of that year Webster was puzzled by the equanimity of New York's business community, which seemed to welcome rather than dread the advent of the independent treasury because of the rush of foreign specie, the circulation of treasury notes, and the increased wartime demand for government expenditure. By February, 1847, a Tennessee Whig congressman was warning that Whig prospects in his state's gubernatorial election were not so bright as others had predicted just months earlier because improved economic conditions resulting from the grain trade helped the Democrats. "Money will be plenty—the Banks easy—Treasury notes in demand and the people prosperous. All these will be claimed as the natural effects of Locofoco measures and the people you know when prosperous, are prone to attribute their prosperity to the direct action of the Administration in power for the time being. Hence I conclude that the Whigs will have heavy work in Tennessee next summer." Significantly, he also concluded that in this situation Taylor was the only man that the Whigs could possibly elect president in 1848.[49]

As the year progressed, Whig hopes of exploiting economic issues

[48]Virtually every economic statistic available bears out this portrait. Exports in merchandise and grain exceeded imports, but imports of gold and silver dramatically exceeded exports in 1847. The value of wheat exports jumped 300 percent in 1847 over 1846. Circulating currency expanded by 15.7 percent in 1847, even though state bank note circulation dropped slightly that year. Government receipts were down and deficits up, but the wholesale price index rose from 83 in 1845 and 1846 to 90 in 1847. For the relevant tables, see *Historical Statistics of the United States*, I, 201, II, 886, 899, 993, 995, 1104, and 1106. For Walker's financing of the war, see James P. Shenton, *Robert John Walker: A Politician from Jackson to Lincoln* (New York: Columbia University Press, 1961), 87–98, and Henry Cohen, *Business and Politics in America from the Age of Jackson to the Civil War: The Career Biography of W. W. Corcoran* (Westport, Conn: Greenwood Publishing Corp., 1971), 40–62.

[49]Sidney Homer to Edmund Burke, November 23, 1846, Burke MSS; Daniel Web-

dimmed perceptibly. In July a worried New Yorker on a business trip to Pennsylvania aptly summarized the party's dilemma:

> It will be necessary to handle the question of the Tariffs of 42 & 46. It is somewhat difficult to meet our opponents before the farmers when wheat is ranging from $1.25 to $2 per bushel. The famine in Europe has produced such an enormous rise in all grains and specie has flowed in on us to such an extent that they have drowned the effects of the Tariff of 46 and somewhat neutralized the effects of the Sub-Try. Besides the mania for Railways in Europe and this country has kept up the price of iron; and the war has called for such enormous supplies of all its materials, and such immense expenditure of money that almost every branch of business has been greatly stimulated. Thus, to the great mass, the country appears to be eminently prosperous.

Only bumper crops in Europe and a prolongation of the war until the government went bankrupt, he concluded, would allow the Whigs to exploit economic issues in the future. In April, 1848, Congressman Meredith Gentry of Tennessee flatly told Webster that it would be a mistake for the Whigs to attempt to repeal the Walker tariff because "a combination of circumstances at home and abroad has made it eminently successful as a revenue measure and less destructive to our home manufacturers than was anticipated." Action against the tariff should be avoided in Congress, he maintained, because it would allow the Democrats themselves to utilize the tariff issue in 1848. They could "insist (plausibly) that the large exports and consequent prosperity of the country combined with heavy receipts at the Customs Houses of the Republick were produced by the Tariff of 1846." Because the Whigs now would be hurt rather than helped by economic issues, running Taylor for president was their only hope in 1848.[50]

It is true that many Whigs in late 1847 accurately predicted in private that the economy would turn downward in 1848 as exports declined, imports increased, and specie flowed outward and that the

---

ster to Robert C. Winthrop, December 18, 1846, Webster MSS; Meredith P. Gentry to William B. Campbell, February 20, 1847, Campbell Family Papers.

[50] Daniel Ullmann to Henry Clay, July 12, 1847, Clay MSS; Meredith P. Gentry to Webster, April 13, 1848, Webster MSS. For an analysis similar to Ullmann's of what happened in 1847, with a similar prediction that continuation of the war and improved economic circumstances in Europe might allow the Whigs to make effective use of economic issues in 1848, see Thomas Wren Ward to Daniel Webster, January 10, 1848, Webster MSS.

Whigs might once again use economic issues. But those trends took time to develop and continued to be disguised during the first months of 1848 by the injection of treasury notes into the economy. Certainly the economy had not flagged sufficiently by June, 1848, when the Whig National Convention met, for Whigs to be sanguine about their prospects of running a traditional champion of Whig economic policies on economic issues.[51] It is little wonder, then, that Whig delegates from northern states like Connecticut, Rhode Island, Pennsylvania, New Jersey, Ohio, and Indiana, where running against Democratic measures had once seemed such a clear track to the White House, would turn to Taylor and Scott in large numbers at that gathering.

Actually, in the summer of 1847 when the effectiveness of economic issues had already waned, the Whigs still retained one compelling issue that unified the party and that might, many thought, bring them victory in 1848. This was opposition to the Mexican War and to any territorial acquisition from it. Antiwar and antiexpansion sentiment was strong among Whig voters everywhere, but especially in the North. Equally important, perceptive Whig politicians like Thomas Corwin of Ohio, Richard W. Thompson of Indiana, Robert C. Winthrop of Massachusetts, William B. Campbell of Tennessee, and John M. Berrien of Georgia realized that the Whigs' "no territory" program offered the best way to hold the party together on the divisive slavery extension issue.[52] By blocking the annexation of any new territory, they could avoid the sectionally rupturing issue of the Wilmot Proviso. One indication of the strength of antiwar, antiextension sentiment was that many Whigs initially opposed Taylor's nomination because he had

---

[51] See the statistical tables cited in n. 48. A different chart, "American Business Activity Since 1790" (37th ed.; Cleveland: Cleveland Trust Company, 1966), shows that indexes of growth increased for every month in 1847 and the first six months of 1848. Beginning in July, 1848, however, the economy declined for the remainder of the year so that by the fall of 1848 economic issues seemed much more viable than they had in the spring of 1848 before Taylor was nominated.

[52] C. B. Lewis to Roger Sherman Baldwin, January 19, 1848, Baldwin Family Papers; Thomas Corwin to Thomas B. Stevenson, December 10, 1847, Thomas B. Stevenson MSS, Indiana Historical Society Library; Corwin to John J. Crittenden, September 2, 1847, Thomas Corwin MSS, Ohio Historical Society; R. W. Thompson to [?], June 8, 1847, draft, Thompson MSS, Indiana State Library; Robert C. Winthrop to John P. Kennedy, January 24, 1848, copy, Winthrop MSS; William B. Campbell to David Campbell, November 20, 1847, Campbell Family Papers; William H. Underwood to John M. Berrien, December 19, 1847, Berrien MSS.

not publicly committed himself to a quick end of the war with no territorial indemnity. Another was the fact that Henry Clay chose to
launch his public bid for the 1848 nomination by denouncing the war
and territorial expansion in a major speech at Lexington, Kentucky,
in November, 1847. As Congress met in December, 1847, therefore, Whigs hoped to unite against the war and expansion and to run on
that platform during the presidential campaign. A Virginia Whig predicted early in February, 1848, that the war would not be terminated
"until the issue of 'Conquest' or 'no conquest' is fairly made and tried
at the polls in the next presidential election."[53]

Once again the Whigs were to be disappointed. As in the case of
the Texas issue in 1845 and economic issues in 1846, the antiwar issue
ran out of steam before it could carry them into power. Polk reluctantly
accepted peace with the Mexicans, and the Senate's ratification of the
Treaty of Guadalupe-Hidalgo on March 10, 1848, effectively killed the
war itself as an issue. Antiwar sentiment remained strong enough to
contribute to Whig victories in Connecticut and Rhode Island in April,
but the Whigs had been stripped of their last substantive issue. Peace,
one Whig congressman had lamented in late February, endangered his
party's chances in 1848; nevertheless Whigs dared not oppose the
treaty.[54] Even worse, the actual cession of Mexican territory in the
treaty negated the Whigs' "no territory" policy and created an urgent
necessity to find some other way to deal with the divisive Wilmot
Proviso question. As virtually everyone in the party recognized by the
spring of 1848, the party would simply be shattered if it were forced
to take a concrete stand for or against the proviso at the national
convention.

Time was of the essence. The Whig National Convention was
scheduled to meet almost exactly three months after Congress ratified
the treaty with Mexico. The Whigs seemed to be stranded in a cul-de-
sac. Every trail they had followed since 1844 had veered away from

[53] The Lexington speech is reproduced in the *Whig Tribune Almanac for 1848*,
7–16; Alexander H. H. Stuart to Richard W. Thompson, February 9, 1848, Richard W.
Thompson MSS, Lincoln National Life Foundation, Ft. Wayne.

[54] On Connecticut, see James F. Babcock to Roger Sherman Baldwin, March 22,
1848, Baldwin Family Papers; Mark Howard to James M. Barnard, April 5, 1848, Mark
Howard MSS, Connecticut Historical Society. The congressman who was alarmed that
peace would hurt the Whigs was Nathan K. Hall of Buffalo. See Hall to Millard Fillmore,
February 23, 1848, Fillmore MSS.

their goal rather than leading them to it. Trying to keep Texas alive or trying to bury it in 1845, openly courting the nativists, attacking Democratic economic policies, and running against the war had all left them short of the mark by March, 1848. And the only substantive route that remained open that spring—exploitation of the slavery extension issue—seemed too hazardous to attempt by a clear party stand. In these circumstances, Whigs from states where they were competitive just like those from states where Whig prospects had always been hopeless turned to the nomination of a military hero for president as the only road to victory in 1848.

Many southern Whigs, of course, had been pushing Taylor's nomination since the spring of 1847 as the best way to neutralize the slavery issue. As one Georgian put it at the end of that year, "Nothing can keep us together & save us but Genl. Taylor—nothing can destroy the Democracy but General Taylor. Under his flag we can give them a Buena Vista drubbing." Some southerners were also attracted to Taylor by the populistic image he had cultivated with his "no party" or "people's" campaign. Georgia's Whigs, for example, desperately needed a weapon to counter the growing Democratic strength among nonslaveholders in the Cherokee District, where the very name Whig was anathema because of its aristocratic connotation. Taylor, and Taylor alone, seemed to provide that weapon. In Kentucky, Maryland, and Virginia, Whigs were accused of being aristocratic foes of the people because they opposed Democratic reforms which would democratize those states' constitutions. Taylor's reputation provided a shield to ward off such charges in all these states. Even in the stronghold of North Carolina, some Whigs feared in early 1848 that the party would need Taylor's coattails to carry the state election in August. The Democrats, they worried, might run a populistic campaign against them in that election, and Democratic gubernatorial candidate David Reid took precisely that tack in May, when he called for eliminating suffrage restrictions in elections for the state senate.[55] Hence in North Carolina, as in other

---

[55] Iverson L. Harris to John M. Berrien, December 15, 1847, Berrien MSS. The argument about the Whig attempt to neutralize attacks on the issue of constitutional reform is inferred from descriptions of the Democratic exploitation of that issue in Harry A. Volz III, "Party, State, and Nation: Kentucky and the Coming of the Civil War" (Ph.D. dissertation in progress, University of Virginia), ch. 1; Stephen Green, "The Collapse of the Whig Party in Maryland" (seminar paper, Yale College, 1973); and Stephen

southern states, Whigs wanted Taylor's nomination in part to offset their disadvantage on a state issue that had little to do with the slavery question. With Taylor as a candidate, Whigs everywhere could run as the true people's party, regardless of their stand on specific issues. As with their handling of the slavery issue in the South, they could counter the concrete platform proposals of their foes with their presidential candidate's image.

It was in the North, however, that the swing of Whig opinion toward a military candidate became most marked in the spring of 1848. Some northern Whigs, of course, had boomed Taylor since 1846, and more joined them after Whig defeats in the fall of 1847. But the predicament that developed after the ratification of the treaty with Mexico transformed the movement toward military candidates into a stampede. For one thing, the end of the war and the acquisition of territory removed one of the major objections to Taylor and Scott. In addition, Taylor's Allison letter of April 22, 1848, mitigated the fears of other Whigs that he did not even belong to their party. Most important, the combined impact of the apparent resolution of traditional issues that might have aided orthodox candidates like Clay and Webster, the fact that Democrats could claim the benefits of a successful war while the Whigs themselves could no longer promise to stop it or expansion, and the naked confrontation with the proviso question simply convinced large numbers of northern Whigs that now only a military hero would do.

Thus it was only nine days after the Senate ratified the Treaty of Guadalupe-Hidalgo that New York Whig Congressman Washington Hunt wrote Thurlow Weed that he, Corwin, John M. Clayton of Delaware, and others now wanted as a candidate a general who had been and could remain mum on the proviso so that the Whigs could run one way in the North and another way in the South on the slavery exten-

---

White, "The Partisan Political Elements in the Virginia Constitutional Convention of 1850–51" (seminar paper, University of Virginia, 1980). On North Carolina, see E. J. Hale to Daniel M. Barringer, January 21, 1848, Daniel M. Barringer MSS, Southern Historical Collection, University of North Carolina; David Outlaw to Emily Outlaw, February 22, 1848, Outlaw MSS; Alex Fleming to M. B. Fleming, June 22, 1848, M. B. Fleming MSS, Perkins Library, Duke University; Alfred Dockery to Robert L. Caruthers, July 25, 1848, Robert L. Caruthers MSS, Southern Historical Collections, University of North Carolina; and Kruman, "Parties and Politics in North Carolina," 116–24.

sion issue.[56] Similarly, Ohio Whig Congressman Robert Shenck, who in 1846 had declared confidently that the Whigs could easily win the presidency on the tariff issue, became a Scott proponent in the spring of 1848. Pennsylvania's Andrew Stewart, a famous exponent of protective tariff doctrine, had moved into the Taylor camp even earlier.[57] Other Pennsylvania Whigs pleaded for the nomination of Taylor because he was the only man who could combine the Native American and Whig forces against the Democrats. Taylor had already accepted the Native American nomination in 1847, and his name on the ticket could therefore cement an alliance with the Native Americans for the October state elections. Such a combination could be achieved, moreover, without overt appeals to nativists, which might alienate immigrants whom Pennsylvania's Whigs were also courting in that election. "With Gen. Taylor as the Whig candidate we gain 15000 Native American voters without being connected with Nativism politically," wrote a frantic Philadelphian in May. "With Gen. Taylor we shall carry the Gen. Assembly and the State Senate we have and thus we shall secure the U.S. Senator to be chosen in place of Mr. Sturgeon." Without Taylor, on the other hand, "the Whig party of this state will be broken up into helpless confusion."[58]

Elsewhere, too, Whigs who had seen their bid to build a perma-

[56] Washington Hunt to Thurlow Weed, March 19, April 17, 1848, Weed MSS. Although New York Whigs like Hunt and Weed wanted a military candidate because of intrastate factionalism and calculations of the national results, the majority of Whigs in the state steadfastly supported Henry Clay. Almost alone among northern states, New York resisted the rush toward military candidates after March. The reason for this atypical loyalty to Clay was, ironically, that New York Whigs by 1848 believed that the rift between the Hunkers and Barnburners was so severe that any Whig could carry the state. By 1848 even a Clay candidacy could not reunite the feuding Democrats.

[57] On Shenck, see John McLean to Salmon P. Chase, May 19, 1848, Salmon P. Chase MSS, Historical Society of Pennsylvania; on Stewart, see N. K. Hall to Millard Fillmore, December 28, 1847, Fillmore MSS.

[58] E. Jay Morris to John P. Kennedy, May 6, 1848, Kennedy MSS. For additional evidence of how the need to combine with the Native Americans influenced Pennsylvania Whig support for Taylor, see George C. Collins to Henry Clay, June 10, 1848, Clay MSS; William J. S. Birken to Millard Fillmore, December 25, 1850, E. G. Lindsey to Fillmore, January 28, 1851, April 7, 1851, Millard Fillmore MSS, Buffalo Historical Society, microfilm ed. For evidence that Pennsylvania's Whigs tried to court immigrants as well as Native Americans in the 1848 state elections, see Michael Fitzgibbon Holt, *Forging a Majority: The Formation of the Republican Party in Pittsburgh, 1848–1860* (New Haven: Yale University Press, 1969), 62–63.

nent majority on the issues of 1846 and 1847 fall short now abandoned former Whig champions and turned to military heroes who alone could draw the additional votes Whigs needed to win. Furious at Clay's last-minute grasp for the nomination in April, an Indiana Whig explained, "The Locos never can be brought into the support of Mr. Clay. We must have a new man, and where can we get a more acceptable man than Gen. Taylor." Fearful that Clay's ambition would disrupt the party and prevent it from rallying behind Taylor, he later complained, "Mr. Clay has been looked on as the embodiment of the Whig party. And if we are defeated again, he will be looked on as the demolisher of the same." Five days after the treaty with Mexico was ratified, another Indiana Whig warned, "The Whigs will have to run either Scott or Taylor or be defeated so badly that you will hardly know we run a candidate. To talk of Clay or [Supreme Court Justice John] McLean is worse than madness." No one, indeed, captured the desperate mood of many Whigs by the eve of their convention better than this same former congressman when, in late May, he again disparaged the thought of a McLean candidacy. "The Whig party would be so dead in a month after his nomination that a galvanic battery could not move a muscle in the whole body. . . . We must have the aid of gunpowder—the fortress of Locofocoism cannot be taken without it." [59]

At the beginning of 1848 the notorious Thomas Dorr of Rhode Island, a Democrat, observed, "The Whigs admit that it was proved in 1844, that it is next to impossible for them to succeed in their own unassisted strength, and that they must come into power, if at all, with the aid of Democratic votes as in 1840. Hence the importance to them of a *taking* candidate. A brave old soldier they think is the man for them." [60] Dorr would prove correct about the eventual decision of the Whig party in 1848, but he was wrong about the process by which they reached it. Not all Whigs had believed that a "*taking* candidate" provided the only route to power after 1844. Whigs in heavily Democratic states quickly gravitated in that direction, but elsewhere the Whigs essayed a number of different roads to recovery. Only when those various

[59] John Edwards to George Dunn, April 3, 27, 1848, George Dunn MSS, Lilly Library, Indiana University; E. W. McGaughey to Caleb B. Smith, March 15, 1848, Caleb B. Smith MSS, Library of Congress; McGaughey to George Dunn, May 23, 1848, Dunn MSS.

[60] Thomas Dorr to Edmund Burke, January 13, 1848, Burke MSS.

sallies failed to reach the target did Whigs in most states adopt a different strategy to defeat the Democratic foe in 1848. Most southern Whigs did indeed turn to Taylor in 1847, largely but not exclusively, because of the slavery issue. But it was only the disappointing results of 1847 and the apparent issue vacuum following the end of the Mexican War in March, 1848, at a time when the economy still flourished, that shifted the majority of northern delegates toward Taylor and Scott. But just as some Whigs had predicted, that issue vacuum proved to be only temporary. By the fall of 1848, after Taylor had already been nominated, the economy had soured sufficiently that Whigs could once again hammer away at the Walker tariff, at the subtreasury, and at large government deficits in key northern states. Those attacks on traditional issues would reinforce the loyalty of most Whig voters in the North to their party. In combination with Taylor's palpable appeal beyond Whig ranks to Democrats, Native Americans, and first-time voters, with his malleability on the proviso issue that allowed the Whigs to run a two-faced campaign on the slavery extension issue, and with the aggravation of the rupture in the New York Democratic party, they would help to give the Whigs their second, and last, chance to occupy the White House.

STEPHEN E. MAIZLISH

The Meaning of Nativism and the Crisis of the Union: The Know-Nothing Movement in the Antebellum North

Starting late in 1853 and continuing for the following three years, a secret movement of nativists, called Know-Nothings, swept the United States. By the time it reached the peak of its strength, the movement could claim over 1.25 million members organized into ten thousand local councils in every section of the country. Working through the American party, Know-Nothings quickly gained control of several northern states, elected representatives to all levels of government, and in 1856 nominated a candidate for the presidency of the United States.[1]

Know-Nothing rhetoric was as explosive as the movement's growth. Employing classic American imagery, one antiforeign tract warned that immigrants taking the form of "a wily serpent" had "approached our Eden with such caution, that even his slimy tracks were invisible, for a long time, to our sight." But "strong hearts," this Know-Nothing publicist proclaimed, had now resolved "to free their soil from the poisonous pollution of its slimy tail." United by a "common devotion to country . . . and the common freedom of men," Americans were determined to block foreign nations from "vomit[ing] . . . their refuse" upon "our shores."[2]

Three decades later America would be glorified as a home for that

---

[1] William E. Gienapp, "The Origins of the Republican Party" (Ph.D. dissertation, University of California, Berkeley, 1980), 601; Michael F. Holt, "The Antimasonic and Know Nothing Parties," in Arthur Schlesinger, Jr., ed., *History of United States Political Parties* (New York, 1973), I, 575–620. I would like to thank William Gienapp for making available to me many of the sources used in this essay.

[2] *Know Nothing Platform: Containing an Account of the Encroachments of the Roman Catholic Hierarchy* (Philadelphia, 1855?), 36–37.

"refuse," but in the 1850s Know-Nothing leaders were able to gather widespread support around a program designed to limit immigration and turn away many of those yearning for the opportunities of American life. "It was reserved for those invisible, noiseless, mysterious, peaceable revolutionists, the KNOW NOTHINGS, to give the finishing stroke to foreignism, and the final blow to demagogism," declared the *Know Nothing Almanac of 1855*. The new movement, warned the *Almanac*, came with "the silence of a zepher, but with [the] crushing force of a tornado."[3]

Although their program varied from state to state, the Know-Nothings' basic demand was for the extension of the naturalization period from five to twenty-one years. For some time native-born Americans had complained that recent immigrants, ignorant of American traditions, were being herded to the polls by corrupt politicians intent upon manipulating the new arrivals to serve their own purposes. The machinery of democracy was complex, argued the Know-Nothings, and people coming from distant countries ruled by despotic regimes needed time to understand and appreciate so unique a system of government before they could participate effectively in it. Thomas Whitney, an early nativist organizer and leading Know-Nothing spokesman, defended the organization's stand on naturalization, explaining that foreigners could never be "invested" with the "*home sentiment and feeling of a native.*" Although Whitney agreed to allow the foreign born to join American society, he insisted that they could never be made a part of the political "family" of the United States.[4] Other Know-Nothings did not want to see foreign settlers accepted into the country on any basis. They favored a head tax on immigrants to limit the entry of at least the poverty stricken and so halt the "abasement" of the citizenry which, many Know-Nothings believed, "such an infusion" would "certainly produce." But however they felt about restricting immigration, all Know-Nothings maintained that to ensure a sound government for those who resided in America, only native-born Americans should wield political power. The purpose of the American party and the Know-Nothing movement, explained Whitney, was the

[3]*The Know Nothing Almanac and True American's Manual for 1855* (New York, 1855), 19.

[4]Samuel Busey, *Immigration: Its Evils and Consequences* (New York, 1856), 5–6; Thomas R. Whitney, *A Defense of the American Policy* (New York, 1856), 135, 140.

"PRESERVATION OF OUR NATIONAL UNION, AND ITS GLORIOUS INSTI-
TUTIONS OF CIVIL AND RELIGIOUS LIBERTY." To accomplish this,
Whitney concluded, "AMERICANS OUGHT TO BE, AND MUST BE, THE
RULERS IN THEIR OWN LAND."[5]

Assisted by such patriotic rhetoric, the Know-Nothings' success in
gaining adherents is not hard to understand. Nevertheless, the movement's growth was erratic and its ascendancy short-lived. It expanded
rapidly in a number of areas with sparse immigrant settlement, while
its progress was slow in some regions with large foreign-born populations.[6] And everywhere its strength evaporated quickly, so quickly
that by 1856 much of the Know-Nothings' influence was gone. So
impressed was British observer Lord Bryce with the speedy disappearance of the nativist organization that he concluded that Americans
must be "a changeful people. The Native Americans, or so-called
Know Nothing party," he explained, "had in two years from its foundation, become a tremendous force rising, and seeming likely for a time
to carry its own presidential candidate. In three years more it was dead
without a hope of revival." Writing prior to the Know-Nothings' collapse, New York *Tribune* editor Horace Greeley noted the same
pattern of Know-Nothing development. The nativist movement, he
claimed, was "as devoid of the elements of persistence as an anti-
cholera or anti-potato rot party."[7]

Recognizing the uneven quality of Know-Nothing growth and the
sharp and sudden nature of the movement's demise, many historians
have questioned the significance of the mid-nineteenth-century nativist outburst. Why, they have asked, did it occur precisely when it
did? Why was it so short in duration? And, finally, what did it mean to
be a nativist in the 1850s if one's commitment to the Know-Nothing

---

[5] *Know Nothing Almanac for 1855*, 20; W. S. Tisdale, ed., *The Know Nothing Almanac and True American's Manual for 1856* (New York, 1856), 22; Whitney, *Defense of the
American Policy*, 320.

[6] Two examples of the uneven nature of Know-Nothing development may be found
by comparing Indiana, which had a low proportion of foreign born in the population and
a strong Know-Nothing movement by the spring of 1854, and Ohio, which had a large
percentage of immigrants but a Know-Nothing organization that took almost a year
longer to develop. See Gienapp, "Origins of the Republican Party," Ch. 5.

[7] Humphrey Desmond, *The Know-Nothing Party, a Sketch* (Washington, 1904),
66–67.

movement was so brief, while the problems of immigration were so persistent?

One of the first groups of historians to attempt an analysis of the unique pattern of mid-nineteenth-century nativist agitation concluded that controversies surrounding the foreign born did not cause instability in Know-Nothing ranks. Rather, both the rise and fall of the Know-Nothings were the consequences of developments outside the realm of immigration politics. "Everywhere," argued Harry Carman and Reinhard Luthin in 1940, "the character of political nativism was shaped by local and national conditions, and events which often had very little connection with nativism itself."[8] In the North, they explained, it was the slavery controversy that was responsible for the Know-Nothing movement's strength.

Although Carman and Luthin were vague about the precise relationship between the sectional crisis and nativism, William Bean, writing sixteen years earlier, had been more specific. He claimed that many northerners joined the Know-Nothing movement because they believed the foreign-born population to be proslavery. Especially in Massachusetts, where the Know-Nothings did particularly well, men became Know-Nothings in order to punish the Catholic church for its support of the peculiar institution of slavery.[9]

Few other traditional interpreters of the Know-Nothings have gone so far as to claim that nativists were primarily motivated by a commitment to an antislavery position, but many have questioned the sincerity of the Know-Nothings' devotion to nativist principles. Unwilling to confront the reality of American intolerance, Allan Nevins at times treated the entire Know-Nothing movement as an embarrassment, while Avery Craven virtually ignored it. Nativist prejudice, according to this traditionalist view, was simply not a central feature of the mid-century American experience. By itself, the Know-Nothings had little lasting political appeal. The slavery issue, the traditionalists argued, crippled both national parties and temporarily gave political nativism an opportunity to flourish. When the continuing slavery controversy

[8] Harry J. Carman and Reinhard H. Luthin, "Some Aspects of the Know-Nothing Movement Reconsidered," *South Atlantic Quarterly*, 39 (April, 1940), 211.

[9] William G. Bean, "An Aspect of Know Nothingism—The Immigrant and Slavery," *South Atlantic Quarterly*, 23 (October, 1924), 322.

succeeded in creating a new system of politics, a system based upon sectionalism, the Know-Nothing organization collapsed.[10]

More recent historians, possessing a heightened awareness of America's ethnic diversity, as well as a greater appreciation of its capacity for bigotry, have come to see nativist outbreaks in every period of United States history as authentic expressions of a fundamental aspect of the national character.[11] These historians argue that ethnic turmoil and division have always plagued America. The Know-Nothing movement of the 1850s was but one more example of the consequences of these ever-present social tensions. It did not arise, these historians insist, as a result of the slavery extension crisis or of any other crisis except that caused by the unparalleled immigration the country was then experiencing. Both the increasing number of foreigners arriving in America and the changing nature of the immigrant population were, in their view, the primary causes of the rise of political nativism in the 1850s.[12]

The number of foreign born in America was indeed rising sharply in the mid-nineteenth century. Between 1845 and 1854 close to three million immigrants entered the United States. This flood of newcomers constituted 14.5 percent of the total American population—the highest proportion of immigrants at any time in the nation's history. And it was not only the size of the new immigration that was unprecedented; the kind of immigrants arriving in America was also unique. By 1850, Catholics from Ireland made up over 40 percent of the foreign-born settlers living in the United States.[13] With unusual church loyalties, ethnic customs, and religious rituals, these immigrants could not be easily ignored by the native-born American population. In 1851, five years after they began to come in large numbers,

[10]Carman and Luthin, "Know-Nothing Movement Reconsidered," 211; Allan Nevins, *Ordeal of the Union: A House Dividing, 1852–1857* (New York, 1947), 328–29, 331; Avery Craven, *The Coming of the Civil War* (Chicago, 1942). Carman, Luthin, and Nevins are the most prominent proponents of this interpretation.

[11]See John Higham, "Another Look at Nativism," *Catholic Historical Review*, 44 (July, 1958), for an early articulation of this view.

[12]For various presentations of this perspective, see Holt, "Antimasonic and Know Nothing Parties" and *The Political Crisis of the 1850s* (New York, 1978); Gienapp, "Origins of the Republican Party"; and Ronald Formisano, *The Birth of Mass Political Parties: Michigan, 1827–1861* (Princeton, 1971).

[13]David Potter, *The Impending Crisis, 1848–1861* (New York, 1976), 241; Ira Leonard and Robert Parmet, *American Nativism, 1830–1860* (New York, 1971), 33.

many of these new arrivals were exercising their right to vote; as they did, native-born citizens became increasingly alarmed.[14]

Know-Nothings quickly took advantage of this popular concern to mobilize opposition to the massive influx of immigrants. Nativist organizer Thomas Whitney, in his book *A Defense of the American Policy*, emphasized the overwhelming Catholic orientation of the country's new residents. Since the start of the nineteenth century, Whitney pointed out, the number of Catholic churches had increased from 90 to 1,824, the number of priests from 68 to 1,704, and the number of bishops from 2 to 40.[15] If allowed to continue uncontrolled, he concluded, immigration would soon lead to a still greater concentration of Catholic religious power in America.

Adding to Whitney's warning, other Know-Nothings charged that the new immigration posed a threat to more than just the religious character of the nation. Know-Nothing Governor Henry J. Gardiner of Massachusetts made clear the common belief that the continued, unrestricted flow of foreigners, especially Catholic foreigners, to America would have serious consequences for the country's social order as well. In his 1855 inaugural address, Governor Gardiner claimed that four-fifths of the beggary, two-thirds of the pauperism, and over three-fifths of the nation's crime originated in the foreign population. Over one-half of the welfare and police costs, he added, came from the care and supervision of the newly arrived immigrants. Numerous Know-Nothing supporters concurred with the governor's estimates. "Crime and pauperism are both evils, injurious to the character and standing either of a community or a government," wrote Know-Nothing propagandist Samuel Busey. "For both of them we are mainly dependent upon immigration." Foreign criminals and paupers outnumbered natives in the same categories ten to one, he declared. Busey's "inevitable conclusion" was "that immigration is an evil, and that it is the principle source of crime and pauperism in this country."[16]

---

[14] Holt, "Antimasonic and Know Nothing Parties," 596, and Gienapp, "Origins of the Republican Party," Ch. 4, both emphasize the importance of the ability of new immigrants to participate in the electoral process in the rise of the Know-Nothing reaction.

[15] Whitney, *Defense of the American Policy*, 116.

[16] Governor Henry J. Gardiner in *Know Nothing Almanac for 1855*, 36; Busey, *Immigration*, 120–21. For additional evidence of the Know-Nothing position on immigration's contribution to social disorder, see *Foreignism Fully Exposed* (Washington, D.C., 1855), 3–7; *Know Nothing Almanac for 1856*, 40; and Sam Crane, *Facts and Figures for Native-*

According to many Know-Nothings, immigrant poverty was leading not only to social disorder, but also to severe hardships for American labor. Destitute immigrants, nativists feared, could easily be hired out for little pay and so depress the wages of American workers. Dramatizing the problem, the 1855 *Know-Nothing Almanac* asked, "Where is the *protection* against the thousands of half-starved pauper-laborers from Europe?" Poverty exists now among American laborers, insisted the *Almanac*, and what was the cause? *"The ruinous competition of imported cheap labor,* DUTY FREE, into the American labor market." A means of keeping poor, foreign labor out of the United States had to be devised, concluded the *Almanac*, or else American workers would be driven in desperation to crime and prostitution.[17]

Clearly immigration itself was creating problems for American society and generating support for the Know-Nothing movement and its program of restriction. Recent historians who have emphasized the impact of these problems on American nativism have contributed significantly to our understanding of the growth and spread of the Know-Nothing movement. Obviously Know-Nothings and their followers felt more deeply about the issues raised by the new immigration than traditional historians have realized. However, to concentrate on these issues alone diminishes our appreciation of the influence other political developments had on the Know-Nothing movement. Without such an appreciation it remains difficult to explain the brief and erratic course of mid-century political nativism. A complex political environment helped shape and define American reaction to the rapid increase in the foreign population. To ignore that total political environment, stressing the role of immigrant issues in the formation of the Know-Nothing movement while minimizing the importance of sectional concerns, fragments our understanding of politics in this period of turmoil.

In the North, nativism, working through the Know-Nothing movement, and opposition to slavery extension, as expressed in the Republican party, were often in competition for the hearts, minds, and votes

---

Born Americans (Ithaca, 1856), 5–8. Crane went so far as to insist that one-half of all the crimes committed in America were committed by Catholics.

[17] Busey, *Immigration,* 76; *Know Nothing Almanac for 1855,* 23. For additional discussion of the problems immigration posed for American labor, see *Know Nothing Almanac for 1855,* 59, 68; and *Know Nothing Almanac for 1856,* 19.

of the electorate.[18] In a number of localities, Know-Nothings and Republicans battled for control of the anti-Democratic forces. Nevertheless, many Americans in the free states held nativist and anti-extensionist beliefs simultaneously. By emphasizing the competition between these two doctrines, we can easily overlook the ways in which together both ideals informed the actions of a majority of the northern population. Only by becoming aware of the interrelationship between antislavery and antiforeign beliefs can we fully comprehend the meaning of political nativism in the antebellum North.[19]

It is not only those who assert the importance of antiforeignism at the expense of the slavery extension controversy who are guilty of distorting political reality in the mid-nineteenth century. Historians who emphasize the crucial significance of the slavery issue in the political ideology of the day also fail to see the continuities between antiforeign and antislavery thought. In his study of Republican ideology before the Civil War, Eric Foner claims that the Know-Nothing goal of restricting immigration conflicted with the antiextensionists' support for the expansion of free labor and economic opportunity. "In a sense," Foner wrote in *Free Soil, Free Labor, Free Men*, "the Republican party's rejection of nativism during the 1850s and 1860s was inherent in its free labor ideology."[20] But nativism was more compatible with Republicanism than Foner would care to admit. Free labor ideology, rather than leading to a Republican rejection of nativism, was to a great extent itself a basic tenet of the nativist system of belief.

While Republican organizers argued that the slave power was hostile to the social values of the free labor North, many Know-Nothing leaders insisted that their main enemy, the Catholic church, was also opposed to a free, progressive, dynamic society.[21] Republicans de-

---

[18] Potter, *Impending Crisis*, 250, offers a recent general overview of this conflict.

[19] Although admitting that individuals could be both Know-Nothings and advocates of slavery restriction, Potter still maintains an emphasis on competition and does not appreciate the significance of their shared beliefs. See also Holt, *Political Crisis*, 170.

[20] Eric Foner, *Free Soil, Free Labor, Free Men* (New York, 1970), 237.

[21] Potter is aware of the parallels between the irrational fears of both the Republicans and the Know-Nothings. In particular he notes the paranoid style of both organizations as well as their shared fascination with the sexual crimes of their respective opponents. But he does not recognize the similarity between specific arguments used by both movements. See Potter, *Impending Crisis*, 252–53.

spised the South's system of labor chiefly because they believed it degraded the value of work and so destroyed ambition and enterprise, creating a community that was backward, stagnant, sluggish, and lazy.[22] Know-Nothings had a similar "free labor" critique of Catholicism. Because Catholics made up by far the largest and least assimilable group of immigrants then entering the country, nativists concentrated their efforts against them. The church of Rome, Know-Nothings argued, like the institution of slavery, destroyed the ambition to advance, but it employed a less direct technique. The Catholic hierarchy, in order to protect its authority, subverted free education; ignorance and superstition were the twin pillars of its rule. Even as they spoke, Know-Nothings believed, Jesuits were "swarming" onto the nation's "shores, penetrating every corner of the Country" with the goal of establishing "universal ignorance."[23] If the public doubted this Know-Nothing charge, Thomas Whitney asked them to consider what was the church of Rome "but a budget of mechanical and ostentatious forms and ceremonies, and a promoter of ignorance and low superstition?" Across the North, Know-Nothings saw the church's efforts to gain public funding for private Catholic schools as further evidence of its desire to block the "spread of intellect."[24] And if Catholicism achieved its goal, what, asked the nativists, would be the result—the paralysis of American industry. Using superstition, the church of Rome would pauperize the country by eliciting donations from the ignorant populace for such trivia as shrines to the toenail of a long-forgotten saint. Then, after crippling the financial ability of the people to progress, the church would rob them of their desire to improve by stifling free, creative thought.[25] Without either the capital or the determination necessary for advancement, American society would soon become hopelessly stagnant.

Most Know-Nothings found the prospect of such social stagnation disturbing. Believing the American people to be above all else energetic and enterprising, and the American nation to be a place where the "bad" was in the past and "what is good is in the future," Know-

[22] Foner, *Free Soil, Free Labor, Free Men*, 40–51.
[23] *Know Nothing Platform: Encroachments of the Catholic Hierarchy*, 17, 30.
[24] Whitney, *Defense of the American Policy*, 64–65, 66.
[25] *Know Nothing Platform: Encroachments of the Catholic Hierarchy*, 14; Whitney, *Defense of the American Policy*, 34.

Nothings could not help but view the possibility of Catholic domination with deep foreboding. A fundamental principle of the American people, argued one tract, was the "right of self-judgement," the right to judge one's own duties to God and to be "answerable for the abuse of that right" to one's "own conscience." This right of self-judgment, this *"holy principle,"* had allowed Americans "to reduce a wilderness to fruitful fields" and "to annihilate by their vigor and industry time and space." By demanding subserviency, "Roman despotism" threatened to end forever the individualism upon which the country's progress had been based.[26] "American Republicanism is the parent of Progress," explained Thomas Whitney. "Romanism is the open foe of progress. . . . Romanism gives to the red man a cross and a rosary; American Republicanism places in his hands a Bible and a hoe." As a final proof of Catholicism's debilitating influence, Know-Nothings often compared what they viewed as the prosperous, enlightened areas of Protestant northern Europe with the declining, ignorant, poor areas of southern Europe and South America.[27] Societal stagnation and Roman Catholicism appeared to be constant companions.

These same areas were not only economically and socially backward but were also politically oppressed, nativists frequently claimed. According to many northern Know-Nothings, the Catholic church, in addition to blocking progress, destroyed human liberty. Roman Catholicism and republicanism were "diametrically opposed." Rather than respecting the rights of individuals, as did a representative form of government, the church was "tyrannical, intolerant, and aggressive."[28] "The simple fact that one is an *absolute* government, and the other a *popular* government, establishes the antipodel," explained Whitney.[29] A clash between freedom and Catholicism was inevitable, insisted another nativist, for "the fundamental principle of popery is, that all power is by devine appointment in the pope; the fundamental princi-

[26] Saunders, *The Progress and Prospects of America* (New York, 1855), 299, 357; *Know Nothing Platform: Encroachments of the Catholic Hierarchy,* 52–53. See also Rev. J. P. Stuart, *America and the Americans versus the Papacy and the Catholics* (Cincinnati, 1853), 3–8.

[27] Whitney, *Defense of American Policy,* 99–101; Saunders, *Progress and Prospects of America,* 152.

[28] Crane, *Facts for Americans,* 9; see also Whitney, *Defense of American Policy,* 71, 90.

[29] Whitney, *Defense of American Policy,* 95.

ple of freedom is that the people are the source of power." The goal of Catholic Europe, concluded many Know-Nothings, was to spread Catholic influence in America "until they reduce this free and enlightened republic to the dominion of the Roman see" and destroy "those institutions which are the beacon lights of civilization and the high hope of the world."[30]

Catholics were particularly well suited to this task of subversion, Know-Nothings argued, for a basic doctrine of the Roman faith was that dissimulation when ordained by the church was justified. Since America's Catholics gave their full allegiance to the pope, any oath they gave to non-Catholics or to the United States government could be easily annulled without penalty by the pope. Catholics could thus never be trusted, not in private transactions nor in their public commitments. "Is there any safety for us with such people in our midst, in any other action except eternal vigilance?" asked one nativist.[31] Given this perception of the reliability of their Catholic neighbors, it is not surprising that Know-Nothings found little reason to resist the conclusion that the papacy was "a desolating curse and its creed antagonistical to human rights and republican institutions."[32]

Alarm over what they believed to be Catholicism's threat to American liberty was, then, central to the nativist reaction against the large Catholic segment of the foreign-born population. Yet the Know-Nothings were not the only ones in the mid-nineteenth century to be concerned about the future of civil liberties in America. Many northerners were at this time also charging the South with the same crime of subverting America's commitment to liberty and representative government. Antislavery men of all shades of belief accused the southern slave power of endangering not only the rights of blacks but those of white Americans as well. Nativists often joined in attacking the South, but whether they did or not, they revealed in their assault upon "Roman despotism," as they had in their critique of Catholicism's opposition to progress, the close relationship between antislavery and antiforeign thought.

---

[30] Enoch Hutchinson, *Startling Facts for Native Americans* (New York, 1855), 66, 96; *Know Nothing Almanac for 1855*, 21.

[31] *Know Nothing Almanac for 1855*, 22; Hutchinson, *Startling Facts*, 50; *Know Nothing Platform: Encroachments of the Catholic Hierarchy*, 13.

[32] Philadelphia *Sun*, quoted in *Know Nothing Almanac for 1855*, 68.

On July 4, 1855, in a speech delivered at the height of Cincinnati's Know-Nothing enthusiasm, the Reverend C. B. Boynton made clear this connection between sectionalism and nativism. He began his oration, as had so many other Know-Nothing lecturers, by calling the papal power the "active foe" of human progress and the enemy of liberty. But Protestantism, he insisted, had a different relationship to these national ideals. "American liberty and Protestantism" had been "nursed" together. The founders of the American settlement had "sought in the western wilderness not only protection from" the "oppressions" of the Old World, "but a spot where liberty could find a refuge, and Protestantism a home and a defense." Now that the papacy was determined to realize its *"one central principle,"* that it was entitled to reign supreme over the entire world, Boynton believed it was necessary to combine "upon the basis of an American nationality" and resist this "politico-ecclesiastical Corporation of priests and jesuits" who were threatening all of America's liberties.[33]

When Boynton spoke of American liberties, he meant much more than simply political rights. The fathers of the Republic, he explained, had intended the American government to be dedicated to freedom as well. They had hoped the nation would "be aggressive upon all forms of human bondage, to give freedom to all men as rapidly as practicable, without distinction of race or color, and . . . to repress and weaken, and finally exterminate that form of oppression which existed in our own country." To argue otherwise was to charge the founding fathers with "deliberate treachery." According to Boynton, the central belief of the new nation was that "all men are born free and equal" and that the government itself "was designed for the overthrow of slavery." "Protestantism and Republican Liberty" were the "watchwords" of America. "Not Protestantism led in chains by a priesthood, nor betrayed by a jesuit, not liberty cherishing and endeavoring to perpetuate a system of chattelism for millions of Americans, but Protestantism with the right will, and power to defend itself, and Liberty seeking deliverance for all." Claiming that the slave power was joining with the pope to subvert American liberty, Boynton insisted that "the American eagle will never dwell in peace with this coiling serpent of slavery.

---

[33] C. B. Boynton, *Address Before the Citizens of Cincinnati, July 4, 1855* (Cincinnati, 1855), 5, 6, 14, 17, 18.

. . . The continent is not wide enough for their common home." He concluded, "Fellow citizens, there are two dangers which threaten our noble Republic. Between these two co-operating foes, the Papacy and Slavery, stands Young America sorely beset." Nevertheless, with God's help America would yet be "Protestant and Free!"[34]

Other Know-Nothing spokesmen shared Boynton's belief that Catholicism and slavery posed a coordinated threat to American liberties. To some, Catholicism was itself a form of slavery, binding men's consciences to a despotic ruler in Rome. Convinced that the church enslaved its own followers, it was not difficult for these Know-Nothings to conclude that Catholics wanted to see slavery strengthened wherever it existed. It was after all under the guardianship of the church, these Know-Nothings pointed out, that the Spanish had established their system of slavery in America. If more evidence of the church's advocacy of slavery was needed, Know-Nothings reminded Americans that the Catholic members of the Democratic party "are yet the public supporters of the infamous breach of public faith in the repeal of the Missouri Compromise, and are aiding with characteristic consistency the universal spread of African slavery over the land." Catholic support for Stephen Douglas' Kansas-Nebraska bill nullifying the Missouri Compromise of 1820 and opening up western territory to slave labor was not without purpose. Catholics, Know-Nothings argued, believed the spread of slavery to be "the surest means of breaking the spirit of free labor and reducing it to the ignorance of beasts of burden," susceptible to control by the church. Using slavery to "degrade the free labor of the Anglo-Saxon on this continent," the church could block the "rapid development of industry, virtue, and intelligence" in America and leave the North's workers "blighted by the withering curse of Romanism."[35]

Still other Know-Nothings claimed the church was using slavery to weaken free society even more directly. Secret emissaries of foreign despots, "jesuits of Rome," "enemies of Republican government," "have seized upon the question of domestic slavery to sow" the "land with dissention" and break the bonds of the Union. Douglas, who

[34]*Ibid.*, 18, 19, 20–22, 24.
[35]*Know Nothing Platform: Encroachments of the Catholic Hierarchy*, 7–8, 11, 12.

through his actions had helped to disrupt that Union, was "a tool of the jesuit priesthood."[36]

Although not convinced that slavery was a papist plot, even Thomas Whitney admitted that it was a "social wrong." "It grates harshly upon the best sympathies of humanity, and casts a blight on the progressive genius of the age." But as with many other nativists, Whitney's real anger was directed not so much against the South's system of slavery as at the repeal of the Missouri Compromise that allowed the institution to spread. The Missouri Compromise, banning slavery north of the 36°30′ parallel in the Louisiana Purchase territory, had almost the character of a treaty, Whitney explained. "It was a pledge—a promise—a solemn guarantee made by the government to the people." Its repeal was therefore "a gross and wanton violation of the national integrity."[37] The dishonesty of the act repealing the compromise is what deeply troubled Whitney and other Know-Nothings. Dishonesty was also a sin which nativists believed Catholics encouraged. It is therefore not surprising that, pictured as an act of national perjury, the repeal of the Missouri Compromise would provoke general opposition among northern Know-Nothings and provide the occasion for articulating their underlying opposition to the South's peculiar institution.

This nativist assault on Douglas' Kansas-Nebraska bill was not limited to Know-Nothing spokesmen. Know-Nothing state organizations throughout the North also openly opposed the lifting of restrictions on the expansion of slavery and in doing so once again indicated the close ties between nativism and sectionalism.

In Indiana, where the Know-Nothings numbered 80,000 by the fall of 1854 and took over the state's anti-Nebraska fusion movement, the organization's 1855 platform declared that neither slavery nor involuntary servitude should be allowed in the western territories. It also opposed the admission of any additional slave state. "Freedom," the party platform declared, "is National. Slavery is a sectional institution for which the Federal Government should not be reponsible." The In-

[36] *A Constitutional Manual for the National American Party* (Providence, 1856), 4–5.
[37] Whitney, *Defense of the American Policy*, 20, 218. See also Erastus Brooks, *Speech of Hon. Erastus Brooks, in the Senate, February 7, 8, and 13, 1855* (New York, 1855?), 3.

diana Know-Nothings insisted too that all their candidates should be men who favored resisting "the aggressions of Slavery, Popery, and intemperance." Members in the state organization also had to prove that they were uncontaminated by the twin evils of slavery and Catholicism. In order to join the party, a man had to demonstrate that he was "Morally and politically opposed to the extension of slavery and . . . free of any alliance with the Roman Catholic Church." Once accepted for membership, the state order administered an oath of allegiance and explained to its new enlistees that the founding fathers "never intended that our Government should either recognize, or sanction human slavery; that it should never become a party to its extension, or be responsible even for its existence." Finally, Indiana Know-Nothings instructed their new members that the primary goal of the organization was "to make this Republic the dwelling place of Freedom, the Polar Star for the oppressed of all nations; to exhibit the glorious spectacle of a government without a king, religion without a Pope; a continent without a slave."[38]

In neighboring Illinois, the Know-Nothing movement was no less opposed to slavery extension. In its 1855 platform, the order disclaimed "all right of the government to interfere with the institution of slavery, as it exists in any of the States of the Union," but it also "distinctly" asserted "that Congress has full power, under the Constitution, to legislate upon the subject in the territories of the United States."[39]

Even in the East, where the Know-Nothings were generally more powerful than in the states of the Old Northwest, there existed a strong antiextensionist commitment among most nativist organizations. In Connecticut, for example, the Know-Nothing movement carried the governorship in 1855 on a platform which proclaimed without hesitation its support for "the unconditional restoration of that time-honored prohibition known as the Missouri Compromise, which was destroyed in utter disregard of the popular will."[40]

[38] Gienapp, "Origins of the Republican Party," 399–400; *Constitution and By-Laws of the Order, adopted, May, 1855* (Indianapolis, 1855), 2, 3, 11, 13.

[39] "1855 Platform of the Illinois Know Nothings," in Roger Williams, *A Short Review of the Illinois Know Nothing Platform* (Petersburg, Ill., 1855), 12.

[40] "Platform of Principles of the American Party in Connecticut, Adopted, June 28, 1855," in Leonard and Parmet, *American Nativism*, 144.

In two of the most important eastern states, New York and Massachusetts, the Know-Nothings' political success also went hand in hand with a firm antiextensionist position. In New York, Know-Nothing gubernatorial nominee Daniel Ullmann came close to victory in 1854, and a year later the party's choice for secretary of state carried the election. In both contests all of the competing candidates, including the Know-Nothing favorites, had taken vigorous positions against repeal of the Missouri Compromise.[41] Given such unanimity on the slavery expansion issue, it is difficult to imagine the Know-Nothing success without their support for antiextensionism.

In Massachusetts, hostility to the expansion of slavery was at least as strong as in New York, and, as in New York, the Know-Nothing success would not have been possible if the party had not endorsed the antiextensionist cause. Throughout its history the popular Massachusetts Know-Nothing party demonstrated a continuing animosity to the South's peculiar institution. Controlling not only the governorship, but almost the entire state legislature as well, the nativist party passed a personal liberty law, petitioned to have a judge who presided at a fugitive slave trial removed from office, and elected to the United States Senate Henry Wilson, a dedicated antislavery man. So important were sectional concerns to Bay State Know-Nothings that conservative nativist Thomas Whitney spoke out in frustration against their "free soil" tendencies.[42]

Whitney's anger over the dominant position antislavery agitation had assumed among Massachusetts Know-Nothings was understandable, yet nativist enthusiasm for antiextensionism clearly was not confined to one state. The relationship between nativism and sectionalism was simply too strong to expect northern Know-Nothings not to advocate a good deal of the antislavery program. But the influence of sectionalism upon nativism went beyond the realm of political doctrine. The sectional crisis also played a critical part in the formation and growth of the Know-Nothing movement. Nativist sentiments throughout the country were genuine and deeply felt, but, as traditional historians have suggested, they gained political expression in the Know-Nothing movement only after the slavery controversy had so weakened

---

[41] See Gienapp, "Origins of the Republican Party," Chs. 5, 7.

[42] Oscar Handlin, *Boston's Immigrants* (Cambridge, Mass., 1941), 202; Whitney, *Defense of American Policy*, 291–92.

the major parties as to enable another political organization to take shape and gain support. Whitney himself admitted that when the Know-Nothings came into being the old parties were already "gradually dissolving into a sectional slime, whose stagnant and fetid odors would have been poisonous to the national health." The Know-Nothings thus arose on the ruins of a party system destroyed by sectionalism. The "national parties," recalled Whitney, "had ceased to exist, except *pro forma*" and sectional division had become the dominant and destructive force when "the American organization opened a new arena to intersectional harmony."[43]

Whitney was not the only one to offer this analysis of the relationship between nativism and the crisis of the Union. Thomas Spooner, Know-Nothing leader in Ohio, came to a similar conclusion. It was the sectional conflict that had allowed the Know-Nothing movement to form, he argued. Repudiation of the Missouri Compromise, a "solemn compact" as he called it, had "aroused the feelings and kindled the spirit so long pent up within the great American heart, and quickened into life and activity the American sentiment that gave birth to our Order."[44]

Spooner spoke for a movement in Ohio that numbered at its peak over 1,000 local councils and 130,000 members. Like state nativist organizations all over the North, Ohio's Know-Nothings combined a determination "to deliver" the "country from the blighting influence of Papacy, Priestcraft, and Kingcraft" with an insistence that "there shall henceforth and forever be no more Slave States."[45] Know-Nothings in Ohio were, then, dedicated to both nativist and antiextensionist positions. This dual commitment reflected not only the fundamental compatibility between sectional and nativist beliefs, but also the significant role antiextensionism played in the development of Ohio's nativist

---

[43]Whitney, *Defense of American Policy*, 286–87. See also *Principles and Objects of the American Party* (New York, 1855), 22. For similar interpretations, see Sister M. Evangeline Thomas, *Nativism in the Old Northwest, 1850–1860* (Washington, D.C., 1936), 132; Leonard and Parmet, *American Nativism*, 78–83; and John Higham, *Strangers in the Land* (New York, 1965), 5–7.

[44]*Report of the President of the State Council of Ohio, June 5, 1855* (Cincinnati, 1855), 7.

[45]*Office President State Council of Ohio, June 2, 1855* (n.p., 1855), 3; Thomas Spooner et al., *Resolutions of the Executive Council of Ohio, June 4, 1855* (n.p., 1855), 1, 2.

movement. The precise role of sectionalism in the rise of nativism differed from state to state, expressing itself in a variety of ways. No one state was typical, but Ohio provides a valuable case study. By examining in detail the importance of the sectional conflict in Ohio's complex pattern of nativist development, we can gain a sense of the process which led to the meteoric rise and the sudden fall of the Know-Nothing movement across the entire North.

The 1854 Kansas-Nebraska Act repealing the Missouri Compromise faced overwhelming opposition in Ohio.[46] Whigs, Democrats, and of course the state's important Free-Soil party joined together in organized resistance to Stephen Douglas' proposal opening new territory in the West to slavery. In July, 1854, just two months after passage of the despised act, the measure's opponents met in a state convention, urged the reinstitution of the Missouri Compromise, and nominated candidates for state supreme court and the board of public works.[47]

The unity of the anti-Nebraska forces left the Ohio Democracy with little room to maneuver. Antagonism toward the South and its presumed extensionist designs was so strong in the summer and fall of 1854 that few Democrats would risk confronting directly the sectional arguments of their opponents. During the fall campaign, loyal Democrats did occasionally question the significance of the territorial issue; but, determined to maintain their own increasingly shaky coalition, they concentrated mostly on discrediting the integrity of the anti-extensionists.[48] Particularly fearful of losing the Protestant-immigrant vote that had so regularly lent them its support, Democrats repeatedly accused the new coalition of being controlled by nativists.

Nativism was no stranger to Ohio politics. It had become especially significant in the chaotic years of the early 1850s, when the disappearance of effective party structures temporarily made the agitation of ethnic prejudices seem politically profitable. In 1853 many Ohioans, concerned about the unusual habits of some of the state's new immigrants, decided that temperance legislation should be the first priority of state government. In that year's October balloting they failed to elect candidates who would support their position. Angered by opposi-

---

[46] Much of this analysis of Ohio politics is taken from my *Triumph of Sectionalism: The Transformation of Politics in Ohio, 1844–1856* (Kent, Ohio: forthcoming).

[47] *Ohio State Journal*, July 14, 1854; Cleveland *Herald*, July 15, 1854.

[48] *Ohio Statesman*, October 4, 1854.

tion from foreign-born Protestants, who saw temperance laws as a threat to their accustomed manner of celebration, these reformers, who had previously objected only to Catholic immigrants, became hostile to all of the state's immigrant population.[49] Assisted by the extreme political turmoil of 1854, they quietly began to organize Ohio's secret Know-Nothing society in order to combat what they considered a serious alien challenge to their American values.

Recognizing the sensitivity of the state's foreign born to such a movement, the Democratic party charged that their anti-Nebraska opponents were dominated by this new nativist order. "Fusion," the Columbus *Ohio Statesman* argued in October, "has been sunk by its leaders into the tombs of a rotten secret agency, where rancor and intolerance breed and revel." Slavery extension, asserted the Cleveland *Plain Dealer*, was a false issue put forward by the opposition to entice the unsuspecting foreign born into what was really a nativist movement. In Cincinnati, where most of the state's immigrant voters resided, the Democratic *Enquirer* echoed this view, cautioning its readers not to be made the "blind tools of this midnight conspiracy."[50]

Undoubtedly much support given to the anti-Nebraska forces came from Ohioans who also opposed what they perceived to be the proimmigrant policies of the Democracy. Antiforeignism was too genuine a phenomenon to be completely absent from any election contest at this time. Nevertheless, as the new anti-Nebraska movement well understood, the Ohio Democratic party's heavy emphasis upon nativism was largely a diversion designed to distract the electorate from the central issue of the day.[51] The real question of the campaign, insisted Free-Soil leader Salmon Chase's *Ohio Columbian*, was "whether the people of Ohio are the enemies of Slavery or the friends of Oppression." The conservative *Ohio State Journal* of Columbus concurred, claiming that

[49] See Jed Dannenbaum, "Immigrants and Temperance: Ethnocultural Conflict in Cincinnati, 1845–1860," *Ohio History*, 87 (Spring, 1978), 125–39, for an analysis of the formation of Know-Nothingism in Ohio.

[50] *Ohio Statesman*, October 10, 1854; Cleveland *Plain Dealer*, October 19, 1854; Cincinnati *Enquirer*, October 4, 1854. See William E. Gienapp, "The Transformation of Cincinnati Politics" (Seminar paper, Yale University, 1969), 57–59, for a more detailed discussion of the fall, 1854, campaign in Cincinnati. Michael Holt, *Forging a Majority* (New Haven, 1969), 143, shows that Democrats used the same tactic in Pittsburgh.

[51] See Cincinnati *Gazette*, October 4, 1854; also *Gazette*, September 29 and 30, 1854.

"scarcely anything else of a political character is talked or thought of by the voters." "IT IS THE QUESTION OF THE CANVASS," concluded the Cincinnati *Gazette*. "Let every man who is in favor of Equal Rights, Northern Manhood and National Honor" show it by voting for anti-Nebraska candidates.[52]

As they went to the polls in the fall of 1854, Ohio's voters had for the first time in years a question of national significance to consider. Their response was unmistakable. The sectionally oriented anti-Nebraska movement gained a stunning victory. Candidates of the new opposition alliance carried every congressional district in the state. In only six counties could the once-powerful Democracy manage to achieve a majority.[53] Attracting important support from Whigs, Democrats, Free-Soilers, and previous nonvoters, the coalition's nominees for the board of public works and state supreme court judge triumphed by wide margins as well. The public works candidate captured an unprecedented 62.5 percent of the votes cast.[54] Never before had any party come even close to such a complete victory. There could no longer be any doubt that sectional issues were primary concerns of Ohio's voters.

The anti-Nebraska press was understandably ecstatic at their overwhelming triumph. "THE PEOPLE ARE AN INSTITUTION IN THIS COUNTRY WHEN THEY SET ABOUT IT," proclaimed the Cincinnati *Gazette*, especially proud of its party's 7,000-vote plurality in normally Democratic Hamilton County. The coalition's success in attracting German Protestants had clearly played a major role in the anti-Nebraska victory in Cincinnati, as even the Democrats were forced to admit.[55] In Cleveland the new movement had also been able to make deep inroads into the Democratic party. "The German 'Freemen' nobly cut loose from parties and voted for the right," concluded the *Herald* with satisfac-

[52] *Ohio Columbian*, October 4, 1854; *Ohio State Journal*, October 7, 1854; Cincinnati *Gazette*, October 8, 1854. See also Cleveland *Herald*, October 2, 1854.

[53] Inter-University Consortium for Political and Social Research, Ann Arbor, Michigan (hereinafter cited ICPSR); Joseph P. Smith, ed., *History of the Republican Party in Ohio* (Chicago, 1898), I, 30. The Democratic counties were Butler, Hocking, Monroe, Noble, Ottawa, and Perry.

[54] Statistics prepared by William E. Gienapp, University of California, Berkeley, 1978.

[55] Cincinnati *Gazette*, October 11, 1854; Cincinnati *Enquirer*, October 11, 1854. See also Gienapp, "Cincinnati Politics," 64–65.

tion. Reminding its Democratic opponents of their accusations of hidden nativist influence in the anti-Nebraska movement, the *Ohio State Journal* remarked, "Our good friends of the Slave Democracy . . . may try to evade the true reading of the verdict, by charging their defeat to this imaginary cause, and to that secret influence; but they should recollect that every effect has a real cause," and in this election "the monstrous legislation of Congress . . . the crowning act of a series of movements on the part of the Slave power," was what determined the outcome of the balloting.[56]

So shattered were the Democrats by their defeat that they hardly seemed interested in seeking an explanation for the debacle. Mockingly, the *Plain Dealer* suggested that perhaps "the Democracy generally mistook the day of the election, and are going to give the Fusionists a brush next week." Quietly, the state party organ in Columbus, the *Ohio Statesman*, did write that "truth and candor compel us to admit, that the repeal of the Missouri Compromise, as to the justice and propriety of which there was an honest difference of opinion among the Democracy of Ohio, has had its effects in producing this temporary disaster to the Democratic party." Although the party organization had united behind Douglas' Nebraska bill, it had clearly failed to carry a significant number of the rank and file with it. Nevertheless, no matter how discredited, the paper would not renounce a party position. Resolutely it insisted that the Democratic principle of popular sovereignty would eventually carry the day, and, hoping to regain the support of Ohio's German Protestants, it maintained that "the election is a thorough triumph of Know Nothingism." Quoting from Ali Baba, the *Statesman* concluded: "'My son, it is only in the night the stars shine out and heaven is revealed.' . . . A secret organization has achieved a triumph by machinations which would shame the devils of the pit. We claim a sort of negative success. The night lowers, but the stars are out, and joy cometh in the morning."[57]

Desperate for any tactic that would allow them to survive the tidal wave of popular opposition to their party's territorial stand, Ohio's Democrats had clearly overdramatized the issue of anti-Nebraskan nativism. Hostility to the foreign born had not determined the out-

[56] Cleveland *Herald*, October 9, 1854; *Ohio State Journal*, October 12, 1854.
[57] Cleveland *Plain Dealer*, October 12, 1854; *Ohio Statesman*, October 17, 11, 1854. See also Cincinnati *Enquirer*, October 11, 1854.

come of the 1854 election. Nevertheless, antiimmigrant feeling was spreading quickly in Ohio and was not completely unrelated to the antiextensionist movement. As early as July, 1854, a conservative Whig reported from Xenia that "the 'Know-Nothings' are increasing rapidly." Although he did not "much like a secret political organization," he had to "confess that the fruits which have so far followed this one, or rather resulted from it, are of decided good flavor, and are ripening very quick. No possible reason can be given why Americans are not at least as *well* qualified to fill the offices and control the affairs of Americans as foreigners." In September, Lewis Campbell, congressman from the Dayton area and a key organizer of the anti-Nebraska opposition, acknowledged that there was a growing assumption that the new nativist society possessed great political power. "How the K.N.'s may strike no one knows," he stated. "I don't have much fear that they will hurt me. They are said to be numerous throughout the Dist; but I don't know."[58] The Cincinnati *Gazette* was more certain of Know-Nothing strength. As the 1854 election approached, the conservative anti-Nebraska paper continued to deny that nativism ruled the antiextensionist coalition, but it did begin to print sympathetic descriptions of Know-Nothing activities.[59] After the election, one Cincinnati observer concluded that at least in his city nativism was as significant as antiextensionism in bringing about the Democratic defeat. "Anti-Nebraska, Know Nothings, and general disgust with the powers that be, have carried this county," reported Rutherford Hayes. Implying that anti-extensionism may have been only a cover for the true basis of many voters' anti-Democratic bias, he wrote, "How people do hate Catholics, and what a happiness it was to thousands to have a chance to show it in what seemed a lawful and patriotic manner."[60]

Clearly, antiforeign prejudice was more important to many 1854 voters than the budding anti-Nebraska coalition cared to admit. But to place too great an emphasis on the role of anti-Catholicism or antiforeignism generally in Ohio's anti-Democratic revolt, as have some

[58]Wm. B. Fairchild to Isaac Strohm, July 2, 1854, and Lewis Campbell to Isaac Strohm, September 9, 1854, Isaac Strohm Papers, Ohio Historical Society.

[59]Cincinnati *Gazette*, September 19, 1854. See also *Ohio State Journal*, July 8, 1854, in Thomas, *Nativism in Old Northwest*, 167.

[60]Rutherford Hayes to Uncle [S. Birchard], October 13, 1854, in Richard Williams, ed., *Diary and Letters of Rutherford Birchard Hayes* (Columbus, 1922), I, 470.

students of 1850s Cincinnati politics, is to confuse the by-product with the root cause.[61] As in 1853, when the devastation of the political system by the sectional conflict enabled ethnic prejudices to enter party contests, so too in 1854 the Nebraska turmoil created an atmosphere in which nativist agitation, preying on deeply felt biases, could spread and become politically significant.[62] The shattering of the remaining bonds of the Jacksonian system left the parties without even a vestige of their old identities. Lost in a world without any recognizable political organization from which to gain shelter, many Ohioans not surprisingly joined a movement that emphasized their American nationality. At least this was something they held in common with others in society. The secrecy and ritualistic aspects of the new Know-Nothing order met well the public's need to belong to a community that was stable, well defined, and committed to battling the surrounding chaos.[63] The Jacksonian parties had once fulfilled this need; until they could be replaced by other political coalitions, many Ohioans found the Know-Nothing movement appealing.

As the Nebraska protest swept the state, the burgeoning secret order followed in its wake. The numbers who joined the new organization were estimated by some contemporaries to have been in the tens of thousands.[64] However, these figures even if accurate do not by themselves show the strength of antiforeignism or the extent of its political influence, for the commitment of these nativists was uncertain. To become an Ohio Know-Nothing in the mid-1850s often had more to do with changes in the political environment than with hostility to the new immigrants, genuine as this feeling may have been. Many of the enlistees were simply temporarily displaced Whigs and Democrats.[65]

---

[61] See Gienapp, "Cincinnati Politics," 65. Gienapp argues that anti-Catholicism was the primary motivation of those Democrats who left their party in 1854 and remained outside it. See also his "Origins of the Republican Party."

[62] Charles Reemelin, *Autobiography* (Cincinnati, 1892), 123; John Sherman, *An Autobiography* (Chicago, 1895), 184.

[63] See David Brian Davis, "Some Themes of Counter-Subversion: An Analysis of Anti-Masonic, Anti-Catholic, and Anti-Mormon Literature," in David Brian Davis, *The Fear of Conspiracy* (Ithaca, 1971), for additional discussion of this idea.

[64] *Ohio Statesman*, March 18, 1855, and *Ohio Columbian*, June 13, 1855, calculated that there were 50,000 Know-Nothings in the state in October, 1854; 120,000 in February, 1855; and 130,000 in June, 1855.

[65] Although holding a different view of the Know-Nothings' role in the transformation of northern politics, Michael Holt shows clearly that in Pittsburgh the nativist order

Soon the Know-Nothing excitement would subside and they would join a more lasting political organization. The demise of Ohio's Know-Nothing order only awaited the stabilization of sectional politics.

The timing of the Know-Nothing outburst clearly indicates its relationship to antiextensionism. The anti-Nebraska alliance was correct in claiming that antiforeignism did not have a controlling influence in the 1854 campaign. The very fact that anti-Nebraska advocates felt free to dismiss nativism so easily confirms the weakness of the secret order at that time. Reminiscing about the 1854 contest, Whig stalwart Oran Follett wrote, "The Know Nothing organization was new and had manifested its power in local elections only; it was on this occasion left out of accounts" by the anti-Nebraska movement.[66] German Protestant participation in the new coalition gives additional evidence of the absence of any significant nativist role in the antiextensionist revolt. The German population would hardly have put its confidence in a party dominated by Know-Nothings. "The American order was just organized," Salmon Chase explained, recalling the 1854 election a year later. "It was sufficiently diffused to be a powerful auxiliary, but not enough was known of it to excite any alarm in the minds of the immigrant population."[67]

A month after the anti-Nebraska triumph, the Know-Nothing movement had grown considerably. In the postelection turmoil, many Ohioans who had continued to hold onto their traditional party loyalties joined those who had already dropped their old ties and were searching for a new political identity. The Know-Nothing order offered them all a welcome haven. Wrote Chase to his lieutenant E. S. Hamlin in November, "I confess I feel more uneasiness about the probable influences of the order on our movement than I did when I saw you last." Still, he believed that the nativists were weak enough for it to be "best not to say any thing [of] them. Wait until it becomes necessary &," he

---

became a temporary home for both lost Whigs who could not immediately bring themselves to join Free-Soil Republicans and dissident Democrats who could not yet ally with their former Whig enemies in the anti-Nebraska movement. Holt, *Forging a Majority*, 141–42.

[66] Oran Follett, "The Coalition of 1855," in Alfred E. Lee, *History of the City of Columbus* (New York, 1892), II, 430.

[67] Salmon Chase to Kingsley Bingham, October 19, 1855, Salmon P. Chase Papers, Historical Society of Pennsylvania.

added hopefully, "it may never become necessary. What is objectionable may cure itself."[68]

Five months later, Chase could no longer afford to be so sanguine. By April, 1855, the nativist reaction was reaching the peak of its strength, threatening to supersede the antiextensionist agitation that had given it a chance to grow. Gaining control of the anti-Democratic coalition in Cincinnati, it succeeded in nominating for mayor James D. Taylor, the violently antiforeign editor of the Cincinnati *Dollar Times*.[69] Fearing a German defection from the coalition over his selection, a Know-Nothing mob entered the foreign wards of the city as the April voting was ending and initiated a riot by destroying a number of ballot boxes.[70] The Democracy, victorious at the polls, angrily labeled the incident "one of the most dastardly and villainous acts ever perpetrated in any community." Thrilled by the opportunity of demonstrating to German Protestants the true nature of the opposition, the *Enquirer* announced that it could "find no language capable of expressing our indignation. . . . Words could but faintly translate the abhorrence we feel that the ark of our safety, the very covenant of our freedom, should be ruthlessly seized by sacrilegious hands, and destroyed before our very eyes." In Columbus the *Statesman* received the news of the Cincinnati disruption with equal satisfaction. Blaming "the reckless, midnight, oath bound order" for the riot, the paper asked sarcastically, "Has the Protestant religion come to so low a condition that it requires such means to give it character and support?"[71]

Neither the Protestant religion nor the Know-Nothing order had grown weak. The antiforeign riot was not a sign of the movement's desperation, but rather an indication of its arrogant self-confidence. Such outbreaks were natural outgrowths of the heightening atmosphere of hostility to the foreign born. Even the usually restrained Cincinnati *Gazette* shared in this antiforeignism. In the aftermath of the riot, the conservative paper revealed that its concern had always been for the "largest degree of intelligence . . . to rule and give tone and character to our institutions." It insisted, "We are not for putting down men be-

---

[68] Salmon Chase to E. S. Hamlin, November 21, 1854, Salmon P. Chase Papers, Library of Congress.

[69] Gienapp, "Cincinnati Politics," 67–72.

[70] Thomas, *Nativism in Old Northwest*, 189.

[71] Cincinnati *Enquirer*, April 3, 1855; *Ohio Statesman*, April 4, 5, 1855.

cause they were born in foreign countries and speak a foreign tongue," but "when the foreign vote shall combine to put down the American vote, the evil day is close upon us." Looking back at the election defeat, the paper concluded that "there is inherent justice in the claims of this [American] party, that men of American sentiments shall govern this country—that native and not foreign nations shall govern our actions, in all matters related to politics." Still dominated by antiforeignism, the *Gazette* stated in June that "the infusion of American nationality into the politics of America, we regard as vital to the stability of our institutions." In Cleveland, resentment against immigrants was no less intense. Following the anti-German riot, the *Herald* proclaimed: "The time has come when the question must be decided whether native Americans can enjoy unmolested the rights purchased by the blood of their fathers, or whether Foreigners shall deprive them of those rights. —Foreigners have set the example of controlling elections with brutal force, and, if needs be, the rights of voters must be secured by the same means."[72]

Clearly nativism was sweeping the state, drawing into its ranks many who had previously contained their antiforeign prejudices. Angered and frustrated by the complete political chaos that surrounded them, these Ohioans now felt no hesitancy in expressing freely their hatred for the strange and incomprehensible foreign-born population. If the aliens could somehow be controlled, then order would be restored to their political universe.

Thus the Cincinnati April riot had revealed the strength of ethnic prejudice in the state, but in time it would also cause a backlash among many previously sympathetic citizens, who soon began to lose their enthusiasm for the secret order.[73] The destruction of ballot boxes and the violence that accompanied it appalled many Ohioans and discredited the Know-Nothing attempt to be recognized as the only political organization that stood for authentic American values. Nativist arguments against a foreign threat were also crippled by the belief of so many Ohioans that the slave South posed a greater danger to their liberties. Overcome by their own hostility to slavery expansion and presumably aware of their declining influence among the electorate, the

[72]Cincinnati *Gazette*, April 4, June 7, 1855; Cleveland *Herald*, June 5, 1855.
[73]See Gienapp, "Cincinnati Politics," 74, and Thomas, *Nativism in Old Northwest*, 176.

state organization, meeting in Cleveland in early June, decided to unite with the new antiextensionist Republican party instead of nominating its own slate of candidates for state office.[74] The order was simply not strong enough to risk engaging as an organization in a confrontation with antiextensionism, and in any case it shared too many beliefs with the new Republican party for there to be a need for a contest between them.

On Friday, July 13, 1855, the sixty-eighth anniversary of the Northwest Ordinance, Ohio's united Republican movement assembled in Columbus.[75] Chaired by Congressman John Sherman, the combined meeting of antiextensionists and nativists resolved to oppose slavery expansion and work to "render inoperative" the section of the Kansas-Nebraska Act "ending freedom" in the western territories. The convention also nominated Salmon Chase for governor and in a show of solidarity selected Know-Nothings for all of the remaining state posts. The platform, however, said nothing about nativism.[76]

Reacting to the convention's decision, many conservative nativists throughout the state grew concerned that a Chase victory in Ohio would lead to a general disruption of the Union. But, despite their discontent, most eventually acquiesced in his selection on a platform free of nativist doctrine. One conservative Whig who had been sympathetic to Know-Nothingism concluded that even though the Free-Soiler's nomination was "an awfully bitter pill . . . the Republican organization is now our only hope against Locofocoism, and personal feeling ought not to interfere with his success."[77] Similarly motivated, the new Republican state central committee secretary argued that, though "I did

---

[74] Cleveland *Plain Dealer*, June 7, 1855; James Ashley to Salmon Chase, June 16, 1855, Salmon P. Chase Papers, Library of Congress.

[75] Smith, *Republican Party*, 39; Sherman, *Autobiography*, 105.

[76] Cincinnati *Gazette*, July 14, 1855. The excellent article by Eugene Roseboom, "Salmon P. Chase and the Know Nothings," *Mississippi Valley Historical Review*, 25 (1938–39), 335–50, correctly concludes that at the convention Know-Nothingism was "swallowed up in the anti-slavery movement and its force dissipated" (p. 345). Another student of the Know-Nothings in this period explains their decision quite simply: "Many Ohio Know Nothings regarded the anti-slavery cause of Chase more favorably than the nativistic cause of Brinkerhoff [the Know Nothing favorite], therefore they supported the former" (Thomas, *Nativism in Old Northwest*, 187).

[77] Wm. Fairchild to Isaac Strohm, September 6, 1855, Isaac Strohm Papers, Ohio

not like Chase . . . my dislike for the continual encroachments of slavery is even greater than for him. . . . With all his faults—and it is not necessary to magnify them—I vastly prefer him to that body of sin, and lump of imbecility, the present incumbent [Democrat]. And although it is but the choice of an alternative, thank God!"[78] Left with few options, most nativists were quietly inching their way into the sectional party.

Not all of Ohio's most conservative nativists would join this movement to Republicanism. Still committed to the Know-Nothing principles which had sustained them during the recent chaos, they could not bring themselves to abandon their ideals and endorse the radical Chase, whatever the consequences. Holding a mass rally in Cincinnati immediately after the July 13 convention, several thousand of these disaffected nativists denounced both the Democratic and Republican gubernatorial nominations. Although also condemning the repeal of the Missouri Compromise, the meeting resolved to challenge the twin threats to the peace of the Union—"abolition" and "nullification." The protesters also agreed to meet in August to nominate a gubernatorial candidate of their own.[79]

Calling themselves the American party, though only a faction of the Know-Nothing or American movement, these dissidents gathered in Columbus August 10 and chose former Whig governor Allen Trimble as their candidate. In their resolutions they once again made clear their opposition to Congress' repeal of the Missouri Compromise and freely acknowledged their attachment to nativist programs "so long as there remains a vestige of that malign foreign influence which threatens our institutions."[80] But their central concern was for the stability of the Union. Fearful that it would soon go the way of other recently devastated political institutions, they wrote Trimble asking him to accept

---

Historical Society. See Rutherford Hayes to S. Birchard, July 15, 1855, in Williams, *Diary and Letters*, 481, for more evidence of "old Whig" discontent with Chase's nomination.

[78] W. B. Thrall to Isaac Strohm, August 20, 1855, Isaac Strohm Papers, Ohio Historical Society.

[79] "Resolves of the Cincinnati Mass Meeting of the American Party," July 19, 1855, Cincinnati *Gazette*, July 20, 1855.

[80] "Resolves of the American Party," *Ohio Statesman*, August 10, 1855.

their nomination and thereby give Ohio "an opportunity to vote for a thorough friend of the Union, and an uncompromising foe to all disunionists." Acceding to their request, Trimble wrote back emphasizing his abhorrence of the current national disruption.[81]

Trimble's candidacy had a significant impact on the election. Chase won, but with only 48.5 percent of the vote, a drop of 14 points from the anti-Nebraska victory a year earlier. Trimble had managed to gain the support of 8 percent of the electorate. Clearly Chase had been hurt by this American defection. In Cincinnati, a stronghold of die-hard nativism, he actually trailed both Trimble and the Democratic incumbent William Medill; in the state as a whole his 15,000-vote margin of victory was more than doubled by the Republican candidate for lieutenant governor, Know-Nothing Thomas Ford, who, running without American opposition, captured 55.9 percent of the ballots cast.[82]

Formidable as it appeared at the time, this American effort soon turned out to have been only the final gesture of a dying political tradition, and in Ohio it rapidly collapsed after the 1855 election. Explained Joshua Giddings, leader of the Free-Soil contingent of the Republican party, "Those who went for Trimble" were "made ashamed of their course and at the same time treated so kindly as to act with us next time of year. The prestige of the K.N.'s is gone, I think forever."[83]

The following year organized nativism, already defeated in the 1855 election, lost most of its remaining political significance. In early January the hard-core elements of the movement, continuing to spew out their antiforeign doctrines, complained that state Know-Nothing president Thomas Spooner was working, as he had the year before, "to transfer the American party, 'body, boots and breeches,' to the Abolition party." Speaking for this group of extremists, Cincinnati *Dollar Times* editor James Taylor also claimed that Spooner was attempting to

[81] Alfred Kelley *et al.* to Allen Trimble, August 9, 1855, and Allen Trimble to Alfred Kelley, August 11, 1855, in Allen Trimble, "Autobiography and Correspondence of Allen Trimble," *The "Old Northwest" Genealogical Society* (1904), 220–22.

[82] ICPSR. See also Scioto *Gazette*, November 2, 1855; Cincinnati *Enquirer*, October 18, 1855. Statistics prepared by William Gienapp, University of California, Berkeley, 1978.

[83] Joshua Giddings to Salmon Chase, October 16, 1855, Salmon P. Chase Papers, Historical Society of Pennsylvania.

"fasten anti-slavery as an issue on the American party."[84] Spooner certainly was working toward this end, but his efforts were supported by an increasing number of Ohio's nativists. The American party, a faction of which had in 1855 rejected Spooner's leadership and fielded a gubernatorial candidate against the Republican coalition, hailed the Know-Nothing president at its January, 1856, state convention for his antislavery stand. At the American national convention in Philadelphia at the end of February, Spooner, along with Lieutenant Governor Thomas Ford and the rest of the Ohio delegation, bolted the convention when it failed to pass an antiextensionist resolution. Happy to see such serious divisions in the nativist ranks, the Republican Cincinnati *Gazette* claimed that after the Ohio delegation's action it was "useless to attempt to disguise the fact that the Slavery question is now paramount to all others."[85]

In March the *Gazette's* claim was confirmed conclusively when a state gathering of American party members not only endorsed the action of their national representatives and repudiated the Philadelphia convention's presidential nomination of Millard Fillmore, but also dropped the fundamental nativist demand that the foreign born be proscribed from positions in government.[86] "The first great fact" of Ohio politics "is the progressive liberality of the Americans," explained Salmon Chase a few days after they had met.[87] Exposed in Ohio to a political environment that for so long had been bombarded by antislavery sentiments of one sort or another, nativists themselves had acquired a strengthened antiextensionist bias. Now, amid the mounting pressures of a sectionally oriented presidential campaign, they had conceded what had been the essence of their program in order to satisfy the needs of the new antiextensionist Republican coalition.

Other state Know-Nothing organizations in the North had followed

[84] Cincinnati *Dollar Times*, January 4, 1856. See also Alexander Latty to Salmon Chase, December 18, 1855, Salmon P. Chase Papers, Library of Congress.

[85] Cincinnati *Gazette*, January 5, March 1, 1856. See also Salmon Chase to Timothy Day, February 29, 1856, in Sarah Day, *The Man on a Hill Top* (Philadelphia, 1931), 154.

[86] "Resolutions of the American State Convention," March 20, 1856, Cincinnati *Gazette*, March 21, 1856.

[87] Salmon Chase to Edward L. Pierce, April 15, 1856, Edward L. Pierce Papers, Houghton Library, Harvard University. See also H. D. Cooke to John Sherman, March 25, 1856, John Sherman Papers, Library of Congress.

different paths of development between 1854 and 1856, but they all agreed with Ohio's nativists that a ban on slavery expansion was necessary. At the 1856 American national convention in Philadelphia and at the national meeting the previous June, northern Know-Nothing orders joined with Ohio's delegation in demanding an antiextensionist stand.

At the June, 1855, gathering of the American party, the news of Ohio's recently adopted state council resolutions favoring a reinstitution of the Missouri Compromise strengthened northern determination to gain a similar commitment from the national convention. Some northern representatives actually suggested that the Ohio resolutions be incorporated into the national platform. Despite their efforts and those of other northern delegates who spoke against slavery expansion, a majority of the committee on resolutions submitted a report urging that the current Kansas-Nebraska law be retained.[88] The committee's minority responded by insisting upon restoration of the Missouri Compromise, and a floor debate ensued. Prominent Ohio Know-Nothing Thomas Ford led a northern attempt to block the majority report. Denouncing the South's "determination to extend by fraudulent and unconstitutional means, the area of human cattledom," he pledged that the "fires of liberty" would burn from "every hill top" in the land "*until Liberty shall be the birthright of every American; until we have a Government without a Despotism; a Religion without a Pope and an Empire without a slave.*"[89] Ford's colleague from Massachusetts, Governor Henry Gardiner, made it clear that he "*would not* be bound by the actions" of the convention if it passed "a declaration of principles that were false to the Constitution, to liberty and to the rights of the humblest citizen of this Republic." Adding a pragmatic note to his idealistic rhetoric, he told the convention delegates that, if they accepted the majority report, the Know-Nothings would be unable to run successfully on the resulting party platform in a single village in New England.[90]

Ignoring the warnings of northern delegates, the American party

[88] New York *Tribune*, June 9, 12, 1855. See also *Report of the President, June 5, 1855,* 9.

[89] "Speech to American Party National Convention," June 13, 1855, Cincinnati *Gazette,* July 18, 1855.

[90] New York *Tribune*, June 13, 1855.

convention passed the majority report endorsing repeal of the Missouri Compromise. With the sole exception of the New York delegation, whose leader was head of the convention, the entire North responded by walking out of the assembly hall. Although some northern delegates simply went home, a number retired to a special rump meeting. Chaired by Massachusetts Senator Henry Wilson, the gathering issued an "appeal to the People" demanding the restoration of the Missouri Compromise, the repeal of which they called "a wrong which no lapse of time can palliate, and no plea for its continuance can justify." Any other solution, the northern Know-Nothings declared, would be unsatisfactory. "The eyes of the whole North are fixed on their representatives here," explained one Massachusetts delegate, "and whoever falters in the cause of Freedom will be held to strict account." Future northern support for the American party cause depended upon the convention's decision on the Missouri issue. Without a restoration of the compromise, the same delegate warned, the American party in the North "is gone forever."[91]

Fearing the accuracy of this representative's contention, state Know-Nothing organizations all over the North rushed to embrace their delegates' action and demonstrate their commitment to antiextensionism. In Indiana a July meeting of the state council backed the walkout by its convention delegation and passed resolutions endorsing the Missouri Compromise and an end to the spread of slavery. In addition, almost every local council joined in supporting the state delegation's action. In Illinois, Pennsylvania, Ohio, Massachusetts, Connecticut, and other northern states, Know-Nothing organizations made similar endorsements. Even New York, whose delegation was the only one from the North not to leave the national meeting over the extension issue, refused to support the convention's resolution on the territorial question. Meeting in August, 1855, the New York state Know-Nothing council rejected the section of the platform which endorsed repeal of the Missouri Compromise. The New York council, like those in other states, had no option but to dissent from their national organization's support of the Kansas-Nebraska Act. Know-Nothing Governor William Minor of Connecticut explained, "The American party would

---

[91] New York *Tribune*, June 13, 15, 16, 1855.

have been blown to atoms in every Northern state" had the 1855 national platform been accepted in the North.[92]

In 1856 the South again dominated the American party's national gathering and successfully resisted attempts to have the Missouri Compromise endorsed. Led, as we have seen, by Ohio, the North bolted once again, this time to join in great numbers the newly organized Republican party.[93]

When forced to choose between their nativist loyalties and their antiextensionist beliefs, most northern Know-Nothings had little trouble deciding where their priorities lay. Slavery was not the only compelling political question facing the United States in the 1850s, but it was, nevertheless, the dominant issue of the day and the Know-Nothing movement was deeply affected by it. This is not to argue, as have some earlier interpreters of political nativism, that the Know-Nothing movement was the creature of the slavery controversy, holding little independent meaning for its adherents outside its relationship to sectionalism. Mid-century nativism was too strongly rooted in American tradition and in the contemporary immigration crisis to be brought so totally under the influence of any other political issue. Still, it is impossible to understand nativism in the 1850s without an appreciation of the central role sectionalism played in it. The ideology, development, and demise of the Know-Nothing movement were inseparably intertwined with the slavery issue. "In a word," wrote Know-Nothing leader Thomas Whitney, "American Republicanism is FREEDOM; Romanism is SLAVERY."[94] Without the surrounding crisis of the Union, mid-nineteenth-century nativism would not have taken the course it did, nor would it have had the same meaning to its loyal enthusiasts across the land.

[92] Gienapp, "Origins of the Republican Party," 640–41, Ch. 7, 750.
[93] See New York *Tribune*, February 2–27, 1856, for an account of the 1856 national American party debate over the slavery extension issue.
[94] Whitney, *Defense of the American Policy*, 95.

JOEL H. SILBEY

The Surge of Republican Power: Partisan Antipathy, American Social Conflict, and the Coming of the Civil War

The secession of eleven southern states between December, 1860, and the spring of 1861 remains the central, traumatic moment in the American historical experience. Recognizing its importance, historians have expended efforts over more than a century detailing and explaining why secession became the chosen course and why it occurred when it did.[1] This historiographic enthusiasm has yet to wane, and studies of the dynamics of secession continue to appear. In recent years, in fact, after a period of decline, there has been a resurgence of interest in the subject. In the last decade Don Fehrenbacher, Kenneth Stampp, William Barney, Steven Channing, the late David Potter, Michael Johnson, David Donald, Mills Thornton, Peyton McCrary, Eric Foner, Michael Holt, and Thomas P. Alexander have all made significant efforts to decipher the complex problem posed by the failure of the constitutional experiment at the beginning of the 1860s.[2]

[1] Thomas Pressly, *Americans Interpret Their Civil War* (Princeton, 1954), is the standard treatment of historiography to its date of publication. For assessments of more recent works, see Eric Foner, *Politics and Ideology in the Age of the Civil War* (New York, 1980), 15–53. In a special, and important, historiographic category is Lee Benson's "Explanations of American Civil War Causation: A Critical Assessment and a Modest Proposal to Reorient and Reorganize the Social Sciences," in *Toward the Scientific Study of History: Selected Essays of Lee Benson* (Philadelphia, 1972), 225–340. I have benefited from the critical and helpful comments of Ronald Formisano, Michael Holt, James McPherson, Phyllis Field, Andrew Rotter, Gerard Bradley, and Steven Fram on earlier versions of this essay.

[2] Don S. Fehrenbacher, *The South and Three Sectional Crises* (Baton Rouge, 1980); Kenneth Stampp, *The Imperiled Union: Essays on the Background of the Civil War* (New York, 1980); William Barney, *The Road to Secession: A New Perspective on the Old South* (New York, 1972); William Barney, *The Secessionist Impulse: Alabama and Mississippi in 1860* (Princeton, 1974); Steven A. Channing, *Crisis of Fear: Secession in South Carolina* (New York, 1970); David Potter, *The Impending Crisis, 1848–1861* (New York,

The list of these recent works is impressively long; their findings are useful and important. They have encompassed explorations of both long-range, underlying causes and immediate considerations affecting specific behavior at critical moments. They have paid a great deal of attention to the internal political and social dynamics of southern society in seeking to uncover and evaluate the raw materials that led to secession. They have applied new ways of looking at and organizing the available evidence: modernization theory, the imperative of republican ideology, the strains of nationalism and of center-periphery tensions. Finally, and most particularly, a number of historians have fully explored the nature and dynamics of elite and mass political behavior. As a result of all this, researchers have illuminated many dark corners of northern and southern society, of antislavery and proslavery movements, and of the American political process generally.[3]

Despite the reach and depth of this work and what has been learned, the story of what brought on the secession crisis remains unfinished. Agreement on causation is still elusive. How the various elements came together to provoke a specific reaction continues to be debated. Disagreements about individual and group motivations and the importance and power of the different forces at play are unabated. Some writers emphasize the threat of internal conflict among southerners themselves, a threat energized by Republican growth and power as "the operative tension in the secession crisis." Secession in this view "was necessary because of the internal divisions within the South, divisions which focused on the degree to which the slaveholding minority could have its way in a government based ultimately on manhood suffrage."[4] Other students, however, stress other southern fears, such as

---

1976); Michael P. Johnson, *Toward a Patriarchal Republic: The Secession of Georgia* (Baton Rouge, 1977); David Donald, *Liberty and Union: The Crisis of Popular Government, 1830–1890* (Boston, 1978); J. Mills Thornton, *Politics and Power in a Slave Society: Alabama, 1800–1860* (Baton Rouge, 1978); Peyton McCrary, *Abraham Lincoln and Reconstruction: The Louisiana Experiment* (Baton Rouge, 1978); Peyton McCrary, Clark Miller, and Dale Baum, "Class and Party in the Secession Crisis: Voting Behavior in the Deep South, 1856–1861," *Journal of Interdisciplinary History*, 8 (Winter, 1978), 429–57; Foner, *Politics and Ideology*; Michael F. Holt, *The Political Crisis of the 1850s* (New York, 1978); Thomas B. Alexander, "The Civil War as Institutional Fulfillment," *Journal of Southern History*, 47 (February, 1981), 3–32.

[3] There are useful assessments of much of this literature, and of the secession process itself, in Stampp, *The Imperiled Union*, esp. 191–245.

[4] Johnson, *Toward a Patriarchal Republic*, xx.

the threat to slavery or the region's inability to expand into new territories. Still other historians articulate their belief in the inevitability of conflict between two distinctly different societies following different courses. One section, they claim, was committed to traditional, pre-bourgeois social and economic patterns; the other section was a vigorous, rapidly modernizing place, the epitome of nineteenth-century bourgeois development. Their profound differences came to a point when they locked horns over northern "modernizing" attempts to integrate "the 'pre-modern' South" into its conception of "a national political and economic system."[5]

There are rich varieties of such historiographic themes with many nuances and differences among them in what Don Fehrenbacher refers to as "the accumulated complexity of the literature on the causes of the Civil War."[6] But what is clear about them is that what happened has neither been fully told nor comprehended in a way that everyone can accept. Nor is there even agreement about where to focus research efforts. The situation has been compared by Willie Lee Rose with being caught in "an entangling morass" whenever we try to account for the causes of the Civil War. "Most of the scholars who have tried to cut boldly through it," she continues, "have had only temporary success. The facts and the variables have proved impossible to account for under any single theory up until now."[7] This traumatic episode remains open and alive to additional historical exploration. Its roots and course, the long-range process and the immediate triggering mechanism, must be considered yet again if we are to understand it fully and accurately.

This last point is particularly highlighted by the recent intrusion into American historiography of a powerful, significant, and new way of understanding politics and the political system in the generation ending in secession, a way that cannot be ignored when we consider what happened in the United States in 1860–1861. Perhaps nothing has been more jarring to students of antebellum politics than the recent findings of those dubbed "new political historians" about the nature of social and political conflict in the decades before the Civil War. According to these historians, far from being intimately, persistently, and

---

[5] Foner, *Politics and Ideology*, 20.

[6] Fehrenbacher, *South and Three Sectional Crises*, xi.

[7] Willie Lee Rose, "Comment" [on Robert Kelley, "Ideology and Political Culture from Jefferson to Nixon"], *American Historical Review*, 82 (June, 1977), 580–81.

directly related to slavery and the sectional crisis, mass political conflicts in the 1840s and 1850s were primarily rooted in a complex interaction of social and political perceptions and religious, national, and racial prejudices and divisions, all brought together under the heading of ethnocultural conflict. As Paul Kleppner sums up the findings, "Nineteenth-century American partisanship was not rooted in economic distinctions. Neither gradations of wealth nor perceived differences in status nor shared orientations toward the work experience were at the core of partisan commitments. Partisan identification mirrored irreconcilably conflicting values emanating from divergent ethnic and religious subcultures." The hostility of Protestants toward Catholics, of pietistic toward ritualistic Protestants, of Anglo-Saxons toward Celts, Germans, and Dutch and other ethnocultural conflicts had more to do with American electoral politics than did arguments over tariffs, territorial expansion, sectionalism, slavery, and executive power. Each political party was deeply involved in this conflict. Party coalitions were based on different grouping of ethnocultural tribes.[8]

Particularly relevant to the process culminating in secession, these ethnocultural variables structured the critical voter realignment of the mid-1850s. Between 1854 and 1856, one of the sharpest turnovers in American politics occurred, resulting in the disappearance of the national Whig party, the ultimate weakening and decline of the Democratic party, and the creation and rise to dominance of a sectionally focused Republican coalition. The Democrats fell from the heights of their sweeping presidential victory in 1852 to a minority position by the presidential election of 1856. Receiving only 45.3 percent of the popular vote that year, they lost control of all but a handful of northern states and their hold on the few states they had won was seriously

[8] Paul Kleppner, *The Third Electoral System, 1853–1892: Parties, Voters, and Political Cultures* (Chapel Hill, 1979), 144. See also Ronald P. Formisano, *The Birth of Mass Political Parties: Michigan, 1827–1861* (Princeton, 1971); Michael F. Holt, *Forging a Majority: The Formation of the Republican Party in Pittsburgh, 1848–1860* (New Haven, 1969); Paul Kleppner, *The Cross of Culture: A Social Analysis of Midwestern Politics, 1850–1900* (New York, 1970); Frederick Luebke, ed., *Ethnic Voters and the Election of Lincoln* (Lincoln, 1979); and Joel H. Silbey, *The Transformation of American Politics, 1840–1860* (Englewood Cliffs, 1967). For the most recent overview of the new political history, see Allan G. Bogue, "The New Political History in the 1970s," in Michael G. Kammen, ed., *The Past Before Us: Contemporary Historical Writing in the United States* (Ithaca, 1980), 231–51.

threatened thereafter. A massive voter reaction to a perceived alien threat to American culture triggered this political upheaval. As Ronald Formisano argues, the rise of the Republicans was primarily due to a long-standing "political evangelicalism" which revived in 1854 and which was further "politicized and broadened by anti-Popery, nativism, temperance zeal and other Protestant moralisms" into a major political revolution that brought down the Democratic party in the northern states.[9]

This ethnocultural element in the realignment politics of the fifties has been well established; however, its recognized importance has raised a serious problem of analysis and interpretation. What do ethnocultural political divisions have to do with secession and the coming of the Civil War—the culminating cataclysm of a decade in which the electoral realignment occurred? "It hardly seems too much . . . to demand of any new sweeping interpretation of the nation's political history," Rose suggests, "that it give a serviceable account of the causes of the Civil War."[10] But how can we possibly integrate the findings of the new political history into an explanation of sectional rupture? "The frenzy of revolution was in the people" at the moment of secession, a southerner recalled twenty years later, but what, if any, was the role of ethnocultural conflict in fomenting that frenzy?[11] Confrontations between Protestants and Catholics and between yankees and Irish, for all their importance in mass voting behavior in the 1850s, seem a long way from a conflict erupting from the clash of different sectional cultures or systems or in response to such immediate matters as the Wilmot Proviso, free-soilism, Kansas, "bleeding" Sumner, John Brown, and the demands of William Lowndes Yancey and his secessionist cohorts. And yet these events, slavery, and the defense of the slave system were ultimately to cause the breakup of the Union.

Most recent students of secession found little place in their explanations for the findings of the new political historians. Some deal with them to a degree, but with obvious difficulty. Others reject these findings out of hand. One reason is the general failure of the new political

[9] Formisano, *Birth of Mass Political Parties*, 330.

[10] Rose, "Comment," 581.

[11] The quotation is from I. W. Avery, *The History of the State of Georgia from 1850 to 1881* (New York, 1881), quoted in Joseph E. Parks, *Joseph E. Brown of Georgia* (Baton Rouge, 1976), 128.

historians to find ways to subsume southern political life within the ethnocultural explanation of antebellum politics. Holt points out, for instance, that "for Dixie, evangelicalism and ritualism, pietism and liturgicalism have definite limitations as analytical concepts. The prophets of the new ethnocultural interpretation, indeed, have largely ignored the South no matter what period they are writing about." [12]

Those who completely reject the findings of the new political history take comfort in such an admission. A few of them even go so far as to regard with disdain the idea that the kinds of ethnocultural conflict described could have had much, if any, role to play in the momentous events of 1860–1861. Too much else was present of a different quality, the focus on slavery too clear-cut, the ethnocultural interpretation not readily assimilable into most explanations in any convincing way. "I tend to think," Rose writes in summary, that "no theory based primarily on cultural voting patterns in the North is going to explain the coming of the Civil War." She concludes by warning historians away "from the treacherous shores of the new determinism that the ethnoculturalists have located through a narrow examination of voter behavior." [13]

Echoing Rose's sentiments, Fehrenbacher, in the most recent attempt to deal with the secession crisis directly, simply ignores the findings of the new political history except for a passing reference at the outset of his book. He finds such efforts to employ new conceptual frameworks to change our focus as "often synthetic and modish . . . reflecting the latest fashions in behavioral science theory and terminology but adding little to the substance of explanation." [14] These are harsh words indeed, which Fehrenbacher follows up with resort to more traditional approaches and explanations. His focus is on the southern secessionists and their fears of what northern Republican voters would demand all right, but what shaped so much of the behavior of those voters, according to the new political historians, does not appear. It is the Kansas-Nebraska bill and debate, not ethnocultural divisions, insists Fehrenbacher, that "more than anything else determined the character of the third party system in its early years." [15]

---

[12] Holt, *Political Crisis of the 1850s*, 8.

[13] Rose, "Comment," 582.

[14] Fehrenbacher, *South and Three Sectional Crises*, 3.

[15] *Ibid.*, 56. Compare his treatment of the birth of the Republican party with that offered by the authors cited in footnote 8.

Finally, one or two historians have suggested, ironically one hopes, that the new political historians would be happy if they could say that the Civil War never happened, because there is nothing in their description of American social conflict or any theories that come out of it that could help to explain divisions based upon a sectional confrontation. The explanation offered by the new political historians, Eric Foner concludes, "has no need for the Civil War. Unfortunately, the Civil War did take place. But the new interpretation leaves a yawning gap between political processes and the outbreak of war." [16]

But this cannot be the end of the story. Secession, a specific political act, cannot be separated from the political world of the time with its everyday concerns, routines, norms, and conflicts. There is, of course, particular irony in noting this, since one area of agreement among almost all students of the secession crisis is that it was the Republican victory at the polls in 1860 that "precipitated the secession of the seven states of the lower South." [17] Why? Because "all the passions of the sectional conflict became concentrated," Fehrenbacher argues, "like the sun's rays by a magnifying glass, on one moment of decision that could come only once in history—that is, the first election of a Republican president." [18] The trigger that ultimately produced separation lay there.

It was the way the political world was developing that threatened the South and drove its leaders to do what they did. But what was it about the Republicans that caused such an action? Fehrenbacher refers to the "expected consequences" of Republican rule, "vague but terrible." [19] In his study of antebellum Alabama society and politics, Mills Thornton describes Alabamians acting, in their "terror," against "frightening" circumstances. [20] What made such vague consequences so terrible, so many good people so terrified? That remains unclear. In dealing with it, however, it seems rash indeed not to consider what we have learned recently about the roots of so much of American political conflict in the 1850s and the political context in which the leaders, both northern and southern, had to operate. The findings about the

[16] Eric Foner, "The Causes of the Civil War: Recent Interpretations and New Directions," *Civil War History*, 20 (September, 1974), 201. See also Eric Foner, *Free Soil, Free Labor, Free Men: The Ideology of the Republican Party Before the Civil War* (New York, 1970), and his recent *Politics and Ideology*.

[17] Johnson, *Toward a Patriarchal Republic*, xv.

[18] Fehrenbacher, *South and Three Sectional Crises*, 63.

[19] *Ibid*.

[20] Thornton, *Politics and Power*, 457.

importance of ethnocultural conflict in shaping political behavior in the pre–Civil War decade unearthed by Lee Benson, Ronald Formisano, Michael Holt, Roger Peterson, Paul Kleppner, Robert Swierenga, Frederick Luebke, and George Daniels, among others, are clear-cut and persuasive. And no one who reads the political idiom of the 1850s can ignore the extensive concern with religious and, more broadly, ethnocultural issues to be found there. As William McLaughlin has remarked, American political rhetoric has often been infused with the metaphors of religious and cultural values. "There has scarcely been an election in American history since 1796 which was not conducted as a fight between good and evil for the power to steer the ship of state toward the millenial harbor."[21]

Moral commitments were particularly strong in the 1850s. Spiritual values, religious metaphors, and ethnic awareness abounded in everyday life. Differences between dissimilar groups in the country had heightened as well. The political realignment in that decade had sharpened and reenergized both. Both permeated the fabric of the American political system and the lives of most Americans. Its full ramifications and meaning may not have been explored or its intensity fully measured, but ethnocultural conflict was obviously not irrelevant, artificial, or temporary in the politics of that time. To articulate its importance does not narrow historical vision simply to voting behavior. The work of the new political historians strongly underlines how much ethnocultural differences and conflicts incorporated a broad conspectus of the political and social processes in the United States generally. We can no more dismiss such conflict than we can the importance of sectional confrontation in explaining America's collapse into internal war.

It is time, in sum, to begin integrating the factors unearthed by students of the new political history into our understanding of the breakup of the Union. Such attempts will not in themselves end the search for the causes of secession and civil war. No one can be that optimistic. But the efforts may at least add important elements to that search. At most they may create a better grasp of the complexities of political choice. And by incorporating those findings we will not omit from our calculations an important aspect of American political history in the 1850s.

[21] William McLaughlin, "Pietism and the American Character," *American Quarterly*, 17 (Summer, 1965), 176.

Unfortunately, few of the new political historians themselves have tried to deal directly with the coming of the Civil War. Their focus has remained on the mid-fifties, primarily on the electoral realignment and the resulting emergence of a third political party system based on how different social groups voted. They ususaly separate these electoral confrontations from the problem of the Union's collapse.[22] It is true that in an intelligent development of the Republican critique of the South, Formisano has shown how a number of apparently diverse and unrelated ideas were brought together. He argues that "nativism, anti-Catholicism, anti-Southernism, anti-slavery and racism did not flow through the political universe in neatly separate streams. . . . Rather, one must understand how racial, ethnic, religious, economic, sectional, and other groups were interwoven symbolically and how issues such as Popery, Slavery, Party, and Rum permeated one another with emotional resonance."[23] Michigan Republicans, he points out, integrated attacks on Catholics with attacks on the slave power into a crusade for white freedom. That crusade united Republicans behind an anti–slavery extension, anti-Democratic program. They saw a relationship between the ethnocultural matters and the expansion of slavery.

Formisano's attempts are critical because he relates the two dominant confrontations of mid-nineteenth-century American politics to each other. But, despite his important effort, the surface of the problem has barely been scratched, particularly in understanding the sectional crisis itself. He tells us what made the Republicans act as they did. But the key to any examination of the crisis of disruption is to explain the behavior of the rest of the political community as well, most centrally and particularly that of the southern secessionists. Why did they act when they did? Why not earlier, in 1850 or 1854? Why not right after John Brown's raid in 1859, as some of them then desired? Any analysis of the crisis must focus on the specific perceptions at the time of the men who committed the overt acts rejecting continuation of the Union. The leaders of the secession movement and those who followed them particularly reflected the fears engendered by the Republican victory. To them, at that moment, Thornton writes, "the

---

[22] Cf. Kleppner, *Third Electoral System.*

[23] Ronald P. Formisano, "To the Editor," *Civil War History,* 21, (June, 1975), 188; Formisano, *Birth of Mass Political Parties.*

Southern future held only horror." Among them "monstrous fears" were feeding on "monstrous realities."[24] Were such inflamed social and political perceptions shaped by the ethnocultural pressures present? If so, why and how, specifically?

It is not that southerners were affected directly in their elections by their own ethnoculturally structured divisions. There is little evidence of that, and the subject needs more investigation. Rather, it is what southerners saw in northern political warfare, highly structured by the ethnocultural cleavages present, that counted to them. To quote Fehrenbacher once more, southern "fear of Republican rule was to no small degree a fear of the unknown."[25] But there was much more to it than that. Secessionists knew some things about the Republicans all too well. Perception and reality intertwined among the secessionists in a particular way. Secession "was intended by Southern political leaders to be a preemptive strike against the threat of a revolutionary take-over."[26] That takeover was based, in their minds, on the plans of the new power group in the nation, the nationally victorious Republican party. When the southern states seceded, they made a strong statement about power. They were frightened by the new political configuration within the nation. It was what they saw in the rise of the Republicans, capped by Abraham Lincoln's election, that led them to take the actions they did.

Fehrenbacher refers to "the surge of Republican power" as "what southerners feared most." It was difficult, he continues, for southerners to view Republicans as "merely a political opposition."[27] But why not? Secessionists certainly saw the Republicans as more threatening toward slavery than any previous political opposition. There was some realism in that. John Rozett emphasizes that the "Republican party did represent to a predominant degree those who, at the very least, had a distaste for the ill treatment of the black man . . . [and that] the South did have something to fear from the election of Abraham Lincoln." Republicans, he concludes, "did adopt a position of limited equality

---

[24] Thornton, *Politics and Power*, 206. The second quotation is from a review by William Freehling, *New York Review of Books* (September 23, 1971), 39.

[25] Fehrenbacher, *South and Three Sectional Crises*, 63.

[26] McCrary, *Lincoln, and Reconstruction*, 65.

[27] Don S. Fehrenbacher, *The Dred Scott Case: Its Significance in American Law and Politics* (New York, 1978), 547; Fehrenbacher, *South and Three Sectional Crises*, 57.

and of moral judgement which the South could neither accept nor tolerate."[28]

Republicans, however, had been going out of their way to play down such commitments and to calm fears thus provoked. They presented several different sides of their nature to the electorate generally and to suspicious southerners in particular. Historians have recognized this well enough. Republicans, in one description, "presented themselves as conservatives," while at the same time they "espoused revolutionary doctrines."[29] But which was reality? Why believe one thing about them and not the other? On one level their future course and policies on slavery matters could not be clear to contemporary observers, yet for the secessionists they were very clear. Southerners did not believe either Republican denials of plans against the South or that party's articulated conservatism. They picked out and emphasized the most dangerous, threatening aspect of the Republican argument. They could not simply play it safe, for that would not convince the electorate they had to sway to their side. Republicans could say what they wanted, but southerners had certain evidence about the nature and intentions of the Republicans which cut through the confusion and ambiguity. The facts that southerners had and the way they viewed them crystallized and clarified their fears and oriented them in a particular way in the frightening political world they inhabited.

To understand the perceptual prism through which secessionists viewed their enemies, it is necessary first to comprehend the role, importance, and outlook of the larger community of which many of them were part. What framed political discourse and action, for all of the sectional tensions present, was an older and still powerful stream of political idiom and belief. There was a continuity to a particular kind of political confrontation in America from the 1830s onward that shaped the way events were seen at the moment of crisis. The political memories of southern secessionists contained crucial influences that interacted with their concerns about slavery and the Union to deepen and intensify their fears.

The secessionist prism was partisan. Southern perceptions were intertwined with their long-standing commitments to a particular politi-

---

[28] John Rozett, "Racism and Republican Emergence in Illinois, 1848–1860: A Re-Evaluation of Republican Negrophobia," *Civil War History*, 22 (June, 1976), 115.

[29] Freehling, *New York Review of Books*, 39.

cal party. The most critical of all subcultures in the antebellum period
were the political parties. This fact is the second major finding of the
new political historians. They argue that parties helped to organize a
vibrant, intense politics, one of great feeling, rhetorical exaggeration,
and deep commitment.[30] Yet parties tend to disappear more than they
should from discussions of secession. There is strong evidence that
they retained their important structuring effect throughout the 1840s
and 1850s despite the rise of sectional tensions. In his presidential
address to the Southern Historical Association, Thomas Alexander
forcefully reminded his audience that "the attachment of the individual voter to party in nineteenth century America was affective, even
religious." Given that, "secession was a step so drastic and so contrary
to the fervor of American nationalism that it could never have been
made persuasive to a majority of voters on the basis of arguments that
individuals could readily associate with their own well being. Only
through the vehicle of the Democratic party was secession possible."[31]

Alexander's partisan religious metaphor is useful and accurate.
Nineteenth-century Americans worshiped at what some labeled "the
shrine of party" right through the secession crisis.[32] Even in a day of
rising sectional differences and confrontations, such worship—that is,
intense partisan commitments and adherence—still ran deep. Almost
half the northern voters remained good and loyal Democrats in 1860
despite the role that Republicans cut out for themselves as the party of
northern white freedom. Party battles remained savage in the North as
well. In the South, too, there is much evidence of the continued importance of partisan traditions and behavior.[33] Furthermore, the major
actors in the crisis of 1860–1861 and most of the other participants as

[30] "The American political culture in the pre-Civil War years was dominated by a
strong national party system, clung to tenaciously and with an intense loyalty for ideological, social and symbolic reasons, with a vigor and devotion revealed on every election
day." Joel H. Silbey, *A Respectable Minority: The Democratic Party in the Civil War Era,
1860–1868* (New York, 1977), 7.

[31] Alexander, "Civil War as Institutional Fulfillment," 14, 20–21.

[32] This phrase or its equivalent was used frequently in political discourse, especially
in the South. For one such usage see the Milledgeville (Ga.) *Federal Union*, January 30,
1849, quoted in Joel H. Silbey, *The Shrine of Party: Congressional Voting Behavior,
1841–1852* (Pittsburgh, 1967), 105.

[33] On this point, for one southern state, see Marc W. Kruman, "Parties and Politics in
North Carolina, 1846–1865" (Ph.D. dissertation, Yale University, 1978). See also Holt,
Political Crisis of the 1850s, and the essay by Alexander in this volume.

well had been politically socialized during the time that the Jacksonian party system had matured and sunk its roots deeply into the American soil. All of these actors had been affected by the powerful force of the partisan imperative that ran profoundly and intensely through the minds and hearts of most concerned Americans.

Political parties brought together in disciplined ranks groups of like-minded individuals, their unity rooted in their common enemies, fears, desires, and attitudes. People caught up in partisan politics were schooled in certain unyielding truths. Parties were always at war with their opponents. Their perceptions of each other and their ideological commitments found expression in a divisive and rousing rhetoric. Like religious converts, the party faithful were forcefully called to their duty and reminded of the dangers they faced if they wavered in their faith and lost the battle. Stump speeches, newspaper editorials, and election pamphlets were the weapons of this warfare. The warfare varied in intensity but it was persistent and always close to the surface of political consciousness. By 1860, both the Democrats and the Republicans had fully developed and articulated clear perspectives about the policies and behavior of their adversaries. These perspectives were highly integrated. They involved all components of current politics stemming from the electoral realignment and its consequences, from antislavery agitation to nativism. Powerfully asserted, they penetrated deeply into both partisan communities. Both elites and masses subscribed to the tenets of their partisan communities. Republicans talked about free soil, free labor, and a crusade for white freedom.[34] But it was what the Democrats talked about in return that was central to the secession episode.

It was, as Alexander notes, the southern Democrats who dominated the movement to leave the Union. They formed its "cutting edge."[35] Its leadership and much of its voting support came primarily from Democratic ranks. One study estimates that two-thirds of the popular vote for secessionist candidates in 1860–1861 came from Democrats.[36] What drove them were the specifics of Democratic perception and commitment. Thus the integrated and national Democratic ideol-

[34] Foner, *Free Soil, Free Labor, Free Men,* and Formisano, *Birth of Mass Political Parties,* spell out the Republican ideology in great detail.

[35] McCrary, Miller, and Baum, "Class and Party," 457.

[36] *Ibid., passim.*

ogy of the 1850s and the framework of party loyalty and partisan belief played critical roles in shaping the perceptions that led southern Democrats to take the actions they did in 1860–1861. The Democratic assault throughout the 1850s furnished southerners with a perspective on their immediate political situation. This perspective provided for the faithful an image of Republicans that guided Democrats in their reaction to the rise of the Republican party, the election of Lincoln, and most specifically to the crisis that followed. In their speeches the leadership constantly invoked traditional partisan usages and symbolism to explain what was at issue. In their political exchanges and in their particular understanding of the Republican threat, southerners demonstrated their absorption of the national Democratic ideology as it had developed. Those partisan components, incorporating the transcendent substance of political warfare, defined for them what was at issue and what, consequently, had to be done.

Southerners gave as much evidence of the Democratic heritage as anyone who lived outside the slave states. Their system of ideas, particularly concerning the Republican threat, resonated with their Democratic ideology. Most observers are so used to seeing southern Democrats pulling away from northern Democrats in the late 1850s that they forget that—despite real and crucial differences over candidates, tactics, and specific policies—there remained agreement over the perceptions of the danger the nation was in and the reasons for that danger. Despite disagreements between them, both sectional Democratic factions shared an integrated vision, a common ideology.

The roots of that ideology lay in the cultural patterns informing American political life. Conflict between different religious, ethnic, and national groups, framed in many different ways, had existed for a long time in the United States.[37] Since the 1830s it had taken partisan form. The resulting battles implanted deep commitments and produced sharp partisan memories even as a generation passed and new issues arose. The political battles of the 1850s had reinvigorated the confrontations and reawakened these memories, always close to the surface. The critical part about the resulting political arguments—encased as they were in the realities and demands of the American politi-

[37] Robert Kelley, *The Cultural Pattern in American Politics: The First Century* (New York, 1979).

cal system with its democratic impulse and vigor, its reductionist rhetoric, and its deeply held commitments—was that they grew into
confrontations of world systems held by quite different cultural blocs.
Evidence taken from specific and often minor episodes—the visit of a
papal nuncio, the burning of a convent, or the rantings of a demented
prostitute—was marshaled and blown into an image of vast conflict.

To Democrats of the late 1850s, ethnocultural conflicts had specific
political meaning. Because of the electoral realignment of the mid-
fifties, a dangerous spirit permeated American politics, a spirit that endangered the freedom of all Americans and ultimately the Union itself.
The "practice of dragging politics into the pulpit" was "rapidly becoming one of the crying evils of the age," they argued. "Religious prejudices are invoked [in] the political arena. . . . The clergy are to be appealed to to take the rostrum. Churches are to be turned into party
conventions." The result was clear to see. "As the pulpit has grown political, the stump has waxed pious." Americans now lived in an age "in
which it is attempted to legislate not with an eye to the rights, the
comforts, the wonts—the well being of *good* citizens" but only with
attention paid to how "the wicked, erring will turn the blessings of
Providence to bad account." Such behavior was profoundly dangerous
to the Union because "persecution is an inseparable concomitant of
sectarian power."[38]

The source of this was clear to Democratic spokesmen. It came
from New England and particularly from the Puritanism that still
abounded there. As the editor of a Texas paper put it in 1856, "The
people of the New England States have been as remarkable in their
history, for the violence of their fanaticism and proclivity to superstition and intolerance on all subjects connected with religion as they
have been for their intelligence, energy and enterprise on all other
subjects."[39] The Democrats particularly feared the sectarian interventionism of the New England divine in the affairs of the nation, the re-

[38] Clarksville (Tenn.) *Jeffersonian*, May 30, 1855; Washington *Daily Union*, June 7,
1854; Edgefield (S.C.) *Advertiser*, November 16, 1854; Athens (Ga.) *Southern Banner*,
August 16, 1855; Mobile *Daily Register*, July 10, 1856, September 13, 1855.

[39] Galveston *Tri-Weekly News*, July 17, 1856; Athens *Southern Banner*, January 25,
1855. Cf. Albany (N.Y.) *Argus*, August 21, 1854. In the discussion that follows, I will
quote from both northern and southern Democratic papers. Most of the time, regarding
this ethnocultural phenomenon, their sentiments were the same, expressed in similar
language.

gion's self-defined crusade to change and uplift people and bring them into conformity with the ideals of the region, indiscriminately, determinedly, and without regard for the desires of those affected.

The descendants of the colonial Puritans, a Tennessee editor suggested during the secession crisis, "retain the salient points which characterized their ancestors, and destroyed the harmony of the earliest settlers of the colonies. The Puritans of today, like the Puritans of 1700, conceive themselves to be better and holier than others, and entitled—by divine right as it were—to govern and control the actions and dictate the opinions" of their fellowmen. New England is "always putting itself forward as the accuser and maligner of its brethren, the marplot and busybody of the confederacy, always crying over its grievances and always arraigning the other states for pretended usurpations. . . . They are unhappy unless they can persecute, either some unprotected class of their own people, or their colleagues in the confederacy." They "first established religious liberty on this continent by hanging and burning all who did not maintain their plan of salvation." An intolerance "social, religious and political leavens the masses there today, the same as when it burnt old women for witches, banished the Quakers, tore down Catholic convents, or gathered together a blue light Hartford Convention." New Englanders arrogantly believed they had a monopoly on truth and exhibited "a fanatical zeal for unscriptural reforms, accompanied by a Pharisaical spirit, which says to brethren heretofore cordially acknowledged, 'Stand back, we are holier than you.'"[40]

But things went further. The importance of all of this rhetoric to Democrats was what such attitudes led New Englanders to do. In a "soil in which every absurdity seems to be indigenous, and is favorable to the growth of every foreign delusion," including sabbatarianism, temperance, abolitionism, "and the other isms imported from Europe," there was devotion to a single purpose: cultural imperialism.[41] New Englanders were so imbued with the fanaticism of religious restrictionism and cultural superiority that they believed they had a "mission" to impose their own values everywhere in the Union. "They

[40] Memphis *Daily Appeal*, February 17, 1861; *Illinois State Register*, September 5, 1856; Albany *Argus*, December 30, 1856, May 5, 1857; Charleston *Mercury*, September 13, 1859; *Arkansas State Gazette and Democrat*, August 11, 1854.

[41] New York *Herald*, October 26, 1860.

persuaded themselves that they had a prescriptive right to impose their politics, their habits, manners and dogmas on the sister States and aspired to convert the whole people of the United States to Yankeedom." The Puritans had demonstrated such commitment again and again throughout American history. They were always at war to shape the future of the nation. They wanted it fundamentally Anglo-Saxon, Protestant, and pietist or Puritan, and not a mixture of diverse ethnic and religious groups which held different values. They proceeded, therefore, "as a central power, dictating to colonies and provinces."[42]

To the Democrats none of this had ever been abstract. The threat by New England was real and frightening. That region abounded with reformers, "people [who] imagine that nothing exists that may not be improved . . . and that they are divinely commissioned agents to accomplish this favorable change." Some of the threat southern Democrats perceived was obviously rooted in differences over slavery, but it involved more than that. In a region where "sectarian hatred outranks even sectional animosity," the persistent "mutual jealousies of New England and the South do not primarily grow out of slavery. They are deeper, and will always be the chief obstacle in the way of full absolute reunion. They are founded in differences of manner, habits and social life, and different notions about politics, morals and religion."[43] Nor was it simply a matter of anti-Catholicism or hatred among different nationality groups. As the Democrats articulated it, this was a war between two cultures, not necessarily sectional in makeup, but in which sectional and regional distinctions played a major role, "of races, representing not difference in blood, but mind and its development, and different types of civilization. It is the old conflict of the Cavalier and the Roundhead, the Liberalist and the Puritan."[44] Whose country is this? was the question asked. The Democrats had one answer, their opponents another.

The threat to a pluralist nation posed by the Puritans, though al-

[42] Washington *Daily Union*, January 27, 1857; Albany *Argus*, January 20, 1857.

[43] Mobile *Daily Register*, October 9, 1857; Richmond *Enquirer* in Washington *Daily Union*, October 24, 1854.

[44] *Atlas and Argus*, February 20, 1857. A part of this quotation is from a famous speech by Clement Vallandigham in 1863, but it reflects a perspective that antedated the war. See Frank Freidel, *Union Pamphlets of the Civil War* (Cambridge, 1967), II, 723.

ways present, had not been that serious in the 1830s and 1840s, although the political battlefield was well marked from the start. Democratic denunciations of their Whig opponents in the 1830s and 1840s often contained attacks on extremism, cultural interventionism, and the great potential for nasty behavior inherent among the Whig descendants of Tory federalism. Fears were always close to the surface. In March, 1850, one New York Democrat succinctly summed up the concern and its cogency. "I fear," James K. Paulding wrote, that "it will not be long before we of the North become the tools of the descendants of the old Puritans, who had not the most remote idea of the principles of civil liberty, and no conception of religious toleration, but the most unrelenting intolerance. The despotism of parsons," he continued, "is taking the place of that of kings. . . . Our freedom is in great danger of becoming sacrificed to the texts of Scripture, and fanatical dogmas."[45]

Still, the Whigs were a nationwide party, never as completely dominated by New England as the Republicans were to become later. Nor had the Whigs, though a robust and competitive party, usually been as potent a political threat. Before the mid-1850s, despite often very close elections, the Democratic party usually dominated the politics of the Union, especially through its control of Congress. (Between 1840 and 1854 they held a majority of the seats in both House and Senate in five of the seven Congresses.) But matters became more dangerous in the early 1850s as two factors threatened, in Democratic eyes, to tip an always present but largely subterranean and controllable conflict of cultural values over into open warfare.

First, the coming of the immigrants in great numbers in the 1840s and 1850s strongly revived rarely quiescent Puritanism and gave it new vigor, direction, and expectations. Second, Puritan extremism had become institutionalized into a dominant position within a narrowly sectional Republican party. Although there had been a Know-Nothing interlude first, embodying much of the spirit of New England cultural imperialism, the Democrats were convinced that many of the Know-Nothings in the North and their ideas were absorbed, as the fifties passed, by the Republicans. The Democrats' "common enemy, composed of Free Soilers, Abolitionists, Maine-Lawites, Free-Negroes

---

[45] James K. Paulding to John C. Calhoun, March 19, 1850, in Ralph M. Alderman, ed., *Letters of James K. Paulding* (Madison, 1962), 515.

and Spirit Rappers," became embodied in the Republican party in "solid phalanx."[46]

It is nothing new to suggest that southerners viewed the Republicans as meddlesome interventionists willing to crusade persistently against the institution of slavery.[47] But what should not be underestimated was the way northern and southern Democrats in the 1850s rooted such meddlesomeness in ethnocultural conflicts which were, in their view, the centerpieces of the Republican advance. As one editor put it, "Abolition is but a small part of their programme and probably the least noxious of their measures." Republican rapprochement with nativist movements in the mid-fifties and acceptance, as the Democrats believed, of the program and goals of the latter had made the larger threat clear. The coming of the immigrant, the Democrats suggested, had caused New England Puritans to revert "to the intolerant fanaticism which marked their early colonial history." The "prevailing leaven [of] Puritanism, the spirit which is almost as deadly hostile to the civil equality of religions at this hour, as when it burned the witches at Salem and whipped Quakers at the cart-tail," had once more become hyperactive and oppressive.[48] And the Republican party was its vehicle. "The principle of republicanism," as seen through the Democratic filter, was "to meddle with everything—to meddle with the domestic institutions of other States, and to meddle with family arrangements in their own states—to force their harsh and uncongenial puritanical creed down the throats of other men, and compel them to digest it under pains and penalties." The Republicans "assail with equal virulence the institutions of the North and those of the South." They "are equally inimical to, and equally to be dreaded by, the North and the South." Their newspapers "boldly" avow "that it is the mission of the Republican party to overthrow Democracy, Catholicism and Slavery."[49]

The Republican party "now proposes to take up arms against one of

[46] Mobile *Daily Register*, October 6, 1855.

[47] See, for example, Avery O. Craven, *The Growth of Southern Nationalism, 1848–1861* (Baton Rouge, 1953).

[48] Washington *Daily Union*, May 20, 1857; *Illinois State Register*, October 4, 1859; Washington *Star*, November 9, 1855.

[49] New York *Herald*, September 21, 1860; Washington *Daily Union*, September 23, 1856, May 20, 1857; Edgefield *Advertiser*, July 1, 1857.

the religious denominations of the country" and "array political parties according to the churches to which their adherents belong, or with which they sympathize." The Republican party, in short, "is a machine to put fanatics into office and preachers into politics." During the presidential election of 1856, Democrats charged that "places of prayer were converted into Republican club rooms, and religious conference meetings into political gatherings, where partisan efforts in favor of the Republican ticket were pressed as a religious duty." The party subsidized the "religious and benevolent press, it smuggles its agents into the pulpit. Most of the professedly religious newspapers and very many of the pulpits of the country preached Republicanism and the duty of voting for Fremont, as a pressing religious obligation." Republicans made "merchandise of the various departments of philanthropy," prostituting "all causes, however sacred they should be against the invasion of politics, to . . . sectional, plundering and treasonable schemes." The Republicans' virulent attack on ethnocultural diversity and their refusal to tolerate "the existence of any institution not according to the puritanical philosophy of New England" added a new, potent, and dangerous dimension to a generalized and usually abstract fear. Democrats had "to combat" not only "the Black Republicans as a political organization," but also "the powerful influence of frenzied religious bigotry" as well.[50]

But there was a second and much more threatening danger: the willingness of the Republican party to use state power to impose the peculiar standards of Puritanism on everyone else. The use of government for such purpose had been a hallmark of early Puritanism, later taken up and advocated by Whigs, but it was now brought to a high pitch by the Republicans. The coercive tradition in American pietism may have been ambiguous as William McLaughlin has suggested, but it did not seem so to the Democrats in the 1850s with their deep fears of Puritanism and intense commitment against government interventionism.[51]

The Republicans, Democrats argued, were fostering an aggressive and uncompromising program of coercive, cultural legislation designed to order and direct individual behavior within the Union.

[50] *Atlas and Argus*, July 22, 1856, September 7, 1857, September 5, 1860; *Illinois State Register*, September 4, 1855.

[51] McLaughlin, "Pietism and the American Character."

Where Republicans ruled in the northern states, restrictive and regulatory laws had quickly been passed because the party believed "men must be legislated into sober habits." They "put the seven deadly sins into a National Platform."[52] Schools came first. As David Nasaw writes, school reformers "were convinced that the only antidote to the diseases of Irish heritage, Catholicism, and poverty was enforced disciplinary training in the common school classrooms." They tried to persuade the newcomers of this, then they "substituted force for persuasion" through state legislation.[53]

More followed. Republicans were "pledged to coercive temperance" and sought "to compass its objects by summary seizures, confiscations and extraordinary punishments upon foregone presumptions of guilt, such as are forbidden by the Bill of Rights." Their commitment to the "temperance swindle" to limit the production and consumption of alcoholic beverages was the "legitimate off-spring" of their "spiritual despotism" as were "the Sunday laws, as well as the anti-slavery agitation and laws to bring the white man to the level of the black."[54]

The "Republican party majority, usurping the prerogatives of God and conscience, decree that all men must conform to their particular puritanical observance of the Sabbath. . . . Sunday is rendered to them a day of sadness and gloom, instead of a day of rejoicing and happiness. The puritanical and straight laced notions imported here from one portion of Europe are forced down the throats of a population from a different part of Europe, who never believed in them[,] and they are compelled to yield obedience to a holy Protestant inquisition."[55] Such social laws will "reduce all sociability to the condition of a Puritan graveyard." Temperance legislation, moves to Americanize school instruction, and other types of social restrictions such as sabbatarian laws were all designed to impress, by whatever means possible, the inexorable values and beliefs of the Puritans on the immigrants and ultimately on all other Americans. To these causes has been brought "the aid of

[52] *Texas State Gazette*, April 16, 1859; *Atlas and Argus*, October 10, 1856, January 3, 1857.

[53] David Nasaw, *Schooled to Order: A Social History of Public Schooling in the United States* (New York, 1979), 73.

[54] *Atlas and Argus*, October 15, 1856; *Congressional Globe*, 34th Cong., 1st Sess., Appendix, 1151; New York *Herald*, September 23, 1860.

[55] New York *Herald*, September 23, 1860.

intemperate action . . . changing into an involuntary and compulsory system [one] which had begun on the principle of moral suasion and an appeal to the better nature of man. . . . Eastern demagogues began to court it as a valuable political adjunct to abolitionism."[56]

The result was predictable. "Whether it shall be a scheme for regulating eating or drinking or the industry of the country, the result will be an effort to govern the World too much." Congress "has heretofore confined itself to punishing the violation of those laws in which it had jurisdiction: counterfeiting, mail robbery, smuggling, etc. Under what clause it finds jurisdiction over the relation of the sexes has never been told." But these "'busy-bodies-in-other-men's matters'" were determined to engineer a Christian society of a particular kind and quality, one in which there would be no room for the kind of values, practices, and beliefs held by a majority of those within the Democratic coalition.[57]

The Democrats obviously had a different view of such issues. First they denied the political relevance of the matters the Puritan-Republicans wanted to discuss. "We never had much faith in promoting the cause of moral reform in any of its different aspects, by linking it with the action of political parties. . . . These parties will give the people better and more intelligent rulers, and a more wholesome administration of affairs, when left to make selections with reference to legitimate political questions." They condemned "the fatuity of . . . dragging into the political arena and subjecting to the vicissitudes of party, the cause of moral reform." The Maine Law and related matters were local questions. They did not "belong in general politics." Concern over such moral legislation was "at war with the real principles of our government as always understood and expounded by the Democratic creed." In sum, "we do not wish to see the Federal government legislating on the marriages or morals of domestic life, and still less on the religion of the people."[58]

Democrats expressed a more general condemnation as well. "In-

[56] New York *Journal of Commerce* in *Illinois State Register*, September 22, 1855.

[57] New York *Herald*, September 28, 1860; *Atlas and Argus*, October 10, 15, 1856, January 3, 1857; Washington *Daily Union*, March 26, 1857; *Congressional Globe*, 34th Cong., 1st Sess., Appendix, 1264.

[58] Washington *Daily Union*, December 13, 1854; *Atlas and Argus*, October 7, 1854, March 26, October 1, 1855, April 28, 1857; Washington *Daily Union*, November 7, 1854.

temperance is an evil," the editor of the *Democratic Review* wrote in 1852, "but for a free government to violate, for any cause, the plainest, most vital and fundamental principles of civil liberty, is also an evil, and one with which the first may not be at all compared." The "heresies of coercive temperance laws, know-nothingism and sectional organizations have their origin in one common error—a desire to interfere with the actions, consciences, and affairs of others." But "the moment . . . democratic principles, that men are to be let alone unless they invade the rights of others, and States allowed to govern themselves— are departed from, we know not what vagaries and inconsistencies communities may run." Clearly "the clergy, in all time, and in all countries, have never interfered in politics or in government without inflicting serious evils or lasting disadvantages upon the people." Let us then, they demanded, "have faith in Democracy! The founders of our government declared that it mattered little if error was left free by government, so long as truth was left free to combat it." Therefore "we will be wise if we learn in time to beware of that political priesthood which . . . commences by arrogating to itself divine attributes, and claiming to speak in the name of God, and ends in the moral and mental degradation and enslavement of its victims."[59]

Many aspects of Republican behavior in their initial national election campaign in 1856 first reinforced and then confirmed Democratic fears. In his massive study of the formation of the Republican party, William Gienapp recounts how quickly Democrats detected the leading role played by Puritan ministers in shaping the direction Republicanism took in 1856 and then in fighting for their party's victory. "We had all the fanatical methodist & Baptist preachers against us hurling their anathemas at us from their pulpits on Sunday and from the stump on week days," one Democrat angrily reported. Another noted that "preachers of all the Presbyterian denominations were out fiercely and fanatically against us."[60]

Gienapp concludes that "the Protestant clergy's support" for the

---

[59]*Democratic Review* (March, 1852), 271; Mobile *Daily Register*, October 12, 1855; Washington *Daily Union*, April 13, 1854; *Atlas and Argus*, January 3, April 28, 1857. Robert Kelley has summed up the implications of the attitudes expressed here very well. The sins that aroused the Democrats, he notes, "were social sins, not so much the sins of personal life." Robert Kelley, *The Transatlantic Persuasion* (New York, 1969), 418.

[60]William Gienapp, "The Origins of the Republican Party, 1852–1856" (Ph.D. dissertation, University of California, Berkeley, 1980), 1172. I am grateful to Professor

Republican ticket "was both vocal and unusual." Ministers "entered the
Frémont campaign with great enthusiasm and more than a little self-
righteousness. . . . Political sermons became standard fare throughout
the summer of 1856, reaching a climax on the Sunday before election
day, when, one Massachusetts Democrat sneered, the fanatical clergy
'appealed to their deluded followers to vote . . . as would enable them
to give an acceptable account at the Day of Judgment!'" [61]

The message of such activities, the rhetoric that accompanied them
and the aura given off, was clear to Democrats. The Republican party
had become proudly and manifestly the repository of all Puritan values
in politics. But, even more than that, the ethnocultural fires of the
mid-fifties had proved to be potent beyond belief: life-long Democrats
of the deepest faith were deserting the party over the matter. The fusion of former Whigs, Free-Soilers, renegade Democrats, and Know-
Nothings into the new Republican coalition had transformed the Democrats' enemies into a powerful and threatening political force. Despite
their sectarian and geographic narrowness, the Republicans posed a
political threat of an enormous magnitude, one unknown before. The
widespread Republican victories in the northern states from 1854 onward underlined the potency of the threat. The swing against the
Democrats in many parts of the North was large and decisive. The
elections to the Thirty-fourth Congress in 1854 were particularly disas-
trous. The Democrats lost seventy of their ninety-two House seats, one
of the greatest turnovers in American political history. They lost such
masses of voters in many localities that they seemed to be reduced
to an uncompetitive rump in key areas. They recovered themselves
somewhat after that, as the realignment sorted itself out, but at much
lower levels of popular support north of Maryland and the Ohio Valley
than they had heretofore enjoyed. In the presidential election of 1856
they held onto national power, but the Republican electoral totals in
the North were the dramatic story of that contest. [62]

The force of the numbers was clear. The Republicans were surging
to power. Although the Democrats remained electorally competitive in

Gienapp for allowing me to see and quote from his unpublished manuscript, which will
become the standard work on the subject of early Republicanism.
   [61] *Ibid.*, 1173.
   [62] The realignment is discussed in *ibid.*; Holt, *Political Crisis of the 1850s*; Fornni-
sano, *Birth of Mass Political Parties*; and Kleppner, *Third Electoral System.*

the northern states, the center of power had shifted significantly. The Democrats were now the minority party outside the South. That fact had a clear meaning for all Democrats to see and digest. From now on, a Republican national victory was very likely. That point, as well as the Republican rhetoric and values that underlay their growth in the northern states, threw a devastating scare into the Democrats, including the southern wing of the party, which had its own particular hobbies to worry about.

In this situation, Democratic rhetoric pinpointing the source of threat grew more agitated and extreme. Their fear was intense. The Republicans were dominated by a seventeenth-century kind of religious fanaticism. And that party of fanatics intended to use the government when it gained control to impose its values by legislation and executive action. Puritan government would be an activist one determined to impose and deny. Republicans were willing to "combat . . . against the people and institutions of half of the States of the Union—stigmatizing them as tainted members of our political family, whose social system is to be stamped with the marks of public reprobation. But let us not stop here. Let us also combine against the political rights and religious freedom of that large class in the Northern States, who were born on European soil."[63]

The Republican commitments, building on the raw materials long present in the political environment and the tendencies among so many of their supporters, had clearly crystallized in the 1854–1856 period in the midst of a turbulent electoral realignment. They might have pulled back slightly since, but not because of any change in their ideological outlook. More likely, any toning down in their appeal was only for tactical reasons. To both northern and southern Democrats, the men who made policy for and dominated the Republicans—that is, that party's power elite—were the ones to be feared, not the simple Republican voters of, say, Wisconsin or Missouri. Even after the Republicans worked to belie their radicalism on the slavery issue, as they did so energetically in 1859 and 1860, they could not hide the legislative proposals and goals of their party which strongly indicated their commitment to interventionism. Occasionally their real attitudes came through tellingly, as with the Republican-led antiimmigrant assault in

[63] *Atlas and Argus*, June 23, 1857.

Massachusetts in 1859, which involved the use of law and the manipulation of the political process to deny deserving immigrants their political rights and access to power.[64] That was real Republicanism speaking. No matter what they said, the Republicans intended to destroy by every means possible the values, institutions, and behavior hostile to their conception of right, from Sunday carousing to tippling in taverns and in private to the holding of slaves. They would let nothing stand in their way. They would use whatever power and means available to them to establish their own view over everyone else. They were defined by their commitment to "the evils of political meddling with morals, religion and the right of distinct communities" and of allowing the government to "invade the territory of the Church" on behalf of one cultural viewpoint within a highly pluralistic nation.[65] They had become a powerful, unyielding monolith, exerting their cultural domination over the rest of the country. Their purifying goals were religious, social, and economic. Where would it all end? In the noncompromising cultural imperialism so often threatened by fanatical New England divines. Puritanism and Republicanism were synonyms. Republicans could not deny it no matter what they said.

This the Democrats argued and firmly believed. Their image of Republicans as manipulators of cultural prejudices convinced them that there was real danger. Certainly, their private communications and the ambience they exuded to both friendly and unfriendly colleagues were little different from their public pronouncements.[66] Their angry and

---

[64] In that year the Republican-dominated Massachusetts legislature passed an amendment to the state constitution restricting—by delaying—the right of foreign-born citizens to vote and hold state office. Dale Baum, "Know-Nothingism and the Republican Majority in Massachusetts: The Political Realignment of the 1850s," *Journal of American History*, 64 (March, 1978), 959–86, argues that the problem was more complex than the Democrats charged and that there was much less Republican support for the legislation than usually claimed. Nevertheless, the Democrats viewed it as a Republican measure and used it against that party in immigrant areas. See Gustave Koerner, *Memoirs of Gustave Koerner, 1809–1896* (Cedar Rapids, 1909), II, 74–76, 89–90.

[65] The first part of the quotation is from a prewar speech by Horatio Seymour of New York, cited in Thomas M. Cook and Thomas W. Knox, comps., *Public Record of Horatio Seymour* (New York, 1868), 21. The second part is from an 1855 speech by Clement Vallandigham, "History of the Abolition Movement," in *The Record of the Hon. C. L. Vallandigham* (Columbia, 1863), 13.

[66] Andrew D. White commented about the great New York Democratic leader Horatio Seymour that "if he hated New England as the breeding bed of radicalism, he loved New York passionately." The symbolism and reality of the Puritan threat became

anguished rhetoric in reaction revealed and codified a set of contrasting beliefs, which fueled the political process and drove it toward dangerous shoals. The Democrats simplified the Republican approach, as was normal in partisan rhetoric. They ignored the tensions among reformers involved in coercive reform and came up with a frightening spectacle. An apocalyptic partisan temper invigorated by a specific aspect of Republican character did its work well. Throughout the period of the electoral realignment and into the secession crisis itself, the partisan confrontation escalated mightily. The noise was bitter and fearsome. As Democrats digested what they heard, they came to fear that the ascension of the Republicans to power would culminate in a drive to restrict and revise the very nature of the Union.

"The Civil War was, at base, a struggle for the future of the nation," Eric Foner has written.[67] Yes, it was. But what was involved in that struggle, and what were the possibilities for the future? The northern attack on the Celtic-Catholic threat, though not at first directly related to slavery, came to be seen by northern and southern Democrats as part of a much larger and quite potent cultural interventionism that knew no bounds in its interfering ways. A common ideology linking all Democrats together still affected the southern Democratic response to the onrushing Republicans. By 1860–1861 they had both internalized a generation of Democratic ideology and perceived an intense increase in the threat the now-triumphant Republicans posed to them. Southern Democrats shared the common partisan image of their enemy and then gave their perception a specific twist and reading of their own, which ultimately caused them to question the value of the Union— unlike their northern colleagues.

All of what was being discussed obviously and repeatedly intertwined with the role and importance of slavery in southern society and the fears of many southerners about its place and safety within the Union. Nothing could have interacted more tellingly. How could the Democrats, southerners in particular, not believe that the Republicans would not force all of the social changes they were convinced that the latter wanted? The history of partisan cultural confrontation since

---

the crucial element ordering and organizing the Democratic ideology. Andrew D. White, *Autobiography of Andrew Dickson White* (New York, 1905), I, 106.

[67] Foner, "Causes of the Civil War," 213.

1854, as the Democrats understood it, proved to them that their opponents would let nothing stand in the way in reshaping America in their own image, whatever their protestations in 1860 about being conservative on such matters. Republicans could not be negotiated with, a Louisiana editor summed up, because they were intransigent extremists intent only on "promulgating the teachings of their accursed fanaticism."[68] A Republican victory would lead to a total war of cultural imperialism. As Maryland Congressman James A. Stewart connected the problems in 1856, "If the Federal Government has the right to dissolve [the relation between master and slave] . . . then it may also declare, that within its territory the marriage contract shall be considered dissolved—prescribe a plurality of wives—enact all the absurdities characterizing fanaticism—may establish Mormonism, Maine-Lawism, spiritualism, witchcraft, a religious test—indeed all the whole code of blue laws. If this Government has the power in one case, and it is left to its discretion, in what will it draw a line of distinction?"[69] The Republican philosophy, in short, threatened a policy of total destruction. The South's future rested on the continuing triumph of pluralist perspectives within the Union; that is, the dominance of traditional Democratic principles. Otherwise slavery was doomed by the same forces that sought to throttle Catholicism and Celtic life-styles.

Clearly, southerners were not reacting to these ethnocultural matters and issues *per se*. What is central is that Democrats, including the southern wing, saw few differences between conflicts over slavery extension and conflicts originating in the coming of the immigrant and Catholic. Ethnocultural matters informed the debate about other things. Slavery was part of the larger matter of cultural hegemony. Neither was trivial; one may have been primary; both were related. The southern Democrats (and their northern counterparts) translated all of this into much more cosmic matters. They moved it to another level: one of a war between cultures. This posed a dangerous problem for the South and for southern slavery. As the editor of one Democratic newspaper put it, "We have found the root of the evil of sectional agitation in the attempt of the moral government to usurp the legitimate jurisdiction of the political government."[70] For forty years, Democrats be-

[68]Baton Rouge *Daily Advocate*, December 3, 1860.
[69]*Congressional Globe*, 34th Cong., 1st Sess., Appendix, 987.
[70]Washington *Daily Union*, January 20, April 16, 1857.

lieved they had been fighting for individual freedom against restriction and coercion. But in the 1850s they were in grave danger of losing the battle. This changed everything, especially for the southerners.

The South was vulnerable to the Republican threat, southern Democrats argued from the mid-fifties on. Republicans were fanatics unable to forego their commitment to regulate and reform. They might speak conservatively about slavery when it suited them and claim to recognize the South's constitutional rights, but how could they be trusted or believed? They would be unable to help themselves once in power. The same power used to defeat drunken Irish Catholics could be used to destroy slavery. Slavery, and every other part of the South's values, could never be safe given the character of the Republican party—whatever its reassurances. The Republican conception of a restrictive-coercive government would be as dangerous to slavery as it was proving to be to freewheeling social habits and religious nonconformity. The Republican commitment to a certain approach to society, social values, politics, and the way government operated threatened all. The South was prepared to believe the worst: not only that the Republicans were antislavery but that they would act as well as agitate. Central to everything, the Republicans could and would act.

After the rise of ethnocultural issues, therefore, no southerner could blink his eyes at alleged threats to slavery or ignore the clear evidence that there was no hope at all for any peculiar values, ideas, or institutions if the Republicans won. Years of partisan warfare told all that was at stake. There was an aura, a sense of purpose, and a commitment to act emanating from the Republicans. Partisan and sectional ideologies converged and sharpened as they interacted in the fifties. Both ethnocultural and slavery-sectional issues defined the Republicans. Both were part of the same parcel, the plans of a small group of regional fanatics to dominate the Union and their willingness to use state coercion not simply in the name of power but in the name of values rooted in a particular and narrow religious perspective.

This was the message that the Democrats offered again and again without respite during the fifties, in the campaign of 1860, and in the months of agony before the Lincoln administration came to power. As Mills Thornton remarks, "Politicians played constantly upon the fear that institutions were conspiring to limit autonomy, and thus to reduce the populace to subservience." They were always looking for something which would be "a symbolic summary" of popular fears.[71] Much of that "symbolic summary" cited here emanated from northern Democrats. But it is almost impossible to find distinctions between the visions of that group and their southern colleagues—except about the value of the Union. They both understood the Republican threat in the same way. Their understanding was shaped by and conveyed in static, unchanging images, no matter how dynamic the situation was in which all of them were caught. On both sides of the Mason-Dixon Line, Democratic spokesmen hammered away at the many faces of cultural interventionism and imperialism. Democratic newspapers and party spokesmen, North and South, maintained without stint the doom-laden, terribly threatening image of the Republicans.

South Carolina's secession convention voted her out of the Union on December 20, 1860. The last secession convention, North Carolina's, completed its work in late May, 1861. There is a rich, full story in the details of the meetings held and the political campaigns that shaped them. Avery O. Craven, Allan Nevins, David Potter, and Don S. Fehrenbacher have each told it very well in recent years.[72] The secession process was dramatic, intense, complex, and often contradictory. Whatever its details, however, at the heart of the actions taken lay the intellectual baggage the delegates brought with them to their meetings. So most historians have stressed, and so it has been stressed here. Clearly the secessionists already had pictures in their minds of what the danger was to themselves and their society thanks to the Republican victory. Those pictures, their perceptions of the enemy, were the motivations behind their subsequent behavior. They were no longer free agents able to consider calmly and likely to have their minds changed by what happened in debates. Matters had gone too far; their perceptual commitments had become too deeply imbedded for that.

It does not wholly matter whether the Democratic-secessionist vision was correct. There was enough evidence around to draw the conclusion they did.[73] Where specific elements of proof were missing, the

---

[71] Thornton, *Politics and Power*, xviii.

[72] Craven, *Growth of Southern Nationalism, 1848–1861*; Allan Nevins, *The Emergence of Lincoln* (New York, 1950), II; Potter, *Impending Crisis* (secession chapters completed and edited by Fehrenbacher).

[73] As Robert Kelley puts it, pietist reformers in the Republican party "were deter-

ideological commitments supplied them and afforded the necessary connecting links. Rhetoric and commitment reinforced, explained, codified, and ultimately helped create perceptions that led to action. To northern and southern Democrats infused with this idiom over a decade of battle for the soul of the nation, the evils associated with the Republicans were not separated into distinct compartments labeled economic differences, slavery, or psychological perceptions. The demonology of secessionist political rhetoric was imbued with and the behavior of southern secessionists was affected by the kinds of ethnocultural perspectives the new political historians have emphasized.

Secessionists constantly made the connection between "black" Republicanism and other peculiar "isms" associated with the electoral revolt of the mid-fifties. All of these were united and integrated, and to southerners especially they were devastating. As secessionists read the political world now unfolding, Republican rule would lead to an unacceptably restrictive society with a dominant, snooping, interfering government forcing conformity to a narrow set of behavioral norms. Cultural divisions and anxieties of this kind were often expressed in the American past even when they were masked as sectional antagonisms, that is, as different concepts of correct behavior and values. But these had been somewhat controlled when the question of values remained outside the purview of the issues discussed and of the powers and responsibility of government. They lurked there but could be managed. The rise of the cultural imperialists in the fifties changed this. Southern Democratic leaders saw the danger as well as did their northern brethren. The long adherence to partisan Democratic values and assumptions provided them with a perspective that fortified and intensified the fears constantly stimulated since 1854 over the future of their institutions, values, and chosen behavior. With Lincoln, the interventionist Republican, about to assume office they acted.

---

mined to use governments—as in the days of the Puritan past—as divine instruments to reshape American life in accordance with the imperatives of the newly recharged faith." And their stance "exuded intransigence." They seemed intent to "'face down'" any southern threats or bullying. Kelley, *Transatlantic Persuasion*, 418; Formisano, *Birth of Mass Political Parties*, 326.